## Principles of Japanese discourse

*Principles of Japanese discourse* offers the first detailed description, in English, of the structure and rhetorical effects observed in various genres of Japanese discourse. Drawing on Japanese *bunshooron* and incorporating results of Western discourse studies, the book covers principles of overall rhetorical organization including *ki-shoo-ten-ketsu*, topic structure, *danraku*, and sentence chaining, and presents a variety of rhetorical strategies frequently used in contemporary Japanese texts.

After presenting these principles in thirty compact entries, Professor Maynard invites the reader to apply the knowledge gained to the comprehension of contemporary authentic Japanese text. Seven selected readings (an essay, narrative, print advertising, a comic, newspaper columns, and a philosophical essay) are presented with vocabulary lists, discourse notes, and other tasks. English translations of Japanese examples/readings, and the readings reproduced in the original format, appear in the appendices.

In this book Professor Maynard has created a new category in the area of Japanese language learning and provided an excellent reference source not only for students but for instructors of the Japanese language worldwide.

日本語

# Principles of Japanese discourse

A handbook

SENKO K. MAYNARD
*Rutgers University*

CAMBRIDGE
UNIVERSITY PRESS

PUBLISHED BY THE PRESS SYNDICATE OF THE UNIVERSITY OF CAMBRIDGE
The Pitt Building, Trumpington Street, Cambridge CB2 1RP, United Kingdom

CAMBRIDGE UNIVERSITY PRESS
The Edinburgh Building, Cambridge CB2 2RU, United Kingdom
40 West 20th Street, New York, NY 10011–4211, USA
10 Stamford Road, Oakleigh, Melbourne 3166, Australia

First published 1998

Printed in the United Kingdom at the University Press, Cambridge

Typeset in Utopia 9/13pt, in QuarkXPress™ [GC]

*A catalogue record for this book is available from the British Library*

*Library of Congress cataloguing in publication data*

Maynard, Senko K.
Principles of Japanese discourse: a handbook / Senko K. Maynard.
p.   cm.
Includes bibliographical references and index.
ISBN 0 521 59095 7 hardback – ISBN 0 521 59909 1 paperback
1. Japanese language – Discourse analysis.   2. Japanese language – Rhetoric.
I. Title.
PL640.5.M396   1998
495.6′0141–dc21   97–3091 CIP

ISBN 0 521 59095 7 hardback
ISBN 0 521 59909 1 paperback

# Contents

# Preface

"I don't get it." That's what a student of Japanese said one day after reading a Japanese essay. "So, what's the point?" Another agreed. Reading Japanese can be frustrating. Even after thoroughly learning most of the basic Japanese sentence structure, one may find it difficult to understand how sentences "make sense" when arranged in discourse. Difficulty in grasping the meaning of sustained Japanese writing – such as units of paragraphs, let alone a lengthy article – is not uncommon among intermediate and advanced students of Japanese.

In reality, to appreciate even the simplest Japanese phrase, one must have a sense of the bigger picture, the discourse framework, and must be able to understand how surrounding sentences and paragraphs hang together as they forward the writer's thoughts. We are aware that even the briefest communication act contains abundant psychological, social and cultural information, some of which cannot be decoded simply by examining the language. Still, much information is expressed through language. Language provides the mechanism not only to communicate meaning but also, and as importantly, to mark connection and, in fact, to signal the very organization of discourse. Larger structural units build discourse further so as to create a cohesive whole. In order to "get it," one must understand how the interlocking strands of a text are tied together and where the critical information appears.

This book is written to provide students of Japanese a useful introduction to the principles of Japanese discourse. It is designed to illustrate how discourse comes together and how such organizational structure is signaled by using an array of strategies. Our task is complex because the rhetorical organization of discourse is based on the organization of ideas. Learning principles of Japanese discourse necessarily forces one to learn more than the meanings directly attributable to language. Given this complexity, a book like this one can provide only a basic reference guide to the principles of Japanese discourse. I have made every effort to present these principles as clearly and explicitly as possible.

Potential users of this book may be wondering about its emphasis on reading, excluding other language skills. My response is that an understanding of discourse principles is requisite to all language skills. And although spoken language is certainly important, it is in written language that we find a more complete representation of discourse structure. Besides, reading involves more than the passive integration of meaning. It requires the reader to construct the discourse anew in such a way that an interpreted text comes to life. Although comprehension of written words and generation of personal talk involve different cognitive and physical skills, the fundamental knowledge required for understanding discourse is identical.

Japanese discourse samples introduced in this book represent the language ordinarily used and readily accepted in Japan today, including both literary and non-literary texts. Ultimately we are interested in learning how to understand others' words, listen to stories, reach new information, expand our knowledge, and share our thoughts and feelings – in Japanese. To that end, I believe that studying the authentic Japanese writings appearing in this book used for explanatory and application purposes will prove useful.

Some of the students who inspired me to pen this book, and who I trust would have benefited from what it offers, have long since left the classroom. But I remain hopeful that they, too, may encounter this book somewhere sometime and, along with present and future students of Japanese, find it to be a useful handbook.

I express my gratitude to the authors and publishers for generously providing permission to use copyrighted materials for pedagogical purposes. My heartfelt thanks to Machi Tawara and Kawade Shoboo Shinsha for Reading 1, excerpt from *Yotsuba no Essei*; Shin'ichi Hoshi and Shinchoosha for Reading 2, *Ari to Kirigirisu*; Asahi Shinbunsha for Reading 3, the *Mado* column, and Reading 6, the *Tensei Jingo* column; Kiyoshi Uramoto and Magazine House for Reading 4, Pro-Keds shoes advertisement; Yoshito Usui and Futabasha for Reading 5, *Kureyon Shinchan* comic; and Tetsuroo Morimoto, Daiamondosha, and Sakuhinsha for Reading 7, *Sabaku e no Tabi*.

I owe Shooichi Iwasaki, Misato Tokunaga, and Kiyomi Nakamura who kindly offered helpful advice and suggestions. Linn Henderson read my manuscript and graciously offered assistance in improving my English. I thank her for spending more than a few precious Chicago summer days combing through my manuscript. I am grateful to Judith Ayling, formerly of Cambridge University Press, for her faith in me and for support and encouragement she so willingly gave at the early stage of this project. I express my deep gratitude to Kate Brett of Cambridge University Press for her constant and timely assistance in the book's editing and the production processes. I am grateful to Rutgers University and the Department of East Asian Languages and Cultures for making funds available to secure the use of some of the copyrighted materials. And as always, I thank my husband, Michael, for his warm and endless support.

# Introduction

The content of this book is best understood when the reader possesses a background knowledge of the Japanese language normally achieved by the end of one or one and a half years of college instruction consisting of between 200 and 250 classroom instruction hours. I assume that the reader is conversant with the inventory of grammatical items covered in basic Japanese grammar. For example, the reader is proficient in interpreting simple and complex sentences with tense variation; is familiar with modal expressions (e.g., *nebanaranai*) and nominal predicates (e.g., *no da*); knows the mechanism of passive, causative and conditional sentences; is familiar with a limited number of connectives and understands different uses of particles and polite levels. The reader is expected to know basic vocabulary ranging between 1,300 and 1,800 items, and is familiar with approximately 300 basic *kanji*.

According to the foreign language proficiency guidelines endorsed by the American Council on Teaching of Foreign Languages, it is at the Intermediate-High level that students begin to possess the ability to comprehend connected sentences and to follow the narrative thread in extended discourse. The content of this book is appropriately used in preparation for or concurrently with the Intermediate-High proficiency level learning. The book also contains reading materials appropriately used by Advanced and Superior level students, and should be useful throughout many years of Japanese language training. I should remind the reader that the proficiency level required for using this book depends not only on the reading materials themselves but also on how the reader uses the book's Part III, especially the tasks and activities suggested.

This book is divided into three parts. In Part I, Preliminaries, I offer brief introductory remarks on Japanese discourse. I introduce the concept of discourse, discuss some of the characteristics of Japanese rhetoric and explain stylistic features including differences between the spoken and written language, as well as differences in predicate styles.

Part II, Principles, the main part of the book, concentrates on rhetorical organization and strategies, two different but related principles of Japanese discourse. First, organizational structures of discourse are presented in Entries 1 to 13. Although many of the organizational principles of discourse are common between Japanese and English, some are not. The rhetorical structure of *ki-shoo-ten-ketsu* is a case in point. Many specific methods of connecting and framing discourse are also particular to Japanese, for example, topic structure, paragraph organization, sentence chaining and so on. These basic organizational principles of Japanese discourse are presented along with some authentic discourse segments.

The second portion of Part II, entries 14 to 30, covers some of the Japanese grammatical and rhetorical features – such as pronouns, demonstratives, tense marking, quotation, and similes – that offer important discourse-related strategies. We study these devices not merely as grammatical items but also, and more relevantly, as meaning–connecting strategies in discourse.

Although later entries are not necessarily more difficult, some build upon earlier entries, and therefore studying the entries in order of presentation is recommended. The index should also make it easy to refer to any entry any time. Some of the entries discuss principles and strategies that are frequently observed, and consequently, are applicable in a wide variety of text genres. Others are more specific and their application is limited to certain genres (these include Entries 8, 9, 13, and 22).

Part III, Selected readings, contains two sections. The first section offers a brief explanation on genres of contemporary Japanese writing. The second section presents seven different pieces of Japanese texts, R(eading)1 to R7. In each of the seven readings, discourse principles introduced in Part II are noted as they are applied in the interpretation of these authentic texts.

In Parts I and II, I use discourse samples, DS1 through DS7, along with additional discourse examples. Portions of R1 through R7 appear in some entries as well. Although every effort was made to choose relatively easy-to-understand texts, given the purpose of the present book, certain complexities are unavoidable. Initially, intensive reading of the sample discourse is not necessary; the skimming and scanning reading methods are satisfactory. Reference to English translation also makes it easier to grasp the gist of the sample discourse under discussion. Full texts of DS appear at different locations (see the end of this section for identifying the location).

English translations of DS1 to DS7 as well as R1 to R7 appear in Appendix 2 and Appendix 3, respectively. These and other translations and summaries are mine unless otherwise noted, and I do not intend them to be the only acceptable versions. Other translations are certainly possible. Translations and summaries are provided only for the purpose of clarifying potential uncertainties.

## Usefulness of discourse principles in learning Japanese

Some of the readers may wonder about the usefulness of learning the principles of Japanese discourse. Let me direct your attention to some of the results of research in language learning that support the usefulness of just such knowledge. Richard D. Kern (1989) reports an interesting experiment involving French instruction at the university level. The findings of his study provide empirical evidence that explicit instruction in discourse-based comprehension strategies can improve intermediate-level French students' ability to (1) comprehend French texts and (2) infer the meanings of unfamiliar words from context. Furthermore, the study found that students who had the greatest difficulty reading in French derived particular benefit from the instruction; improvement was more significant among poor readers of French. I should add that other studies as well – for example, Patricia Carrell (1984) – advocate the use of discourse knowledge in the learning of foreign languages.

The discourse knowledge is also found to be useful in our first language. For example, as reported by a psycholinguistic study (Segal, Duchan and Scott [1994]), connectives carry meaning and they connect textual meanings at both sentence and discourse levels. They mark discourse continuity and discontinuity both in the text and as inferred by the reader. In this manner, connectives help shape the interpretation of the ensuing clause and guide its integration into the overall discourse.

In the 1995 Japanese best-seller titled *Choo-Benkyoohoo* "Ultra Learning Methods" Yukio Noguchi cites the comprehension of overall framework as one of the three cardinal rules of learning. Knowing the overall organization of the comprehension task helps one's understanding of smaller units; in terms of language, knowing discourse organization helps understand clauses and words. This insight is particularly important for foreign language learners. Foreign language readers often process a text "bottom-up" focusing on surface structure features and building comprehension through analyses and syntheses of visual input. Language learning research has revealed that foreign language readers tend to be more linguistically bound than native language readers. This is partly because foreign language readers' word recognition skills are not quite satisfactory until advanced levels of study, and as a result they are often unable to allocate sufficient cognitive resources to effectively carry out discourse-level interpretive processes. Therefore, explicit training in discourse principles helps connect the missing link.

Moreover, language learners are known to incorporate knowledge of various kinds – from lower level knowledge such as vocabulary and word-level grammar, extending to middle level knowledge of sentence grammar, and further reaching higher level knowledge of discourse organization. When the reader lacks certain knowledge, other level knowledge compensates for it; the reader completes the task through an interaction among multiple levels of knowledge. In Japanese language learning so far, some of the higher level knowledge (e.g., principles of discourse) has been under-utilized. This book focuses precisely on this discourse-level learning.

## Orthography

This book assumes the reader's competence in elementary Japanese which includes knowledge of *hiragana*, *katakana* and recognition of some 300 basic *kanji*. Although ideally all Japanese materials should be presented as they appear in the original source, to avoid potential frustration of not being able to read *kanji*, in Parts I and II of the book, I present some materials in Romanized transcription either with or without Japanese orthography. Romanization follows the Hepburn style, except long *a*, *i*, *u* and *o* are doubled and long *e* is written *ei* (for words of Chinese origin) and *ee* (for words of Japanese origin). The syllabic *n* is spelled as *n'* when followed by a vowel or a semivowel, *y*. When I use Romanization, I divide words for the purpose of facilitating reading only; they do not necessarily reflect grammatical divisions.

In Part II, when the full text of the discourse sample appears, it is presented sentence-by-sentence in the Japanese orthography as it appears in the source, along with a vocabulary list. Other examples use *tooyoo kanji* when presented in Japanese orthography. As a rule Japanese texts longer than two sentences are also presented in Japanese orthography. In Part III, Readings 1 to 7 are given in (1) sentence-by-sentence reproduction of the text, and (2), later in Appendix 1 in the way they appear in the authentic original texts. For sentence-by-sentence reproduction of the text, beyond the standard Japanese font style used throughout the book, I use another style in R4 and R5, resembling their original font style. It is hoped that the reader is familiarized with different font styles used in the Japanese publishing industry.

## Parts of speech and abbreviations

The parts of speech designation given in vocabulary lists follows the Japanese (not translated English) categories. When multiple phrases appear together as a vocabulary item, as a rule, no designation is given. The following abbreviations should be noted: adj (adjective), adv (adverb), conn (connective), dem (demonstrative), exc (exclamatory expression), n (noun), pn (pronoun), prop (proper noun), and v (verb). An asterisk (*) is used to signal attention, or to mark an ungrammatical form. Three dots, unless they immediately follow phrases, indicate that a portion of the text is deleted.

## Location of discourse samples

The full text and the vocabulary list of the discourse samples appear in different entries as given here: DS1, a passage on frustration, in Entry 1; DS2, "Once Burned, Always Burned," in Entry 2; DS3, a passage on copying, in Entry 3; DS4, "Color and Human Life," in Entry 4; DS5, "Noisy Departure," in Entry 8; DS6, a poem "The Deer," in Entry 11; and DS7, part of a poem "Do Not Bundle Me," in Entry 18.

# To the instructors

Although this book may be used as a reference handbook and as a Japanese reader for individual use, its effectiveness increases when used as one of the textbooks for Intermediate-High, Advanced, and Superior levels of Japanese language courses. Parts I and II offer bite-size units for students to read at home in preparation for classroom discussion. If students find no difficulty in comprehending the entries at issue, there is no need to spend precious classroom time dwelling on them.

In reading courses when students are confused about certain aspects of Japanese discourse, explicit explanation is helpful. Leaving too many issues unresolved and only loosely understood should be avoided. Students are known to indicate an understanding of the material they don't actually have simply to please the instructor. Although this desire to please moves the class along, ultimately it only leads to the students' frustration. By directing students to the entries in Part II, instructors can take a proactive approach; it offers a solution to the problem in its earliest stage so as to reduce its negative consequences.

Part III can be used either as primary or supplementary reading material. Readings were selected from different genres of contemporary Japanese so that students will familiarize themselves with a variety of styles. In terms of content, those writings emphasizing human experience and emotion common to students everywhere were chosen. Topics that touch upon Japan and Japanese culture are already abundantly available elsewhere; materials selected for this book are expected to emphasize commonality among peoples while offering meaningful food for thought. I hope students will read not merely to learn the Japanese language but also, and more importantly, read to think, to feel, to wonder and to ask questions.

In developing reading materials for Part III, I made every effort to refer to, wherever relevant, the content of the entries covered in Part II. Applying principles and strategies of Japanese discourse to authentic texts affords an effective method for improving reading skills. All readings contain the following items: introduction, pre-reading tasks, text with a vocabulary list, discourse notes, discourse activities, and post-reading activities. Some redundancy appears in the vocabulary list. It contains words many of the students are familiar with, and the list also includes items appearing in earlier readings. This accommodates readers with different proficiency levels who may select those readings most interesting and suitable to them. The instructor will note the absence of grammar notes in Part III.

Although knowledge of basic grammar should be sufficient to comprehend the material, depending on the students' proficiency level, some explanation may be necessary. Tasks and activities suggested may also need to be revised depending on the students' ability.

Reading authentic texts such as those selected for Part III requires special knowledge since every text assumes cultural knowledge. Reading culturally distant texts challenges everyone, and it becomes necessary to incorporate a variety of supplementary materials for facilitating comprehension. For example: additional *tanka* by Machi Tawara and Bokusui Wakayama for R1; other Aesop's fables and short stories by Shin'ichi Hoshi for R2; introduction to the format of Japanese newspaper discourse and internal organization of newspaper columns for R3; discussion on loan words and spoken language for R4; learning about homonyms for R5; introduction to *Hanasaka Jijii* and other Japanese old tales for R6; and the song *Tsuki no Sabaku*, philosophy of Tetsuroo Watsuji, and Japanese proverbs for R7; and so on.

Although I use English in my explanation and instruction, I am aware that instructors should use as much Japanese as possible in the classroom. We all determine, based on our own pedagogical beliefs, how much English should be spoken while teaching the Japanese language. Depending on the skill being taught, use of Japanese to a greater degree than this book does is recommended. At the same time I caution against the tendency for instructors to hide behind their Japanese competence leaving the students in the dark at the mercy of incomprehensible (to students) explanations in Japanese.

When choosing reading materials for Japanese courses, each instructor will have a preference for certain topics and genres. Students' interests also vary, from one group to another and from one year to the next. Readings are sometimes selected to complement content of other Japan-related courses. Materials chosen in Part III, therefore, are offered as samples only. I hope that the manner of incorporating principles and strategies of Japanese discourse in the reading task will provide a useful idea or two on how the instructor might develop an assemblage of choice reading materials.

*Part I*
## Preliminaries

Intuitively we know that when using language, we construct sentences by combining various units of linguistic signs, such as words, phrases and clauses. Although thoughts are usually expressed in sentence units, we rarely use the sentence in isolation. Rather, most linguistic expressions we experience consist of multiple sentences. Multiple sentences, when written, are often grouped together to form meaningful paragraphs, paragraphs to form chapters, and so on. We call this semantically connected unit of linguistic expression a "discourse" or "*bunshoo*." I will also use the term "text" to refer to discourse, but with an emphasis on actual written pieces of discourse.

How are multiple sentences, a segment of discourse, connected to convey meaning? A random string of sentences lacks cohesion and is consequently meaningless. When reading, we expect thoughts to be organized and arranged in cohesive units. But how are these units organized in Japanese texts? Are the Japanese ways of understanding and expressing discourse organization and connection identical, similar to or different from those of English? If we define discourse and *bunshoo* as "connected units of linguistic expression," how are these units actually connected? What strategies are used to signal such connection in Japanese?

In traditional Japanese language studies, the term *bunshoo* has been used synonymously with the term discourse. A number of Japanese scholars in *bunshooron*, studies of *bunshoo*, have gained knowledge that we will be relying upon in this book (Tokieda 1977, Ichikawa 1981, Nagano 1986, Hinata and Hibiya 1988, Nagara and Chino 1989, Kaneoka 1989, Kubota 1990, Nishida 1992, and so on). In Japanese *bunshooron*, topics such as *bunmyaku* "threads of discourse," sentence chaining, *danraku* "paragraph" structure, and the categorization of *bunshoo* genres have been primary areas of research. Studies of discourse and text (e.g., discourse analysis and text linguistics) in the West have also produced useful results. For example, in English, a variety of expressions have been identified as connection devices (e.g., conjunction, repetition, substitution, and topic continuity) and different types of discourse organization are known (e.g., narrative structure, required sections in academic theses, and topic hierarchy). We will be studying all these concepts in detail.

So far I have used the expressions "connected" and "cohesive." However, what one means by these terms may not be as clear as it first appears. Although the principal basis of connected discourse is the logical property – in that it "makes sense" – sociologists and anthropologists have long known that logic, in terms of language, is a cultural phenomenon. The Japanese language has been called "illogical" or simply "alogical," and consequently often "vague."

This stereotypical view, however, is misleading in two ways. First, when comparing Japanese ways of rhetoric with Western ways, the so-called Western "logical" foundation normally refers to a logical syllogism which occurs only in limited cases in everyday rhetoric. In the tradition of Western rhetoric (for example, Aristotle's), what is advocated is the rhetorical syllogism (enthymeme) in which the premises and conclusion are only ordinarily probable, not necessarily logically valid. In reality, not all English writings make statements with supporting reasons introduced by *for*, *because* or *since* or an *if . . . then* statement.

Secondly, the Western logic-based prescription is suitable for certain types of discourse only – both in the West and Japan. As we will find out in the course of this book, Japanese writers utilize, although in different ways when compared with English, logical progressions in certain texts. The difference lies in that depending on genres, Japanese texts show evidence of using a variety of rhetorical structures including and beyond deductions (enthymemes) and inductions (use of examples). One can make a similar statement regarding English texts, but the degree of freedom Japanese writers exercise in writing seems greater. Furthermore, certain methods for creating connected discourse are found to be both effective and ideal in Japanese but not in English. This gives an impression that Japanese texts are difficult to understand, too subjective and often lacking in cogent arguments, and that the writer's intention is ambiguous at best.

I should also mention that alleged ambiguities arise in part from the reader's expectation of what a particular reading piece should contain. In general, when compared with English, the distinction in Japanese genres is less clear and genre-specific discourse principles and strategies are less forcefully practiced. The gap between what an English-speaking reader expects and actually finds in a piece of Japanese text can be grave in some cases. It will be our aim to clarify some of these myths and difficulties.

In real-life pages of written text, Japanese writings show multiple types of discourse organization and connection, and often these mechanisms are mixed and multifold. The conclusion may not be stated until the very end of the essay, only after seemingly unnecessary steps, or the conclusion may be only indirectly suggested. Reading Japanese requires knowledge and awareness beyond what English readers already possess. It is our task to learn principles and strategies particularly important for comprehending Japanese texts.

Although we are going to study Japanese as written texts only, we know that the spoken style appears often in written discourse. In fact some contemporary texts employ a style that gives the impression of the writer talking directly to the reader. (A good example is advertising copy introduced as R4 later.) And even if a text may predominantly follow the written style, direct quotations of spoken language appear frequently. Thus, in order to "read" Japanese we need to understand spoken Japanese as well.

Just as in other languages, it is between the written and spoken styles that the most basic stylistic distinction can be drawn among varieties of the Japanese language. In writing one creates a planned discourse addressed to a reader distant in time and space, while in speaking one normally creates unplanned discourse addressed directly to the partner. Spoken language uses an increased level of fragmentation, and it frequently employs expressions emotionally appealing to the partner, including exclamatory expressions, interactional particles and so on. Discourse organization in casual conversation, for example, is usually less complicated. On the other hand, written language features a prepared presentation of thought, often accompanied by complex sentence structures, sometimes with multiple subordinate clauses into which information is richly packed. Complex discourse organization which spans over a long stretch of discourse is mostly limited to writing.

In addition to the general differences described above, which are common across languages, one particular difference between the written and spoken language in Japanese is worth noting. Japanese vocabulary is of two basic kinds; synonymous words come in pairs of native and Chinese-derived words. The native vocabulary called *yamatokotoba* (or *wago*) consists of a string of consonant plus vowel syllables which have staccato sounds and are written in *hiragana* or in *kanji-hiragana* combination. Chinese-derived words, *kango*, often take "n" sounds and long vowels. *Kango* appears mostly in two-character compounds and falls into the grammatical category of noun. The list below illustrates a comparison between the two types of vocabulary.

| kango | yamatokotoba (wago) | meaning |
|---|---|---|
| nin-gen | hito | person |
| koo-i | okonai | conduct |
| ryo-koo | tabi | travel |
| hin-kon | mazushisa | poverty |

*Kango* vocabulary is larger, and its relatively precise and analytical quality makes it a suitable means for expressing abstract thoughts. *Yamatokotoba* is more appropriately used to express emotion and feelings. Different discourse genres use varying levels of mixture of these two types of vocabulary. Casual speech, for instance, shows restricted use of *kango* while an academic thesis uses *kango* more abundantly. According to the National Language Research Institute study quoted in Yutaka Miyaji (1985: 99), the proportional distribution of different kinds of vocabulary in written Japanese (magazines) and in spoken Japanese show the following results. *Yamatokotoba* and *kango* appear in approximately 54% and 41% of the total vocabulary, respectively, in magazines while in spoken Japanese *yamatokotoba* is more dominant (occurring approximately 72% of the total) than *kango*, which appears only in 24% of the total vocabulary. (The remaining 4% falls into Western words and mixed vocabulary.)

We find different distributional tendencies among different kinds of written texts as well. We can compare two brief discourse segments in which either *yamatokotoba* or *kango* is the dominant vocabulary. First, examine three sentences taken from R1, an essay by Machi Tawara (1988). We find no cases of *kango* in this text.

*R1: Sentences 8–10*

8.　空の青からも、海の青からも、染め残されたカモメ。

9.　カモメのようなあなた。

10.　あなたはかなしくないですか。

8. Sora no ao kara mo umi no ao kara mo somenokosareta kamome.
(The sea gull, left alone without being touched by the blue of the sky, or the blue of the sea.)

9. Kamome no yoona anata.
(You are just like a sea gull.)

10. Anata wa kanashikunai desu ka.
(You aren't sad, are you?)

Compare these sentences with a passage from the Preface of the Japanese Constitution as presented below (NTT 1996). *Kango* phrases are underlined.

(1)    日本国民は恒久の<u>平和</u>を<u>念願</u>し、<u>人間相互</u>の<u>関係</u>を<u>支配</u>する<u>崇高</u>な<u>理想</u>を深く<u>自覚</u>するのであって、<u>平和</u>を愛する<u>諸国民</u>の<u>公正</u>と<u>信義</u>に<u>信頼</u>して、われらの<u>安全</u>と<u>生存</u>を<u>保持</u>しようと<u>決意</u>した。

*Nihon kokumin* wa, *kookyuu* no *heiwa* o *nenganshi, ningen soogo* no *kankei* o *shihaisuru suukoona risoo* o fukaku *jikakusuru* no deatte, *heiwa* o aisuru *shokokumin* no *koosei* to *shingi* ni *shinraishite*, warera no *anzen* to *seizon* o *hojishiyoo* to *ketsuishita*.

We, the Japanese people, desire peace for all time and are deeply conscious of the high ideals controlling human relationship and we have determined to preserve our security and existence, trusting in the justice and faith of the peace-loving peoples of the world.

Although it is possible to recognize differences between written and spoken language, these two categories are not mutually exclusive. Certain writings incorporating the mixture of both written and spoken styles may be called an "in-between" style. We must not ignore the fact that a written text is a creative work; writers are free to express themselves as they wish as long as the created text is comprehensible and discernible. Mixing spoken and written styles is a strategy often used to create desired expressive effects. Magazines targeted to Japanese youth offer a good example since their articles and reports often adopt colloquial speech style. Perhaps it is closer to reality to think of styles as more or less written or spoken resulting in a variety of in-between styles, instead of understanding them as two mutually exclusive categories.

Beyond the written and spoken (and in-between), we recognize an additional style dimension, the so-called *da, desu/masu* and *dearu* predicate styles. First in order is a review of some stylistic differences we are familiar with, formal (*desu/masu*) and informal (abrupt, *da*) styles.

*1. formal style:*

(2.1)  Sensei ga kyooshitsu ni haitte **kimashita.**
(The teacher came into the classroom.)

(2.2)  Suruto kodomotachi wa shizukani **narimashita.**
(Then the children became quiet.)

*2. informal (abrupt) style:*

(3.1)  Sensei ga kyooshitsu ni haitte **kita.**
(The teacher came into the classroom.)

(3.2)  Suruto kodomotachi wa shizukani **natta.**
(Then the children became quiet.)

Most elementary Japanese language textbooks primarily use the formal *desu/masu*-style for both spoken and written discourse. Students of Japanese are also exposed to the *da*-style in casual speech and in some writings. In casual speech, the *da*-style rarely appears by itself; rather, particles and other expressions normally accompany it. Casual speech takes the style as given in (4) with fragmented utterances marked with particles.

(4.1)  Sensei ga kyooshitsu ni haitte **kite sa,**
(The teacher came into the classroom, and,)

(4.2)  soide kodomotachi wa **saa,** shizukani **natta n da yo.**
(then, the kids became quiet, you know.)

The *da*-style as depicted in (3) appears in some writings, especially when the writer addresses the reader not as an individual person but as a group. Novels, essays, and newspaper reports are mostly written using *da,* although sometimes mixed with *desu/masu* as well. Formal personal letters and official announcements are normally written in the *desu/masu* style.

The *dearu*-style

There is an additional style called *dearu*-style, which is restricted to written language (and very formal speech). The *dearu*-style in an abrupt form is often used as a dominant predicate style in persuasive and argumentative discourse, such as criticism, articles, editorials, and academic theses as well as in laws and regulations. Formal expressions of *dearu*-style are rarely used; they appear in very formal speech or in a formal narrative style. The *dearu*-style takes verb forms identical to the *da*-style, except that in place of affirmative forms of the "be" verb (i.e., *da*), *dearu* and its conjugated forms are used as shown below.

**Dearu forms**

| | |
|---|---|
| abrupt non-past | *dearu* |
| abrupt past | *deatta* |
| abrupt speculative | *dearoo* |
| formal non-past | *dearimasu* |
| formal past | *dearimashita* |
| formal speculative | *dearimashoo* |

(The *da* under discussion includes those that accompany *na*-type adjectives. Thus, *shizuka dearu, shizuka deatta, shizuka dearoo, shizuka dearimasu, shizuka dearimashita* and *shizuka dearimashoo* are used.)

## Three basic styles of written Japanese

1. *desu/masu*

(5) Tookyoo e **ikimasu**.
(other forms: *ikimasen, ikimashita, ikimasen-deshita*)
(I'm going to Tokyo.)

(6) Ano hito wa Tookyoo shusshin **desu**.
(other forms: *dewaarimasen, deshita, dewaarimasen-deshita*)
(That person is from Tokyo.)

2. *da*

(7) Tookyoo e **iku**.
(other forms: *ikanai, itta, ikanakatta*)
(I'm going to Tokyo.)

(8) Ano hito wa Tookyoo shusshin **da**.
(other forms: *dewanai, datta, dewanakatta*)
(That person is from Tokyo.)

3. *dearu*

    (9)  identical to (7) above

    (10)  Ano hito wa Tookyoo shusshin **dearu**.
    (That person is from Tokyo.)

In discourse segments without a be-verb, one cannot tell whether the style used is *da* or *dearu* since all other verbs take identical forms. It is also true that the be-verb may not be used explicitly in discourse. Nouns and noun phrases by themselves may be considered as full sentences. In this case, one cannot tell the stylistic difference between *da* and *dearu*. These three styles are sometimes mixed in Japanese writings; we will study the style mixture later in Entry 14.

*Part II*

## Principles

# 5    Rhetorical organization

## Prelude: cohesion and coherence

Although we study organizational principles, as in other languages, not all Japanese written texts strictly follow them. Some writings (e.g., formal letters, newspaper reports, and academic theses) follow organizational principles more closely than creative writings (e.g., novelistic writings, advertising copy and poetic texts). Many options are available to writers, and the end result is often a combination of various discourse schemes. Despite this complexity, knowing basic organizational principles is useful for identifying overall internal structures of discourse. For example, one may be able to predict the kind of information appearing in different parts of discourse.

I am not claiming that all the readings the reader will be exposed to can be explained in terms of the discourse organizational principles we will be studying. Creativity and conformity, both important ingredients, go hand-in-hand in writing. Although creativity often calls on surprises, surprises are surprises because we know the ordinary and the expected. I am saying, therefore, that learning conventional and prescribed principles of Japanese discourse is useful in the end.

Important in understanding Japanese beyond the sentence is that Japanese writings in certain genres, especially short essays, follow the organizational principle called *ki-shoo-ten-ketsu*. Under the *ki-shoo-ten-ketsu* organization, the writer presents the conclusion toward the end in somewhat roundabout ways. Generally, a reversal in the form of a surprise turn occurs immediately before the conclusion. It is also important to understand how text is first divided into segments – such as paragraphs (or *danraku* in Japanese) – and is then reconnected to form a coherent and meaningful whole. We will also pay attention to how one identifies the "point," the central message, of discourse. The resultant knowledge will make it easier to examine the entire text from a bird's-eye view enabling the reader to appreciate the meaning attributable to the entire text.

Two basic notions must be clarified at this point. First is "cohesion," which broadly refers to cases where one interprets two or more elements in discourse through associated meanings. Such semantic connection is expressed in language in many different ways. In a sequence of sentences such as "A girl came out. She was wearing a black coat," "she" is thought to be the same person referred to as "a girl" in the preceding sentence. This "connects" two sentences in terms of meaning since both describe the same girl. In a sequence of sentences such as "Finally a girl came out. So we walked up to her and asked a few questions," the connective "so" overtly joins the sentences in terms of cause and result. The incident described in the first sentence offers a condition which facilitates the action depicted in the second. Again, two sentences are connected. Cohesion is realized as a tie, that is, a meaning-based connection among items in discourse.

The second important ingredient in discourse is "coherence." While cohesion broadly refers to the connection among items in discourse, coherence refers more narrowly to the logical connection – the organization of logical progression of thought that "makes sense." In the example above, "Finally a girl came out. So we walked up to her and asked a few questions," in addition to the connective joining the two sentences (a case of cohesion), we find coherence since the two sentences are connected logically, that is, a cause–result relationship. Cohesion refers to concrete cases of semantic connection in a broad sense whereas coherence refers to the narrowly defined logically motivated progression in discourse. In actual texts cohesion and coherence may overlap and they may be simultaneously marked by a number of principles and strategies.

Cohesion and coherence, not being mutually exclusive, focus on different aspects of discourse. While cohesion is generally associated with connection observed in the local area across a limited number of sentences, coherence is generally associated with an overall organization of text. For example, in some academic writings a preferred rhetorical progression may be: premise, hypotheses, analytical or experimental results, argument, discussion, and conclusion, in this order. When discourse is created so as to convey logically acceptable progression of thought, such text is said to be coherent. The concept of coherence is often applicable across languages in certain genres, but not applicable in all genres in all languages equally. In what follows we examine some of the basic organizational principles in a variety of genres in Japanese.

Entry 1 **Three-part organization**

The most basic discourse structure in Japanese is the three-part organization, consisting of the initial, middle, and final parts. The three-part organization is common among many languages including English, and this simplest organization is frequently used. These three parts, though bearing labels other than *joron*, *honron*, and *ketsuron*, apply in their broadest sense to the internal structure of expository, persuasive, descriptive, and narrative discourse. Although real-life text – such as an essay, a newspaper column, a short story, or a novel – contains various sub-parts which in turn contain additional sub-parts, and so on, the overall three-part structure as shown below can be observed at some level in most readings.

Three-part discourse organization
     *joron* (initial, introductory part)
     ↓
     *honron* (middle, main part)
     ↓
     *ketsuron* (final, concluding part)

Now examine DS1, a brief expository text, paying special attention to its organizational parts.

*DS1* (Ishimori *et al.* 1985b:40)

1. 私たちは、心の中に不満や心配事があるとつい
   ひとりごとを言ってしまう。
2. なぜひとりごとを言うのだろうか。
3. それは、ひとりごとを言うことによって、いく
   らか気持ちが落ち着くからである。
4. 私たちは、腹が立った時、石を蹴飛ばして気持
   ちを鎮めることがある。
5. これは、直接の原因ではないものに怒りの行動
   を向けて、気持ちを発散させる代償行為である。
6. 無意識の代償行為は、人間に与えられた一つの
   生きる知恵なのである。

<u>Vocabulary</u>:

1.

| | | | |
|---|---|---|---|
| 心 | こころ | n | heart |
| 不満 | ふまん | n | dissatisfaction, discontent |
| 心配事 | しんぱいごと | n | worries |
| つい | | adv | inadvertently, involuntarily |
| ひとりごと | | n | monologue, talking to oneself |

3.

| | | | |
|---|---|---|---|
| 気持ち | きもち | n | feeling, mood, emotion |
| 落ち着く | おちつく | v | to calm down, to recover one's composure |

4.

| | | | |
|---|---|---|---|
| 腹が立つ | はらがたつ | v | to be angry, to be outraged |
| 石 | いし | n | stone |
| 蹴飛ばす | けとばす | v | to kick away |
| 鎮める | しずめる | v | to quiet down |

5.

| | | | |
|---|---|---|---|
| 直接の | ちょくせつの | | direct, immediate |
| 原因 | げんいん | n | cause |
| 怒り | いかり | n | anger, rage |
| 行動 | こうどう | n | act, action, conduct |
| 向ける | むける | v | to direct, to aim |
| 発散する | はっさんする | v | to emit, to release |
| 代償行為 | だいしょうこうい | n | compensatory act |

6.

| | | | |
|---|---|---|---|
| 無意識の | むいしきの | | unconscious |
| 人間 | にんげん | n | human beings |

| 与える | あたえる | v | to give, to bestow |
| 生きる | いきる | v | to live |
| 知恵 | ちえ | n | wisdom |

*Translation*

1. When we find discontent and worries inside our hearts, we inadvertently say (mumble) things to ourselves.

2. Why do we mumble to ourselves?

3. It is because by mumbling to ourselves, we calm our emotions down a little.

4. When angry, we sometimes kick at stones and calm our emotions.

5. This is a compensatory act which channels anger into things other than the direct cause, thus releases one's feelings.

6. This unconscious compensatory act is life's wisdom given to human beings.

One can divide DS1 into three parts. The initial part (sentences 1 and 2) begins the exposition by mentioning a specific kind of human behavior (mumbling when being discontent). The middle part (sentences 3, 4, and 5) develops this topic by explaining why such behavior occurs. In this process, an additional example is given (in sentence 4) to support the meaning of such behavior. The last sentence offers a final part which makes the concluding point of the discourse.

Entry 2  **Five-part organization**

Beyond the basic three-part organization, certain texts are more readily divided into five parts known in Japanese traditional (Buddhist) rhetoric. The five-part organization applies primarily to expository and persuasive discourse. These elements are:

```
Five-part discourse organization
    okori        beginning
    ↓
    uke          leading
    ↓
    hari         main point
    ↓
    soe          supplement
    ↓
    musubi       conclusion
```

For example, study DS2, a brief essay, *Kogeguse*, by Kuniko Mukooda.

**DS2 (Mukooda 1984:101)**

焦げ癖

A:

1.　新しいフライパンや支那鍋をおろすときは新しいドレスをおろすときよりも緊張する。

B:

2.　十分にカラ焼きをして、少しさましてから古い油を入れ、また熱くして油を捨てる。

3.　これを三回ほど繰り返して、野菜の切れっぱしをいためて使い勝手を研究する。

4.　もちろん、これも捨てるのである。

5.　もったいないが、これから先何年もお世話になる台所の片腕を仕上げてゆくのだから、このくらいは大目にみてもらわなくてはならない。

C:

6.　こんなに気を使っていても、やはり焦がしてしまうことがある。

7.　　鍋の焦げたのは交通事故と一緒で、ほんの一瞬
　　　の油断で事は起き、あと何ヶ月も泣かなくては
　　　ならない。

D:

8.　　丁寧に焦げを落とし、もう大丈夫と思っている
　　　と、また同じところが焦げてしまう。

9.　　一度悪い癖がついてしまうと、それが本当にも
　　　とにもどるには、大変な時間と努力がいる。

E:

10.　　これは人間も同じかもしれない。

Vocabulary:

| | | | |
|---|---|---|---|
| 焦げ | こげ | n | burn mark |
| 癖 | くせ | n | habit |

1.

| | | | |
|---|---|---|---|
| フライパン | | n | frying pan |
| 支那鍋 | しななべ | n | wok |
| おろす | | v | to use for the first time, to break in |
| ドレス | | n | dress |
| 緊張する | きんちょうする | v | to be nervous, to be under stress |

2.

| | | | |
|---|---|---|---|
| 十分に | じゅうぶんに | adv | sufficiently |
| カラ焼き | からやき | n | frying the pan empty |
| さます | | v | to cool down |
| 油 | あぶら | n | oil |
| 熱くする | あつくする | | to heat |
| 捨てる | すてる | v | to throw away |

3.

| | | | |
|---|---|---|---|
| 三回 | さんかい | | three times |
| 繰り返す | くりかえす | v | to repeat |

| 野菜 | やさい | n | vegetable |
| 切れっぱし | きれっぱし | n | cut end-pieces |
| いためる | | v | to stir-fry |
| 使い勝手 | つかいかって | | manner of handling, usage |
| 研究する | けんきゅうする | v | to study |

5.

| もったいない | | adj | wasteful |
| 何年 | なんねん | | many years |
| お世話になる | おせわになる | | to receive assistance from |
| 台所 | だいどころ | n | kitchen |
| 片腕 | かたうで | n | a right-hand help |
| 仕上げる | しあげる | v | to complete |
| 大目にみる | おおめにみる | | to forgive, to tolerate |

6.

| 気を使う | きをつかう | | to be careful, to be sensitive |
| 焦がす | こがす | v | to burn (something) |

7.

| 鍋 | なべ | n | pan |
| 焦げる | こげる | v | to be burned |
| 交通事故 | こうつうじこ | n | traffic accident |
| 一緒 | いっしょ | n | same as |
| ほんの | | | just, only |
| 一瞬 | いっしゅん | n | one second |
| 油断 | ゆだん | n | carelessness |
| 何ヶ月 | なんかげつ | | many months |
| 泣く | なく | v | to cry |

8.

| 丁寧に | ていねいに | adv | with much care, thoroughly |

| 落とす | おとす | v | to get rid of |
| 大丈夫 | だいじょうぶ | adj | fine, secure |
| 9. | | | |
| もとにもどる | | v | to return to its original condition |
| 努力 | どりょく | n | effort |
| いる | | v | to be necessary, to require |
| 10. | | | |
| 人間 | にんげん | n | human beings |
| 同じ | おなじ | adj | same |

**Translation**

*Once Burned, Always Burned*

    A:

1. When I break in a new frying pan or wok for the first time, I am more nervous than when I put on a new dress.

2. After amply heating up the pan, and letting it cool a while, I pour in a little used oil, heat it and then empty the pan.

    B:

3. After repeating this three times, I stir-fry (unusable) vegetable end-pieces and examine how the pan is cooking.

4. Of course, I throw the contents away.

5. Although it is a bit wasteful, since I am rearing my right-hand assistant in the kitchen from whom I will receive assistance for some years to come, I suppose this extent of waste should be tolerated.

    C:

6. Even though I go to this much trouble, I sometimes end up burning the pan.

7. Burned pans are similar to traffic accidents; the accidents occur in a moment's carelessness and one suffers the consequences for many more months.

    D:

8. I clean the burns with great care and just when I think, "Now perhaps everything is working out fine," I end up burning the same spot again.

9. Once a bad habit is formed, enormous time and effort is required before it (corrects itself and) returns to complete normalcy.

E:

10. Human beings may be the same.

In the original print, DS2, is divided into five short paragraphs as indicated by A to E. Table 1 summarizes how each paragraph contributes to the organization of the essay.

**Table 1** The five-part organization of DS2, with paragraph summary

| paragraph | *five-part organization* | *paragraph summary* |
|-----------|-------------------------|---------------------|
| A | *okori* (beginning) | Author's nervous feelings when using new pans. |
| B | *uke* (leading) | Process of carefully seasoning the new pan as explained in detail. |
| C | *hari* (main point) | Sometimes making unfortunate mistakes of burning the pan, nonetheless. |
| D | *soe* (supplement) | Difficulty of recovering from the mistake. |
| E | *musubi* (conclusion) | Similarity to human life: once a bad habit formed, hard to get rid of. |

When reading Japanese, it helps to scan over the document, taking in the units such as a single paragraph, multiple paragraphs, sections and/or chapters from a bird's-eye view. Whether it primarily follows a three-part organization or a five-part organization, by identifying structural parts, i.e., the building blocks of the entire discourse, we are able to speculate as to how the pieces of information hang together within a larger cohesive whole. Grasping the overall framework of the text helps compensate for any lack of specific knowledge. For example, it is easier to speculate on the meaning of any one word when the general framework is already understood.

Entry 3  **Ki-shoo-ten-ketsu**

In addition to the basic three-part and five-part organizations, the Japanese use a four-part organizational principle called *ki-shoo-ten-ketsu*. *Ki-shoo-ten-ketsu* originates in the structure of four-line Chinese poetry and is frequently referred to in Japanese as a model rhetorical structure of expository (and other) writings.

---

**Ki-shoo-ten-ketsu organization**

| | |
|---|---|
| *ki* | (topic presentation) presenting topic at the beginning of one's argument |
| *shoo* | (topic development) following *ki*, developing the topic further |
| *ten* | (surprise turn) after the development of the topic in *shoo*, introducing a surprising element, indirectly relevant, related to or connected with *ki* |
| *ketsu* | (conclusion) bringing all of the elements together and reaching a conclusion |

---

A classic example of this four-part organization is a well-known four-line description about Itoya's daughters, taken from Masaru Nagano (1986:102).

(1.1)　大阪本町糸屋の娘。
(1.2)　姉は十六、妹は十五。
(1.3)　諸国大名は弓矢で殺す。
(1.4)　糸屋の娘は目で殺す。

*ki* (topic presentation)
　　　(1.1) Oosaka Motomachi Itoya no musume.
　　　(Daughters of Itoya [the thread shop] in the Motomachi of Osaka.)

*shoo* (topic development)
　　　(1.2) Ane wa juuroku, imooto wa juugo.
　　　(The elder daughter is sixteen, and the younger one is fifteen.)

*ten* (surprise turn)

> (1.3)  Shokoku daimyoo wa yumiya de korosu.
>
> (Feudal Lords kill [enemy] with bows and arrows.)

*ketsu* (conclusion)

> (1.4)  Itoya no musume wa me de korosu.
>
> (The daughters of Itoya "kill" [men] with their eyes.)

Note the pun on the word *korosu* "to kill," which is introduced in *ten*, a kind of a side track. Suddenly the story line switches to the feudal lords' "killing" at *ten*, which is re-connected to the girls "killing" (attracting) men with their eye gazes in *ketsu*.

Let us study another text, DS3, by paying attention to the discourse organizational parts, especially in terms of *ki-shoo-ten-ketsu*.

**DS3 (Ishimori et al. 1985b:38–39)**

1.  昔は書物の中から情報を取り出して保存したい時には、それを手で書き取ったものである。

2.  うっかりすると書き誤ることもあった。

3.  今は複写機が利用できるので、新聞、雑誌、書物などから、文字も図も誤りなく、しかも素早く写し取ることができる。

4.  ところで、旅をする時に感じることだが、車で駆け回ると、少ない時間で多くの場所に行けて便利だが、行った土地の様子があまり印象に残らない。

5.  これに対して、自分の足で歩くと、景色や人々の様子を身をもって感じ取ることができる。

6.  情報を集める場合も同じで、機械で複写するのは確かに便利だが、自分の手で書き取ったほうがよいことも多い。

7.  必要な情報がいつまでも記憶に残って、あとの利用に役立てることができる。

<u>Vocabulary</u>:

1.

| | | | |
|---|---|---|---|
| 昔 | むかし | n | ancient times, old days |
| 書物 | しょもつ | n | books |
| 情報 | じょうほう | n | information |
| 取り出す | とりだす | v | to take out |
| 保存する | ほぞんする | v | to keep, to preserve |
| 書き取る | かきとる | | to write down |

2.

| | | | |
|---|---|---|---|
| うっかりする | | v | to be careless, to be absent-minded |
| 書き誤る | かきあやまる | | to make mistakes in writing |

3.

| | | | |
|---|---|---|---|
| 複写機 | ふくしゃき | n | copier, copying machine |
| 利用する | りようする | v | to use, to make use of |
| 文字 | もじ | n | letter(s), character(s) |
| 図 | ず | n | drawing, chart |
| 誤り | あやまり | n | mistake, error |
| 素早く | すばやく | adv | quickly |
| 写し取る | うつしとる | | to copy down |

4.

| | | | |
|---|---|---|---|
| ところで | | conn | by the way |
| 駆け回る | かけまわる | v | to run around |
| 場所 | ばしょ | n | place, location |
| 便利 | べんり | adj | convenient |
| 土地 | とち | n | locality, place, region |
| 様子 | ようす | n | the state of affairs, circumstances |
| 印象 | いんしょう | n | impression |
| 残る | のこる | v | to stay, to remain |

5.

| | | | |
|---|---|---|---|
| これに対して | これにたいして | | in contrast to this, as opposed to this |
| 景色 | けしき | n | scenery |
| 人々 | ひとびと | n | people |
| 身をもって | みをもって | | firsthand, experientially, personally |
| 感じ取る | かんじとる | | to experience and to feel |

6.

| | | | |
|---|---|---|---|
| 機械 | きかい | n | machine |
| 複写する | ふくしゃする | v | to duplicate |
| 確かに | たしかに | adv | certainly |

7.

| | | | |
|---|---|---|---|
| 必要な | ひつような | adj | necessary |
| いつまでも | | adv | for a long time |
| 記憶 | きおく | n | memory |
| 利用 | りよう | n | utilization, use |
| 役立てる | やくだてる | v | to make use of |

For the purpose of understanding the internal organization of DS3, summary statements for each sentence are given below.

*Sentence-by-s3entence summary*

1. In olden times, copying information by hand was necessary.

2. Some mistakes were made.

3. Copying machines made it possible to make quick and accurate copies.

4. Traveling by car is convenient, but one has little impression of localities.

5. Walking makes it possible to enjoy the localities firsthand.

6. Although copying machines are convenient, copying by hand is sometimes better.

7. Information remains in one's memory longer and can be used later.

**The four-part organization of DS3**

| | |
|---|---|
| *ki* (topic presentation): | sentences 1 and 2 (inconvenient method of copying in olden times) |
| *shoo* (topic development): | sentence 3 (convenient and accurate copying made possible by copying machines) |
| *ten* (surprise turn): | sentences 4 and 5 (traveling by car is convenient, but leaves little impression; walking makes the traveling experience richer) |
| *ketsu* (conclusion): | sentences 6 and 7 (information copied by hand stays in one's memory longer and is therefore more useful) |

Two points are important regarding DS3. First, at the stage where *ten* appears, a topic shift (from "copying" to "traveling") occurs. This shift is likely to puzzle the reader. But a knowledge of the *ki-shoo-ten-ketsu* structure prepares the reader for this seemingly straying text. Second, the "point," or the central message of the discourse (that is, conclusion), appears at the very end. Only at the *ketsu* stage does the reader discover the reason for the discourse development observed up to that point. Given the conclusion, DS3 can in fact be interpreted as a criticism against the modern way of life (for example, lamenting excess technology as reflected by mindless copying and de-humanizing fast-paced automobile travel). All the preceding sentences function as tools for reaching this interpretive conclusion. Comprehending any text involves more than knowing the discourse structure, but knowing the *ki-shoo-ten-ketsu* structure may aid the reader who may be frustrated in the process of reaching the final *ketsu*.

Another text readily understandable in terms of *ki-shoo-ten-ketsu* is DS1.

| | |
|---|---|
| *ki* (topic presentation): | sentence 1 (people often mumble when worried) |
| *shoo* (topic development): | sentences 2 and 3 (why mumble?; can calm emotions a little) |
| *ten* (surprise turn): | sentences 4 and 5 (people kick stones when angry; such is a compensatory act) |
| *ketsu* (conclusion): | sentence 6 (compensatory acts represent human wisdom) |

Beyond the three-part organization of *joron* (sentences 1 and 2), *honron* (sentences 3, 4 and 5) and *ketsuron* (sentence 6), DS1 shows the *ki-shoo-ten-ketsu* organization. The surprise turn taken by sentences 4 and 5 makes DS1 an appropriate candidate for the four-part organization.

The organizations presented so far are not necessarily mutually exclusive. Depending on the text, one or more than one structural forces may be at work. In the case of DS2, neither the three-part organization nor the *ki-shoo-ten-ketsu* structure applies. It closely and exclusively follows the five-part organization.

Regardless of the organizational principle, Japanese writings (essays and expository writings in particular) present the conclusion toward the end. This exhibits a striking contrast with English deductive writing style. According to John Hinds (1990), English readers usually assume deductive discourse, and if that assumption fails, they will assume that the discourse follows an inductive process. Deductive writing presents its thesis statement (or, conclusion, opinion, and view) in the initial position whereas inductive writing makes the thesis statement in the final position. Hinds (1990) states that Japanese writing – specifically newspaper essay but with implication to other kinds of writings as well – is neither deductive or inductive; rather it is "quasi-inductive" (Hinds' term). In quasi-inductive discourse, (1) the presentation of the writer's purpose is delayed, (2) pieces of information contained in the writing are related loosely to a general topic, and (3) the concluding statement is not necessarily directly based on the preceding statements.

In some Japanese writings, the task of the writer is not necessarily to argue, convince and persuade the reader. Rather, the task is to stimulate the reader into contemplating an issue or issues that might not have been previously considered by providing a number of observations and perspectives. The reader is expected to draw his or her own conclusions based on the reading. Hinds (1990) notes that this reader-involving writing style is found in languages such as Chinese, Korean and Thai. I should also add that Finnish writing is also known to follow the non-deductive style (attributed to Tirkkonen-Condit and Liefländer-Koistinen [1989]).

In the light of the open-ended rhetorical style of the *ki-shoo-ten-ketsu* principle, and the quasi-inductive method, when reading Japanese, one should anticipate differences from how thoughts progress when reading

English discourse. Knowing what a Japanese text is likely and not likely to provide helps in one's overall comprehension of the text.

Additional information

The *ki-shoo-ten-ketsu* practice which places the conclusion at the very end of the discourse has become the target of increasing criticism from Japanese scholars, specialists and the public. Takeshi Shibata (1992) suggests that the contemporary information age necessitates placing the conclusion at the beginning. Especially in practical discourse (e.g., business documents, mass communication and academic theses), making the point clear at the beginning is strongly recommended. Lamenting that Japanese writings tend to be essay-like and often meander to no end, Shibata recommends a reordering of the original *ki-shoo-ten-ketsu* so that some writings follow *ketsu-ki-shoo-ten-ketsu*. Despite the lament, however, the *ki-shoo-ten-ketsu* style thrives, especially in brief essays and short stories.

## Entry 4 **Topic structure**

Topic, when we focus on its appearance with corresponding comment within a sentence, is called a sentence topic. In text, multiple sentence topics operate together and organize a hierarchical network of discourse topics. In a topical network, the main discourse topic operates as a pivotal point of reference, providing the starting point for related topics. Particular to Japanese is the availability of various overt topic markers, such as *wa, mo,* and, *to ieba,* which mark topical phrases. Although topics and topic markers do not always appear on the surface, when they appear they are useful for identifying discourse topics and sub-topics.

The reader should be warned that the concept of topic discussed here differs from the topic sentence often introduced in English rhetoric. The topic sentence summarizes the content to follow and often specifies the concluding main point. Presenting a topic in Japanese discourse merely identifies the items and issues the ensuing text discusses.

Topics are marked by a variety of expressions (e.g., particles, connectives, and adverbs) in Japanese, some of which are listed below.

(1)    明日の誕生日は友達を三人招待します。
(2)    かな子さんも来ますよ。
(3)    人間の感情とは何と複雑なものか。
(4)    男って案外感情的なものね。
(5)    海外旅行といえばやはりハワイ旅行が一番人気があり
       ますね。
(6)    明日の会議ですが、何時ごろ出ましょうか。
(7)    今度こそがんばろう。
(8)    僕だっていつか海外旅行に行く。
(9)    野球なんかつまらないよ。
(10)   その男、うわさどおりのプレーボーイなんだ。

(1) Asu no tanjoobi **wa** tomodachi o sannin shootaishimasu.
(On my birthday tomorrow, I am inviting three friends.)

(2) Kanakosan **mo** kimasu yo.
(Kanako is also coming.)

(3) Ningen no kanjoo **towa** nanto fukuzatsuna mono ka.
(Human emotions are such complex things!)

(4) Otoko **tte** angai kanjootekina mono ne.
(Men are surprisingly emotional, aren't they?)

(5) Kaigairyokoo **to ieba** yahari Hawai ryokoo ga ichiban ninki ga arimasu ne.
(Speaking of travel abroad, as expected, Hawaii is the most popular destination of all.)

(6) Ashita no kaigi desu **ga**, nanji goro demashoo ka?
(About tomorrow's meeting, what time shall we leave?)

(7) Kondo **koso** ganbaroo.
(This time, let's do our very best.)

(8) Boku **datte** itsuka kaigai ryokoo ni iku.
(Someday I will travel abroad!)

(9) Yakyuu **nanka** tsumaranai yo.
(Baseball is no fun at all!)

(10) [no topic marker; presentation of topic at the sentence-initial position, often followed by a comma, read with a pause]

Sono otoko, uwasa doori no pureebooi na n da.

(That guy, as the rumor has it, he plays around with women quite a bit.)

Topic phrases represent different grammatical categories; topics are grammatical subjects in (2), (3), (4), (8), (9), and (10); adverbial phrase in (1) and (7). (5) and (6) are examples where one uses topic markers specifically for introducing topics.

While topic markers above identify topical phrases within sentences, topics also function to provide cohesion in discourse. DS4, titled "Color and Human Life," is a kind of text useful for illustrating how discourse topics/sub-topics (often marked by *wa*) are hierarchically organized. In order to facilitate the discussion, a summary of each paragraph follows.

**DS4 (Hayashi 1987:5)**

色さいとくらし

A:

1.  にぎやかな町の通りを歩いているとき、わたしたちは、ふと店先に足を止めることがある。

2.  そこには、赤、青、黄、緑、さまざまないろどりの洋服、かばん、ぼうし、ハンカチなどが、きれいにならんでいる。

3.  その美しいいろどりを見ていると、楽しい気持ちになる。

4.  これらの色は、たいていは、人間が作って着色したものである。

B:

5.  むかしは、今のように自由に色を作り出すことができなかった。

6.  草のしるや鉱物をくだいたものなど、自然にあるものの色をそのまま利用して、ほかのものに着色していた。

7.  ところが、19世紀の半ばに、イギリスで、コールタールからむらさき色がつくられた。

8.  それ以来、色を合成することができるようになった。

9.  今では、何万色もの色が作り出せるようになっている。

C:

10.  色は色合いによって、人にあたえる感じがちがう。

11.  わたしたちは、それぞれの色の持つ感じをうまく利用して、色さいを生活の中に生かしている。

D:

12.  赤は、見る人を強くしげきし、真っ先に人の目につく色である。

13.  それで、郵便ポストや消防自動車、火災報知機などは赤くぬってあるし、交番や病院の入り口には、赤い色のランプがつけてある。

14.  町の交差点などに立っている信号機では、赤は「とまれ」を示す約束の色になっている。

E:

15.  青は、冷たく、すずしい感じがする色で、見る人の心に落ち着きをあたえる。

16.  それで、細かい仕事をするための事務づくえや作業台を、うす青くぬることがある。

17.  電車の運転室なども、全体がうす青くぬってあることが多い。

F:

18.  黄色は、明るく、広がっていくような感じをあたえる色で、ものをはっきりと目立たせる。

19.  それで、子どもたちの通学用のぼうしやかさなどに、黄色を用いることが多くなった。

G:

20.　色を組み合わせると、さまざまな効果を生み出すことができる。

21.　黄色のような明るい色と黒とが組み合わされると、はっきりと人目につくようになる。

22.　道路標識に黄色と黒とでかいたものがあるのは、そういう効果を利用しているのである。

23.　また、赤と緑、だいだいと青などの組み合わせは、おたがいに相手の色を強め合うので、あざやかに見える。

24.　緑の木立の中に赤い屋根があると、遠くからでもあざやかに見える。

H:

25.　色さいは、ひとびとにいろいろな感じをあたえ、生活に役立っている。

26.　色さいを上手に使って、わたしたちのくらしを、いっそう楽しく、豊かなものにしていきたいものである。

Vocabulary:

| 色さい | しきさい | n | color, hue |
| くらし | | n | living, life |

list of color terms:

| 赤 | あか | n | red |
| 青 | あお | n | blue |
| 黄 | き | n | yellow |
| 緑 | みどり | n | green |
| むらさき | | n | purple |
| 黒 | くろ | n | black |
| だいだい | | n | orange |

1.

| ふと | | adv | by chance, unintentionally |
|---|---|---|---|
| 店先 | みせさき | n | storefront |
| 足を止める | あしをとめる | | to stop by |

2.

| さまざまな | | adj | various, varied |
|---|---|---|---|
| いろどり | | n | (many) colors |
| ハンカチ | | n | handkerchief |
| ならぶ | | v | to form a line, to be neatly arranged |

4.

| 色 | いろ | n | color |
|---|---|---|---|
| たいてい | | adv | mostly |
| 着色する | ちゃくしょくする | v | to color, to dye |

5.

| 自由に | じゆうに | adv | freely, at will |
|---|---|---|---|
| 作り出す | つくりだす | v | to create, to produce |

6.

| 草 | くさ | n | grass, weed |
|---|---|---|---|
| しる | | n | juice, extract |
| 鉱物 | こうぶつ | n | mineral |
| くだく | | v | to break into pieces, to smash |
| 自然 | しぜん | n | nature |
| 利用する | りようする | v | to use, to make use of |

7.

| 19世紀の半ば | 19せいきのなかば | n | mid-nineteenth century |
|---|---|---|---|

| | | | |
|---|---|---|---|
| コールタール | | n | coal tar |

**8.**

| | | | |
|---|---|---|---|
| 合成する | ごうせいする | v | to synthesize, to compound |

**9.**

| | | | |
|---|---|---|---|
| 何万色 | なんまんしょく | | tens of thousands of colors |

**10.**

| | | | |
|---|---|---|---|
| 色合い | いろあい | n | hue, tint |
| あたえる | | v | to give |

**11.**

| | | | |
|---|---|---|---|
| 生かす | いかす | v | to make the best use of |

**12.**

| | | | |
|---|---|---|---|
| しげきする | | v | to excite, to stir up, to stimulate |
| 真っ先に | まっさきに | adv | at the very first, first of all |
| 目につく | めにつく | v | to attract one's attention |

**13.**

| | | | |
|---|---|---|---|
| 郵便ポスト | ゆうびんポスト | n | mailbox |
| 消防自動車 | しょうぼうじどうしゃ | n | fire engine |
| 火災報知機 | かさいほうちき | n | fire alarm |
| ぬる | | v | to paint |
| 交番 | こうばん | n | police box |
| ランプ | | n | lamp |

**14.**

| | | | |
|---|---|---|---|
| 交差点 | こうさてん | n | intersection |
| 信号機 | しんごうき | n | traffic light |

| とまる | | v | to stop |
| 示す | しめす | v | to show, to point out |
| 約束 | やくそく | n | rule, promise |

15.

| 心 | こころ | n | heart |
| 落ち着き | おちつき | n | calmness |

16.

| 事務づくえ | じむづくえ | n | (clerical) office desk |
| 作業台 | さぎょうだい | n | work table |
| うす青く | うすあおく | adv | in pale blue |

17.

| 運転室 | うんてんしつ | n | operator's control room |
| 全体 | ぜんたい | n | the whole, entirety |

18.

| はっきりと | | adv | clearly |

19.

| 通学用 | つうがくよう | | used for going to school |
| 用いる | もちいる | v | to use |

20.

| 組み合わせる | くみあわせる | v | to combine |
| 効果 | こうか | n | effect |

21.

| 人目につく | ひとめにつく | | to attract people's attention, to be noticeable |

22.

| 道路標識 | どうろひょうしき | n | road sign |
| 利用する | りようする | v | to utilize, to use |

23.

| おたがいに | | adv | each other |
| 相手 | あいて | n | partner, the other party |

| 強める | つよめる | v | to strengthen |
|---|---|---|---|
| あざやかに | | adv | brightly |
| 24. | | | |
| 木立 | こだち | n | (a cluster of) trees |
| 屋根 | やね | n | roof |
| 25. | | | |
| 役立つ | やくだつ | v | to be useful |
| 26. | | | |
| くらし | | n | living, life |
| いっそう | | adv | increasingly more, that much more |
| 豊かな | ゆたかな | adj | rich |

**Paragraph summary**

*Color and Human Life*

A: Various colors (red, blue, yellow, green) add to our lives; these colors are manufactured.

B: Historically, only natural colors were used; since the nineteenth century on, manufactured colors are used.

C: Colors give different feelings; we use the effects of colors in our lives.

D: Red is stimulating; used as critical signals in society (mailboxes, fire engines, fire alarms, as well as red lights for police boxes and hospitals, and so on).

E: Blue is calming (and soothing); used to paint conductors' rooms, for example.

F: Yellow is bright, attracts attention; used for children's hats and umbrellas.

G: Combining colors is effective; for example, yellow and black for traffic signs; other striking color combinations include red and green (red house among green trees), orange and blue.

H: Color is useful; we should make use of colors in order to enrich our lives.

One can identify the discourse topic structure of DS4 by tracing the *wa*-marked phrases, as shown in Figure 1.

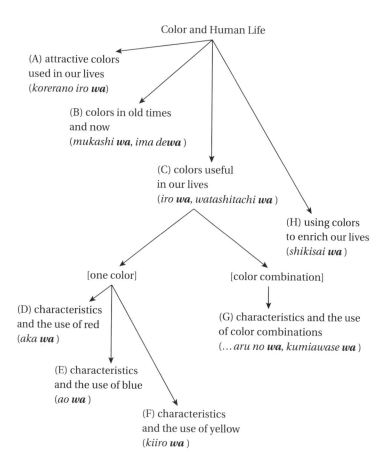

**Figure 1** Topic structure of DS4 based on *wa*-marked phrases. (Arrows indicate relationships among topics, leading from higher-level topics toward lower-level sub-topics.)

As shown in Figure 1, DS4's main (and highest level) topic is given in the title "Color and Human Life." By tracing phrases marked by topic markers and by arranging them in terms of how they relate to each other (i.e., which topic subsumes which), one can draw a topic hierarchy such as the one presented. Each paragraph is grouped around an identifiable topic, making it possible for us to understand the text as illustrated. DS4 contains, immediately below the top-level topic, four sub-topics (those represented in paragraphs A, B, C, and H). Paragraphs D, E, F, and G fall under the topic framework of C, while D, E, and F are constituents of the third-level topic (they refer to characteristics and the use of three separate colors), and another third-level topic presented by G (characteristics and the use of color combinations). Topic structures are useful for comprehending how different topics and related paragraphs are structured within discourse and consequently for reaching an accurate interpretation of the text.

Since DS4 exclusively uses the topic marker *wa*, let me present another discourse example (11), whose content is similar to DS4, but where different topic markers appear.

(11.1) 色さいは人々にいろいろな感じをあたえる。

(11.2) あたたかくやさしい感じのするものといえば、まずピンクがあげられる。

(11.3) オレンジ系の色もあたたかい感じをあたえる。

(11.4) 病院の中でうすいピンクやオレンジ色のまざったカーテンを見るだけでほっとすることもある。

(11.5) このように色さいは人間の生活にうるおいをあたえてくれるものである。

(11.1) Shikisai **wa** hitobito ni iroirona kanji o ataeru.
(Colors stir a variety of emotions in people.)

(11.2) Atatakaku yasashii kanji no suru mono **to ieba** mazu pinku ga agerareru.
(Speaking of those colors that stir warm and tender feelings, first we can mention pink.)

(11.3) Orenjikei no iro **mo** atatakai kanji o ataeru.
(Orange and related colors also give warm feelings.)

(11.4) Byooin no naka de usui pinku ya orenjiiro no mazatta kaaten o miru dake de hotto suru koto **mo** aru.
(There are some occasions when one feels relieved in the hospital just to see draperies in colors mixed with pale pink or orange.)

(11.5) Kono yooni shikisai **wa** ningen no seikatsu ni uruoi o ataetekureru mono dearu.
(In this manner, colors enrich human life.)

This example shows the use of topic markers *wa* in (11.1) and (11.5), *to ieba* in (11.2), and *mo* in (11.3) and (11.4).

Entry 5 **Organizational markers**

By organizational markers I mean particles, connectives, adverbs and idiomatic phrases which overtly specify discourse organization including the topic organization. There are at least five different kinds of organizational markers; (1) topic marking, (2) topic development, (3) topic shifting, (4) sequencing, and (5) general conclusion. Some examples of organizational markers follow.

(1)    鎌倉といえばやはり大仏が有名である。

(2)    ここで問題点をはっきりさせておきたいと思う。

(3)    いじめは確かに複雑な問題だ。そこで、次の点にしぼって考えてみよう。

(4)    それでは、皆様お体を大切に。また会える日を楽しみにしています。

(5)    さて、五月におたずねした大阪の学会の件ですが...

(6)    ところで、駅前にまた駐車場ができたそうだ。

(7)    まだいろいろ問題はあるが、それはさておき、会議の準備をすすめよう。

(8)    日本語を勉強するうえで大切なことはいくつもある。第一に、基本的な文法をしっかり学ぶこと。第二に、早い時期にひらがなやカタカナを学ぶことである。

(9)    まず、用語の定義からはじめよう。

(10)   次に、この新しい概念が日本でどのように理解されてきたかについて述べよう。

(11)   最後に、簡単に私の見解を述べる。

(12)   このレポートを書こうと思ったのには二つの理由がある。一つは事件の重要性があまり知られていないこと。もう一つは殺された田辺氏に対する追悼の念とでも言おうか。

(13)   この会社からは同じ車種のツードアとフォードアが輸出されている。前者はヨーロッパで、後者はアメリカでおもに販売されている。

(14)　勉強するつもりで大学に入る者は二割にも満たない。つ
　　　まり、学生が考えている大学生活とは、学問以外の経験
　　　をすることなのである。

*1. topic marking*

Topic markers include those introduced in Entry 4 – *wa, mo, towa, tte, to ieba,* the connective *ga, koso, datte,* and *nanka.* One example will suffice here.

*to ieba* (talking of, speaking of)

(1)  Kamakura **to ieba** yahari daibutsu ga yuumei dearu.

(Speaking of Kamakura, after all, the Great Buddha is famous.)

*2. topic development*

*kokode* (here, at this point)

(2)  **Kokode** mondaiten o hakkirisasete okitai to omou.

(At this point I would like to clarify the issues involved.)

*sokode* (so now)

(3)  Ijime wa tashikani fukuzatsuna mondai da. **Sokode**, tsugi no ten ni shibotte kangaete miyoo.

(Bullying is certainly a complex problem. So now, let us think by focusing on the following points.)

*soredewa* (then, well then)

(4)  **Soredewa**, minasama okarada o taisetsuni. Mata aeru hi o tanoshimi ni shiteimasu.

(Well then, everyone, take care of yourself. And I look forward to seeing you again.)

*3. topic shifting*

*sate* (now)

(5)  **Sate**, gogatsu ni otazuneshita Oosaka no gakkai no ken desu ga . . .

(Now, regarding the Osaka conference I asked you about in May . . . )

*tokorode* (by the way)

(6)  **Tokorode**, ekimae ni mata chuushajoo ga dekita sooda.

(By the way, I hear that another parking lot opened in front of the station.)

*sore wa sateoki* (putting it aside, in the meantime, aside from that)

(7)  Mada iroiro mondai wa aru ga, **sore wa sateoki**, kaigi no junbi o susumeyoo.

(There are many problems left, but putting those aside, let's get ready for the meeting.)

*4. sequencing*

*daiichini – dainini* (first-second)

(8) Nihongo o benkyoosuru ue de taisetsuna koto wa ikutsumo aru. **Daiichini**, kihontekina bunpoo o shikkari manabu koto. **Dainini**, hayai jiki ni hiragana ya katakana o manabu koto dearu.

(There are many important things related to studying Japanese. First, to learn the basic grammar. Second, to learn *hiragana* and *katakana* early on.)

*mazu* (first of all)

(9) **Mazu**, yoogo no teigi kara hajimeyoo.

(First of all, let me start with the definition of technical terms.)

*tsugini* (next)

(10) **Tsugini**, kono atarashii gainen ga nihon de donoyooni rikaisarete kita ka nitsuite nobeyoo.

(Next, let me state how this new concept has been interpreted in Japan.)

*saigoni* (lastly)

(11) **Saigoni**, kantanni watashi no kenkai o noberu.

(Lastly, I will state my personal view.)

*hitotsu wa – moo hitotsu wa* (for one thing – for another thing)

(12) Kono repooto o kakoo to omotta no ni wa futatsu no riyuu ga aru. **Hitotsu wa** jiken no juuyoosei ga amari shirareteinai koto. **Moo hitotsu wa** korosareta Tanabeshi ni taisuru tsuitoo no nen to demo ioo ka.

(There are two reasons why I thought I would write this report. For one thing, the significance of the case is not sufficiently known. For another, should I say it is a mourning for the murder victim, Mr. Tanabe.)

*zensha – koosha* (the former – the latter)

(13) Kono kaisha kara wa onaji shashu no tsuudoa to foodoa ga yushutsusareteiru. **Zensha** wa yooroppa de, **koosha** wa Amerika de omoni hanbaisareteiru.

(From this company the coupe and the sedan of the same model of cars are exported. The former is sold primarily in Europe, the latter in the United States.)

*5. general conclusion*

*tsumari* (in other words)

(14) Benkyoosuru tsumori de daigaku ni hairu mono wa niwari nimo mitanai. **Tsumari**, gakusei ga kangaeteiru daigakuseikatsu towa, gakumon igai no keiken o suru koto na no dearu.

(Those who enter universities for the purpose of studying are less than 20% [of the students]. In other words, the university life students imagine is experiencing things other than academics.)

The following text (similar in content to DS1) illustrates the use of these organizational markers in discourse.

(15.1) 私たちは心の中に心配事があるとついひとりごとを言う。

(15.2) ひとりごとを言うのにはどんな意味があるのだろう。

(15.3) ひとりごとは気持ちを落ち着かせてくれる。

(15.4) ところで、私たちは腹が立った時、石をけって心を鎮めることがある。

(15.5) まず腹が立った時は何かしたくなる。

(15.6) 次に何かすぐできることをさがして行動する。

(15.7) 例えば近くのものを投げたり、けったり、まわりの人にあたったりする。

(15.8) つまり、これらの行為は原因ではないものに怒りを向ける代償行為なのである。

(15.9) それによって気持ちを鎮めるのだ。

(15.10) 要するに、このような代償行為は人間に与えられた一つのストレス解消法とも言えるものなのである。

(15.1) Watashitachi **wa** kokoro no naka ni shinpaigoto ga aru to tsui hitorigoto o yuu.
(Worries inside our hearts make us inadvertently say [mumble] things to ourselves.)

(15.2) Hitorigoto o yuu no ni**wa** donna imi ga aru no daroo.
(What does it mean to mumble to ourselves?)

(15.3) Hitorigoto **wa** kimochi o ochitsukasete kureru.
(Mumbling to ourselves calms our emotions.)

(15.4) **Tokorode**, watashitachi **wa** hara ga tatta toki, ishi o kette kokoro o shizumeru koto ga aru.
(By the way, when angry, we sometimes kick at stones and calm our emotions.)

(15.5) **Mazu** hara ga tatta toki **wa** nanika shitaku naru.
(First, when angry, we want to take some action.)

(15.6) **Tsugini** nanika sugu dekiru koto o sagashite koodoosuru.
(Next, we choose something we can do immediately and behave accordingly.)

(15.7) **Tatoeba** chikaku no mono o nagetari, kettari, mawari no hito ni attattari suru.
(For example, we may throw things nearby, kick objects, or lash out at people nearby.)

(15.8) **Tsumari**, korera no kooi **wa** gen'in dewanai mono ni ikari o mukeru daishookooi na no dearu.
(In other words, these are compensatory acts which target one's anger toward things other than the direct cause.)

(15.9) Sore ni yotte kimochi o shizumeru no da.
(By doing so, we calm our emotions.)

(15.10) **Yoosuruni**, kono yoona daishookooi **wa** ningen ni ataerareta hitotsu no sutoresu kaishoohoo tomo ieru mono na no dearu.
(In short, such compensatory acts can be said to be a way of releasing stress.)

When reading real-life texts, it is useful to be on the lookout for organizational markers. These markers are cues for understanding (1) what topic-organizational role a particular sentence plays in the overall discourse structure, and (2) how the writer sequentially organizes his or her flow of information and thoughts.

## Entry 6  *Bunmyaku* – threads of discourse

The term *bunmyaku* "thread(s) of discourse" is used in a somewhat general sense in Japanese *bunshooron* "studies of discourse." It refers to an idea that discourse is connected in terms of identifiable processes or stages of linear progression. Depending on text genres, *bunmyaku* may be specifically called plot (in narratives) or logical sequences (in academic theses). In Japanese, we recognize three different kinds of *bunmyaku* – (1) situational, (2) psychological, and (3) logical.

The situational thread involves the consistency and the sequential chaining of situations, in terms of both time and space, which the writer describes or in which the discourse is situated. One finds the situational thread in many genres. For example, an important situational thread in a narrative is the chronologically connected time sequence where events happen following the chronologically sequenced narrative framework. Another type of situational thread within a narrative may be based on the location where various incidents take place. There is much commonality across languages in the narrative threads in terms of time and space.

Now, the location in the broad *bunmyaku* context may be where the verbal interaction occurs or the situation where relevant events happen. The place may also be abstract, for example, an imaginary place (a framework) within which one makes a logical judgment or argumentation as in academic theses. There is more variability in this kind of *bunmyaku* across languages.

The psychological thread also applies to a variety of sequential connections found in many discourse genres. It includes such things as psychological and emotional positions that the writer takes toward what he or she describes (including the so-called perspective and point of view in literary theories) as well as how the writer's and characters' feelings sustain themselves through many transitions and developments. (More about this in Entry 9 which discusses the narrative point of view.)

Logical threads are of several types which can be further combined. They are similar to Western logical progressions and play a critical role in academic theses and articles. Following Takaaki Nagao's (1992:30) work, we identify several variations of the progression of logical arguments as listed below.

---

**Logical threads in Japanese discourse**

1. problem → reference/data leading to evidence → conclusion
2. proposed opinion → evidence based on reference/data → confirmation of proposed opinion
3. concrete examples → problem statement →supplementary evidence based on reference/data → conclusion
4. definition/explanation → concrete examples → further consideration → opinion/claim
5. problem statement → reference/data leading to evidence → hypotheses → supplementary reference/data leading to evidence → conclusion
6. concrete examples → problem statement → speculation/hypothesis → supplementary reference/data leading to evidence → conclusion

These types of linear progression are similar to English logical progressions, especially in academic theses including (1) problem statement → hypothesis → testing → results → discussion/conclusion, and (2) problem statement → evidence → solution/claim.

In reality, a piece of discourse can be read in terms of a multiple and mixed progression of threads. Beyond the three types of threads mentioned above, we should note a particular way Japanese discourse marks information associated with threads of discourse. Topic markers identify two types of sequential connections in Japanese – the agent topic and the non-agent topic threads of discourse. Due to the distinct topic-marking system in Japanese, the writer can overtly maintain the sequential relationship in terms of agent, which often coincides with topic, as well as in terms of non-agent topic. In other words, the thread may be based on the topic consistency of the agent involved (who does what) as well as of the topic continuity of what is being talked about. This is true in English as well, but in Japanese, partly due to the availability of the overt topic marking system, the non-agent topic thread of discourse is prominently displayed.

The agent topic versus non-agent topic thread is illustrated by segments (1.1) to (1.4), and (2.1) to (2.4), respectively.

(1.1)　私の同僚はうそをつくことがある。

(1.2)　しかも(彼は)重大なことに関してうそをつく。

(1.3)　(彼は)別に悪いことだとは思っていないらしい。

(1.4)　(彼は)うそをつくことについて反省もしないし後悔もしない。

(2.1)　私は時々うそをつくことがある。

(2.2)　うそをつくなどということはまっとうな人間がするべきことではない。

(2.3)　だからなるべく（そういうことは）さけるようにしている。

(2.4)　しかし、うそをつくことは時と場所によってはものごとをまるくおさめる手段でもある。

(1.1) **Watashi no dooryoo wa** uso o tsuku koto ga aru.
(My colleague sometimes tells lies.)

(1.2) Shikamo (**kare wa**) juudaina koto ni kanshite uso o tsuku.
(Moreover, he lies about important things.)

(1.3) (**Kare wa**) betsuni warui koto da towa omotteinai rashii.
(It seems that he doesn't think it is particularly a bad thing to do.)

(1.4) (**Kare wa**) uso o tsuku koto nitsuite hansei mo shinaishi kookai mo shinai.
(He neither reflects on nor regrets telling lies.)

(2.1) **Watashi wa** tokidoki uso o tsuku koto ga aru.
(I sometimes tell lies.)

(2.2) **Uso o tsuku nado to yuu koto wa** mattoona ningen ga surubeki koto dewanai.
(Telling lies is not something that a moral person should do.)

(2.3) Dakara narubeku (**sooyuu koto wa**) sakeru yooni shiteiru.
(So as much as I can I try to avoid it.)

(2.4) Shikashi, **uso o tsuku koto wa** toki to basho ni yotte wa monogoto o maruku osameru shudan demo aru.
(However, depending on the time and place, telling lies offers a means for avoiding conflict.)

In (1) the agent or the person telling lies is the topic and maintains the thread. In (2) the non-agent topic of telling lies is the thread-carrying element and is marked by a topic marker.

Given an understanding of threads of discourse, let us examine the multiplicity of *bunmyaku* in DS4, "Color and Human Life." The logical *bunmyaku* of DS4 can be characterized as a modification of the second type, as shown below.

introduction:
      introductory: A (attractive colors used in our lives)
      background: B (colors in old times and now)
      ↓

proposed opinion
        main: C (colors useful in our lives)
        ↓
evidence, concrete examples:
        example: D (characteristics and the use of red)
        example: E (characteristics and the use of blue)
        example: F (characteristics and the use of yellow)
        supplementary: G (characteristics and the use of color combinations)
        ↓
conclusion, confirmation of opinion:
        conclusion: H (using colors to enrich our lives)

One also understands DS4 in terms of the situational thread by using the concept of space as follows. Paragraph A relates to the specific concrete place of "city," while B moves to an in-memory historical location in the mind. Paragraphs C through G are located in a conceptual and topical region that centers on "color" and related issues. The final paragraph then leads us back to a more concrete place, the all-encompassing human life. One may also identify, although less prominent, a psychological thread that runs through the discourse. Paragraphs A, C, and H represent the writer's personal view, opinion, or thought, while the other paragraphs represent observation and description, being psychologically more distant than the former.

Depending on the genre, different threads serve more or less critical paths to the creation of coherent and cohesive text. A travel diary, for example, may be organized around the actual locations or the time sequence (developing along the situational thread) while a psychological novel is likely to be developed along the psychological states of the characters.

I should make it clear at this point that the ease or difficulty of identifying *bunmyaku* depends on the text. Since this book contains several examples of relatively clear *bunmyaku*, let me cite one example of *bunmyaku* that is rather unclear. The text presented in (3) consists of sentence summaries of a newspaper column called *Mado* "Window" from *Asahi Shimbun*. The column's title is *Horaa* "Horror" and contains ten paragraphs and seventeen sentences.

A:

(3.1) Who writes the scariest story?

(3.2) Such a contest was held in the year 1816.

(3.3) The poet (George G. N.) Byron started the contest; (Percy B.) Shelley and his wife, among others, participated.

B:

(3.4) As a result of this contest, Mrs. Shelley's "Frankenstein's Monster" was born.

(3.5) This, it can be said, is the origin of the modern horror stories.

C:

(3.6) I recently took a look at Japanese horror stories.

(3.7) "Parasite Eve," "Ring" and "Spirals."

D:

(3.8) All involve the leading edge of science and beyond.

(3.9) The world of the supernatural was also included.

E:

(3.10) Modern horror stories feature genetics, viruses, and micro-organs.

F:

(3.11) Mrs. Shelley's horror story also dealt with life.

(3.12) Tragedy resulted from the young scientist who conquered the mystery of life.

G:

(3.13) The scientist ended up creating an unbearably ugly creature.

H:

(3.14) In the twentieth century, Mrs. Shelley's creation began to walk with those recognizably awkward steps.

I:

(3.15) Micro-monsters of today lurk in the human body and wait for the opportune time to strike.

(3.16) Horror no longer depends on sight; rather one perceives horror through some tactile sensation.

J:

(3.17) Today's horror originates in the shapelessness of the menace.

*based on* Horaa, *Asahi Shimbun, Oct. 22, 1995, p. 3*

Although one can appreciate this newspaper column, the *bunmyaku* is a bit obscure. For example, the writer does not present a logical progression nor a psychological thread. The *bunmyaku* development seems to meander. Paragraphs A, B and C follow *ki-shoo-ten*, and paragraphs D and E suggest the conclusion. Paragraph F repeats *shoo*. Paragraphs F and G add to the content of paragraph B. Paragraph H adds an additional perspective to B. I and J, i.e., *ketsu*, offer a mild concluding information. The topic of the column provides cohesion, but sub-topics are varied and lack a clear organizational structure. This becomes evident when compared with DS4, for example. When faced with a text lacking in a clear sense of organizational thread, looking toward the end of the column for a general conclusive point is useful; one can use this information when working backward through the text.

One must be aware that not all writings have specific points to make. Some articles are written for the general purpose of sharing information, as this column turns out to be. The column title *Mado* "Window" suggests an open forum where different kinds of text may appear. The reader does not expect to receive the writer's explicit views; rather, the enjoyment of reading comes from learning more, or having one's own knowledge or thought confirmed. Some texts may not even provide new information. It may be a poetic essay offering an occasion where readers appreciate empathetic emotional experience. One also finds similar cases in English, but in Japanese the genre distinction is often blurred, and writing may easily become something related to an essay, an exposition or an opinion piece.

### Additional information

In contemporary Japanese language education, partly to meet society's demand for clearer and explicit presentation of thoughts, logical sequences are emphasized. For example, in a high school textbook (Ishimori *et al.* 1985a:121–122), the structure of *ronsetsubun* (editorials, opinion pieces) is specified as the following. Here the use of examples for analogical purposes is the key.

> *joron* (introductory remarks): presentation of the issues raised, examination of past approaches
>
> ↓
>
> *jirei no teiji* (examples): presentation of examples used for developing the writer's opinion, pointing out mistakes of others (e.g., wrong examples)
>
> ↓
>
> *ronri no teiji* (cohesiveness, logical explanation): statement of new discovery, rules and theory based on the new evidence
>
> ↓
>
> *ketsuron* (concluding remarks): statement as to how the new discovery changes the old view and how the new view increases and deepens one's understanding of things

These four elements can be incorporated into the three-part organization we studied earlier: (1) *joron*, (2) *honron* which includes *jirei no teiji* and *ronri no teiji*, and (3) *ketsuron*. In a broad sense these four categories also match the *ki-shoo-ten-ketsu* construction as well. Ishimori *et al.* (1985a: 123) contains an example of such text, a piece taken from a series of writings by Torahiko Terada titled *Hahen* "Fragments." The *bunmyaku* of the example piece goes as follows:

(1) (*joron*) There are richly decorated cabins in today's cruise ships.

(2) (*jirei no teiji*) One thing missing in these cabins is the window. Windowless rooms, like prisons, cannot even come close to humble rooms with an open view.

(3) (*ronri no teiji*) Once we are on cruise ships, airplanes, and trains, we are deprived of the freedom to get off wherever we want, but as long as we can see outside, we can identify our relationship to the world. When spending a night in windowless rooms we have no means to locate ourselves except to depend on our memory.

(4) (*ketsuron*) Thinking this, we must open as many "windows of the heart" as possible and open them as widely as possible.

The use of examples in (2) and (3) offers a logical basis that leads, through analogy, to the conclusion.

## Entry 7 **Connectives**

Connectives (conjunctions and connective phrases) are primary devices for overtly marking coherence in discourse. What follows is an example text in which connectives appear.

**Text using connectives: (content similar to DS3)**

(1.1)　昔は書物から情報を得たい時にはそれを手で書き取ったものである。

(1.2)　そのため、うっかりすると書き誤ることもあった。

(1.3)　しかし、今はコピー機が利用できる。

(1.4)　だから誤りなく写し取ることができる。

(1.5)　しかも、素早く、何枚でもコピーすることができる。

(1.6)　一方、簡単にコピーできることがマイナスになる面もある。

(1.7)　コピーが余りに簡単なのだ。

(1.8)　従って、内容を忘れてしまいがちになるのである。

(1.1) Mukashi wa shomotsu kara joohoo o etai toki niwa sore o te de kakitotta mono dearu.
(In the old days when they wanted to gather information from books, they used to copy it down by hand.)

(1.2) **Sono tame**, ukkarisuru to kakiayamaru koto mo atta.
(Because of this, they sometimes made mistakes in their copying.)

(1.3) **Shikashi**, ima wa kopiiki ga riyoo dekiru.
(But today we can use copying machines.)

(1.4) **Dakara** ayamarinaku utsushitoru koto ga dekiru.
(Therefore we can copy down things without mistakes.)

(1.5) **Shikamo**, subayaku, nanmai demo kopiisuru koto ga dekiru.
(In addition, we can copy quickly and produce multiple copies.)

(1.6) **Ippoo**, kantanni kopii dekiru koto ga mainasu ni naru men mo aru.
(On the other hand, being able to copy easily has some negative aspects.)

(1.7) Kopii ga amarini kantanna no da.
(Copying is too easy.)

(1.8) **Shitagatte**, naiyoo o wasurete shimaigachini naru no dearu.
(Accordingly, we tend to forget the content.)

The text above represents an extreme case, created simply to illustrate how connectives may be used. In the real text, connectives appear more sparingly. Too many connectives give an impression of being redundant. DS3, taken from an authentic source and similar to (1) in content, contains only two connecting phrases, the connective *kore ni taishite* (in sentence 5) and the organizational marker *tokorode* (in sentence 4). The reader may notice expressions connecting clauses within a sentence. These include: *node* in sentence 3, *ga* in sentences 4 and 6, and the *te*-form of the verb in sentence 7.

Although connectives appear in the discourse context where cohesive relationships are recognized, these relationships are often socioculturally and psychologically determined. For example, depending on the kind of social norm one assumes, different or even opposite connectives may appear.

(2.1) その時 5 時半。

(2.2) 退社時間から 15 分すぎたところだった。

(2.3) しかし（そのため）そこには誰も残っていなかった。

(2.1) Sono toki goji han.
(It was five-thirty.)

(2.2) Taisha jikan kara juugofun sugita tokoro datta.
(It was fifteen minutes past the quitting time.)

(2.3) **Shikashi** (or, **Sono tame**) soko niwa daremo nokotteinakatta.
(But [or, therefore] nobody was there.)

If one expects, based on what usually happens in a particular situation and society, that everyone should leave immediately after five-fifteen, then *sono tame* is appropriate; if one expects (again following the situational and social norm) that workers usually stay after five-fifteen, then *shikashi* would be more appropriate.

Connectives also add much more to discourse than merely marking the cause–result relationship. For example, compare the following sentences with sentences 1 and 2 of the text presented earlier in (1).

(3.1)　昔は書物から情報を得たい時にはそれを手で書き取ったものである。
(3.2)　しかし、うっかりすると書き誤ることもあった。
(3.3)　しかし、書き誤ることは余りなかった。

(3.1) Mukashi wa shomotsu kara joohoo o etai toki niwa sore o te de kakitotta mono dearu.
(In the old days when they wanted to gather information from books, they used to copy it down by hand.)

(3.2) **Shikashi**, ukkari suru to kakiayamaru koto mo atta.
(However, they sometimes made mistakes in their copying.)

(3.3) **Shikashi**, kaki ayamaru koto wa amari nakatta.
(However, they rarely made mistakes in their copying.)

The connection between (3.1) and (3.2) differs from that shown in (1); here a but-connection is used instead of an and-connection. Additionally, note that although (3.2) and (3.3) both start with the but-connective *shikashi*, opposite positions are taken in the consequent statements. Depending on what the writer expects, the writer's use of connectives differs. Put differently, the reader understands the expectation of the writer through the use of connectives. Here we find cases where the functions of connectives differ due to (1) different assumptions the writer has about relevant situation and society, and (2) whether or not the writer's expectation is met (that is "and") or not (that is "but").

If there were no connectives, the reader would have to interpret the relationship between the two sentences in whatever possible way the textual context suggests. Connectives appear in texts, to signal different personal expectations and assumptions the writer has toward the events described. In other words, the relationship between two sentences that connectives connect involves a logical relation and socio-cultural information as well as the writer's attitude toward events.

I should also add that in spoken Japanese, speakers use connectives not so much for the purpose of cohesive connection as for characterizing the speech itself. For example, *shikashi* can be used in conversation as a speech prefacing device (as in *Shikashi atsui nee, kyoo wa.* "But, it's so hot today, isn't it?"). Just as in English one may use the connective *so* in "So, what's up?" we must be aware that this use is sometimes carried over into written discourse.

Another frequently used connective *dakara* also functions similarly in varied ways in conversation. *Dakara* is used not only to connect cause and result but also (1) to add explanation relevant to what was previously mentioned and (2) to mark the end of the speaker's turn in conversation. As I reported elsewhere (Maynard 1993), in conversational discourse, *dakara* used for explanation is fairly frequent (36.62%) in contrast with the cause–result *dakara* (57.75%). *Dakara* used to mark the end of the speaker turn occurs less frequently, 5.63% of the time.

A related issue the reader may be interested in is the frequency – how frequently are connectives used in Japanese? Suzuko Nishihara (1990) found, after comparing thirty articles of identical content appearing in *Newsweek* magazine in Japanese and in English, that Japanese texts use connectives slightly more frequently (once in 5.82 Japanese sentences compared with once in 7.69 English sentences). Although one often finds deletion in Japanese text, connectives, especially those which confirm the sequential connection in discourse (rather than those that clarify causal and conditional relationships), seem to appear more frequently than in English.

Japanese connectives have been categorized in many, and slightly different, ways. For example, Masaru Nagano (1986) lists the following manners in which sentences are connected in discourse.

*1. expansion*

The second sentence is an expansion, for example a more detailed description of the first. (Clue words include connectives such as *sorede* and *dakara*.)

*2. opposition*

The second sentence expresses an opposing view toward the first. (Clue words include connectives *ga, shikashi* and *tokoroga*.)

*3. addition*

A related statement is added to the first sentence. (This is achieved by the verb -*te* form and other connectives, such as *de, soshite* and *sono ue*.)

*4. apposition*

The first and the second sentence both describe the identical item. (This is marked by connectives such as *tsumari* and *tatoeba*.)

*5. supplement*

The second sentence is a supplement to the first. (*N(o) da* and *wake da* sentences provide explanation / cause for the first sentence.)

*6. contrast*

The second sentence represents a view or meaning contrasting with the first. (The contrastive use of *wa* and particles expressing alternation such as *ka, matawa* are used.)

*7. diversion*

The second sentence diverts from the first. (Sentential adverbs and connectives including *tsugini* and *tokorode* are used.)

English connectives are often divided into four categories: additive (e.g., and, or, nor, furthermore, incidentally), adversative (e.g., but, yet, however, on the other hand), causal (e.g., so, therefore, because, for, as a result), temporal (e.g., then, next, at first, finally, at this moment). Following this system I list some of the frequently used connectives in Japanese. Refer to additional connectives functioning as organizational markers we studied in Entry 5.

(4)    デパートでいろいろ買い物をした。そして六階のティー ルームでコーヒーも飲んだ。

(5)    忙しい。それにお金もない。とても海外旅行に行ける状 態ではないのだ。

(6)    映画につれていってもらった。そのうえ中華料理もごち そうになった。

(7)    彼はすぐれた医者である。また小説家としても有名であ る。

(8)　この戸は風で開いたのだろうか。または誰かが開けたのだろうか。

(9)　その器具はそこにあると思ったのだが。あるいは実験室に置いてきたのかもしれない。

(10)　友達はなかなか来ない。電車が遅れたのだろうか。それとも電車に乗り遅れたのだろうか。

(11)　日本料理といわれるものはいろいろあります。例えば、すし、すきやき、てんぷらなどです。

(12)　あの国会議員は政治家にしてはめずらしく正直だと言われる。反対に、正直というより、正直に見せかけているだけだという意見もある。

(13)　この仕事は男性にも女性にも向いている。しかし誰でもいいというわけではない。

(14)　金がないから楽しくないという考えの人が多い。だが金がなくても人生を楽しむ方法はいろいろある。

(15)　会えるかもしれないと思って行ってみました。けれどもやはり先生はいらっしゃいませんでした。

(16)　まだ5月です。でも今日は真夏のような日ざしです。

(17)　あした試験がある。だから今夜のパーティーには行かない。

(18)　土曜日も日曜日も休まず働いた。その結果、家族で始めた小さな会社が10年で従業員150人の会社となった。

(19)　朝刊を読んだ。それから食事をして会社へ行った。

## 1. additive

*soshite* (and)

(4) Depaato de iroiro kaimono o shita. **Soshite** rokkai no tiiruumu de koohii mo nonda.

(We did a lot of shopping at the department store. And [we] had coffee at a coffee shop on the sixth floor.)

*soreni* (added to that – often used for providing additional reason or cause for the consequent statement)

(5) Isogashii. **Soreni** okane mo nai. Totemo kaigai ryokoo ni ikeru jootai dewanai no da.

([I]'m busy. Added to that, I have no money. I'm no way in a situation where I can afford to travel abroad.)

*sono ue* (on top of that, in addition to that, moreover – implies that the additional incident or state exceeds normal expectation)

(6)  Eiga ni tsurete itte moratta. **Sono ue** chuuka ryoori mo gochisoo ni natta.

([He kindly] took me to the movies. Moreover, [he kindly] treated me to a Chinese dinner.)

*mata* (also)

(7)  Kare wa sugureta isha dearu. **Mata** shoosetsuka to shitemo yuumei dearu.

(He is an excellent doctor. Also, he is famous as a novelist.)

*matawa* (or)

(8)  Kono to wa kaze de aita no daroo ka. **Matawa** dareka ga aketa no daroo ka.

(I wonder if this door was opened by the wind. Or, I wonder if someone opened it.)

*aruiwa* (or, either or, whether this or that)

(9)  Sono kigu wa soko ni aru to omotta no da ga. **Aruiwa** jikkenshitsu ni oite kita no kamoshirenai.

(I thought that instrument was there, but . . . Or, perhaps I've left it in the lab.)

*soretomo* (or, or else)

(10)  Tomodachi wa nakanaka konai. Densha ga okureta no daroo ka. **Soretomo**, densha ni nori okureta no daroo ka.

(My friend is late. I wonder if the train was delayed. Or, did she miss the train?)

*tatoeba* (for example, for instance)

(11)  Nihonryoori to iwareru mono wa iroiro arimasu. **Tatoeba**, sushi, sukiyaki, tenpura nado desu.

(There are a variety of dishes that are called Japanese cuisine. For example, *sushi, sukiyaki, tempura*, and so on.)

*hantaini* (opposing [this])

(12)  Ano kokkai giin wa seijika ni shitewa mezurashiku shoojiki da to iwareru. **Hantaini**, shoojiki to yuu yori, shoojiki ni misekaketeiru dake da to yuu iken mo aru.

(That Diet member is said to be unusually honest as a politician. Opposing this, there is an opinion that he is simply pretending to be honest rather than being truly honest.)

## 2. *adversative*

*shikashi* (however, still)

(13)  Kono shigoto wa dansei ni mo josei ni mo muiteiru. **Shikashi** dare demo ii to yuu wake dewanai.

(This work is appropriate for both males and females. However, it is not the case that anyone can do it.)

*daga* (yet, however)

(14)  Kane ga nai kara tanoshikunai to yuu kangae no hito ga ooi. **Daga**, kane ga nakutemo jinsei o tanoshimu hoohoo wa iroiro aru.

(Many people think that life is no fun because they don't have money. Yet, there are many ways to enjoy life without money.)

*keredomo* (but)

(15)  Aeru kamoshirenai to omotte itte mimashita. **Keredomo** yahari sensei wa irrasshaimasendeshita.

(I went there thinking that I might be able to see (him/her). But, as expected, the teacher wasn't there.)

*demo* (even so, still)

(16)  Mada gogatsu desu. **Demo** kyoo wa manatsu no yoona hizashi desu.

(It's still May. Even so, today the sunlight is just like that of mid-summer.)

*3. causal*

*dakara* (because of that, so, therefore)

(17)  Ashita shiken ga aru. **Dakara** kon'ya no paatii ni wa ikanai.

(Tomorrow I have an exam. Because of that I'm not going to a party tonight.)

*sono kekka* (as a result)

(18)  Doyoobi mo nichiyoobi mo yasumazu hataraita. **Sono kekka**, kazoku de hajimeta chiisana kaisha ga juunen de juugyooin hyakugojuu-nin no kaisha to natta.

([He] worked Saturdays and Sundays without a break. As a result, a small company started with family members became a company with 150 employees in 10 years.)

*4. temporal*

*sorekara* (and, and then)

(19)  Chookan o yonda. **Sorekara** shokuji o shite kaisha e itta.

([I] read the morning newspaper. And then [I] had breakfast and left for the company.)

## Entry 8  **Narrative structure**

This entry concentrates on narratives, which include *mukashi banashi* "old tales," *minwa* "folktales," fairy tales, short stories, and the general genre of fiction. Two issues related to the narrative discourse are discussed; its internal structure in this entry, and the narrator's and character's point of view in the next entry.

All narratives contain a beginning, a middle and an end in multiple combinations. In general we identify the following essential elements in the narrative.

---

**Structural elements of narrative**
1. Setting (place, time, characters)
2. Episode (events, happenings, problems/conflicts leading to resolution)
3. Ending remarks

---

Often the narrative initial sentence contains information that defines the setting. A typical example from old tales and folktales goes something like:

(1)  Mukashi mukashi aru tokoro ni ojiisan to obaasan ga sundeimashita.
(Once upon a time, in a [faraway] place, there lived an old man and an old woman.)

In (1), the reader is told of the story's time, place and main characters.

Let us study DS5, the first few paragraphs of the first chapter, "Noisy Departure," in Jiroo Akagawa's mystery novel titled *Kumo ni Kieta Akuma* "The Devil that Disappeared into the Clouds."

**DS5 (Akagawa 1995:7–10)**

にぎやかな出発

A:
1.　　バスの中は、至ってにぎやかだった。
B:
2.　　まあ、ありがちなことではある。
3.　　これから修学旅行へ出かける、なんてときには、往きのバスの中は、一種の興奮状態に包まれるのが普通である。

C:
4.    「——ちょっと！静かにしてよ」
5.    と、矢吹由利子が怒鳴った。
6.    「眠れないじゃないの」

D:
7.    「こんな所で眠ろうって方が無理」
8.    と言ったのは、バスで隣の席に座っている親友
      の桑田旭子。

E:
9.    「眠いのよ」

F:
10.    いつもなら、由利子だって、一緒になってはし
       ゃぐのである。
11.    しかし——まあいい。
12.    夜ふかしの事情は色々ある。

G:
13.    といって、由利子の場合は、恋人と二人で過ご
       したからではないことは確かだった。
14.    17歳で、もちろん年齢相応に女っぽくなってい
       る（つもり）とはいえ、まだまだ、色気より食
       い気の由利子。
15.    いや、その点では、隣の旭子も同じことだ。

H:
16.    バスは、ひたすら走り続けている。
17     羽田空港へと向かって。
・・・

I:
18.    ——さて、と改まるほどのこともないが、バス
       に乗っているのは、私立花園学園の女子高校二
       年生。

J:

19.  これから、＜スキー学校＞へでかけるところで
     ある。

・・・

K:

20.  この辺で「あれ？」と思われる読者もおられる
     かもしれない。

L:

21.  矢吹由利子、桑田旭子に加えて、もう一人、甚
     だユニークな仲間、弘野香子がいるんじゃない
     の、と。

Vocabulary:

| | | | |
|---|---|---|---|
| にぎやかな | | adj | noisy (with chatter) |
| 出発 | しゅっぱつ | n | departure |

1.

| | | | |
|---|---|---|---|
| 至って | いたって | adv | very much, exceedingly |

2.

| | | | |
|---|---|---|---|
| ありがちな | | adj | likely |

3.

| | | | |
|---|---|---|---|
| 修学旅行 | しゅうがくりょこう | n | school excursion |
| 往き | いき | n | on the way to |
| 一種の | いっしゅの | | a kind of |
| 興奮状態 | こうふんじょうたい | n | excited state |
| 包む | つつむ | v | to wrap, to surround |
| 普通 | ふつう | n | ordinary |

5.

| | | | |
|---|---|---|---|
| 怒鳴る | どなる | v | to shout, |

6.

| | | | |
|---|---|---|---|
| 眠る | ねむる | v | to sleep |

7.

| 無理 | むり | adj | impossible |

8.

| 座る | すわる | v | to sit down, to be seated |
| 親友 | しんゆう | n | best friend |

9.

| 眠い | ねむい | adj | sleepy |

10.

| はしゃぐ | | v | to make a racket |

12.

| 夜ふかし | よふかし | n | staying up late |
| 事情 | じじょう | n | circumstances, reasons |

13.

| といって | | conn | however, but |
| 恋人 | こいびと | n | boyfriend, girlfriend, lover |
| 確か | たしか | adj | certain, sure |

14.

| 年齢相応に | ねんれいそうおうに | | as expected for one's age |
| 女っぽい | おんなっぽい | adj | feminine |
| 色気 | いろけ | n | desire/appetite for love affair |
| 食い気 | くいけ | n | desire/appetite for food |

16.

| ひたすら | | adv | steadily, continuously |

17.

| 羽田空港 | はねだくうこう | prop | Haneda Airport |
| 向かう | むかう | v | to head toward |

18.

| さて | | conn | well now |
| 改まる | あらたまる | v | to be formal |
| 私立 | しりつ | n | privately owned/financed |

| 花園学園 | はなぞのがくえん | | [name of high school] |
| 女子高校 | じょしこうこう | n | girls' high school |
| 19. | | | |
| スキー学校 | スキーがっこう | n | ski camp, ski school |
| 20. | | | |
| この辺で | このへんで | | at this point |
| 読者 | どくしゃ | n | reader |
| おられる | | v | [honorific form of *iru*], to be |
| 21. | | | |
| 加える | くわえる | v | to add |
| 甚だ | はなはだ | adv | considerably, quite |
| ユニークな | | adj | unique, unusual |
| 仲間 | なかま | n | member (of a clique) |

**Translation**

A:

1. Inside the bus it was very noisy.

B:

2. Well, that is something often expected.

3. They are going on a school excursion; on such occasions, it is usually the case that the inside of the bus on the way to the destination is filled with an air of excitement.

C:

4. "Hey, be quiet!"

5. Yuriko Yabuki yelled out.

6. "I can't sleep."

D:

7. "Trying to sleep here is ridiculous,"

8. said Akiko Kuwata, (Yuriko's) best friend who was seated next to her on the bus.

E:

9. "But, I'm sleepy."

F:

10. Usually Yuriko would make a racket together with her.

11. But . . . oh well.

12. There are various reasons for staying up late.

G:

13. Surely it wasn't because Yuriko had spent the night alone with her boyfriend.

14. Yuriko was seventeen; she thought she was as feminine as one would expect for her age, but still she was motivated by a desire for food over a desire for a love affair.

15. No, in that regard, Akiko, sitting next to her, was the same.

H:

16. The bus is moving steadily.

17. Heading for Haneda Airport.

. . .

I:

18. Well (perhaps there is no need to be formal here), those riding the bus are juniors at Hanazono Gakuen, a private girls' high school.

J:

19. They are now on their way to a "ski school."

. . .

K:

20. At this point some of the readers may think, "Wait!"

L:

21. "In addition to Yuriko Yabuki and Akiko Kuwata, isn't there another rather unusual (clique) member, Kyooko Hirono?"

In this initial segment of a mystery novel, we find the following narrative structure.

| | |
|---|---|
| Sentence 1: | Inside the bus (← place) it was very noisy. |
| Sentence 3: | They are going on a school excursion (← time). |
| Sentence 5: | Yuriko Yabuki (← character) yelled out. |

Regarding the overall narrative structure of Japanese old tales and folk-tales, let me first introduce a story of *Kaguya-hime* "Princess Kaguya," whose plot develops as follows (based on Tokunaga 1977).

### Princess Kaguya

Once upon a time an old couple lived in a village not too far from the cap-ital. The old man went to the bamboo patch to harvest bamboo from which he made baskets. One day he found a bamboo with its bottom glittering. When the old man cut down the bamboo, he found a beautiful baby girl inside. He took the little baby home and lovingly raised her with his wife. After that time whenever the old man cut down a bamboo, he found a gold coin inside it. The old couple became rich.

The little baby grew up to be a beautiful young woman in six months and people named her *Kaguya-hime* "Princess Kaguya." Even the emperor learned about her beauty and wanted to see her. But she stayed home with the old couple. Three years passed by and the couple noticed that *Kaguya-hime* began to weep on nights of the full moon. One night the princess told the couple that she was from the Moon-world, and she had to return to her world on the night of the full moon in August.

The emperor sent three thousand armored men to guard her, but when one hundred Heaven-people appeared riding on white clouds accom-panied with beautiful music, all the men lost their will to fight. Princess Kaguya, now wearing a gossamer *kimono*, joined the Heaven-people and left the village being lifted quietly into the night sky.

*based on Tokunaga 1977:198–215*

The structure of this old tale resembles many other stories, and Yoshihiko Ikegami (1982:374) finds in this and similar types of traditional folktales a structural pattern of encounter-and-separation. Ikegami identifies the narrative structure in terms of a juxtaposition between (1) events consist-ing of the encounter followed by separation, and (2) participants who are humans and supernatural creatures.

Another frequently occurring narrative plot in traditional Japanese folktale is what Toshio Ozawa (1982) calls a story of one night's event. The underlying narrative plot in these stories displays first the lack of, and then the regaining of, social stability as it most frequently relates to mature or older folks. The event that disrupts the social order is often caused by a mythical creature who comes from the supernatural world, and the regaining of the social order is achieved through human effort. This scenario differs from often recognized Western folktales and fairy tales in which an unhappy or unfortunate young protagonist gains social status and power by the time the story reaches its final happy ending (e.g., *Cinderella*). Ozawa maintains that Japanese narratives, in general, concern themselves with the social order more than an individual's rise in social status. The *Kaguya-hime* story may be interpreted in the following way. First, change is brought to the couple (with the arrival of a beautiful supernatural daughter), and the consequent return to their original (now enriched) life, embedded within an undercurrent of the narrative movement, the encounter followed by the unavoidable separation.

## Entry 9  **Narrative point of view**

At least three characters may interact in the narrative text – author, narrator, and character(s) – each speaking in different voices. Depending on from whose point of view the text is produced, linguistic expression takes a different form. Moreover, the location of the narrator – in terms of (1) how distant from or close to the events the narrator places himself or herself, and (2) how the narrator talks to the reader – becomes critical.

In the segment of a mystery novel, given as DS5, "Noisy Departure," we identify two basic, related but distinct, narrative points of view.

*1. the narrator's omniscient point of view*
>    1.  characters' points of view (description of things or direct quotation of characters, e.g., sentence 4)
>
>    2.  the narrator's point of view (description of characters and things or comments related to them, e.g., sentence 1)

*2. the narrator-as-a-friend point of view*
>    1.  The narrator directly speaks to the reader, e.g., sentences 20 and 21.

Different points of view in the narrative are often marked by specific linguistic devices. Tense is one clue for identifying the narrator's viewing position. If the narrator is in the very scene where the event takes place, the verb is usually marked by non-past tense. (Here non-past refers to both present and future tenses which take common -*ru* and -*u* forms. Past tense refers to -*ta* and -*da* forms.) If the narrator describes the event as something that happened in the past, something that has been completed, or something that happens as the speaker had hoped for, the narrator is likely to choose the past tense. Other strategies such as *n(o) da* predicate are in non-past tense through which the narrator directly talks to the reader, and they play a part in manifesting different narrative points of view.

For now, we study all the sentences appearing in DS5 based on different points of view and how they are related to the linguistic form – tense marking, in particular. Table 2 illustrates this. (Sentences 17 and 21 are subordinate clauses to 16 and 20, respectively; this is indicated by parentheses.)

**Table 2** Narrative point of view as reflected in the tense of sentence-final expressions of DS5. ("n" is an abbreviation of "narrator's" and "c" of "character's.")

| paragraph | sentence | final expression | narrative point of view | tense |
|---|---|---|---|---|
| A: | 1. | *nigiyaka datta.* | n description | past |
| B: | 2. | *koto dewa aru.* | n comment | non-past |
|  | 3. | *futsuu de aru.* | n comment | non-past |
| C: | 4. | *shite yo.* | c direct quotation | non-past |
|  | 5. | *donatta.* | n description | past |
|  | 6. | *janai no.* | c direct quotation | non-past |
| D: | 7. | *muri.* | c direct quotation | non-past |
|  | 8. | *Kuwata Akiko.* | n description | (non)-past |
| E: | 9. | *nemui no yo.* | c direct quotation | non-past |
| F: | 10. | *hashagu no dearu.* | n comment | non-past |
|  | 11. | *maa ii.* | n comment | non-past |
|  | 12. | *iroiro aru.* | n comment | non-past |
| G: | 13. | *tashika datta.* | n description | past |
|  | 14. | *Yuriko.* | n description | (non)-past |
|  | 15. | *onaji koto da.* | n description | non-past |
| H: | 16. | *tsuzuketeiru.* | n description | non-past |
|  | 17. | *(to mukatte.)* | (n description) | |
| I: | 18. | *joshikookoo ninensei.* | narrator-as-a-friend | non-past |
| J: | 19. | *dekakeru tokoro dearu.* | n description | non-past |
| K: | 20. | *omowareru kamoshirenai.* | narrator-as-a-friend | non-past |
| L: | 21. | *(janai no to.)* | (narrator-as-a-friend) | |

Sentences 8 and 14, which lack overt verbs marking tense, may be interpreted either as past or non-past. Given the immediate discourse context, sentence 18, which also lacks an overt main predicate, is interpreted as representing the non-past tense.

Studying Table 2, we find that (1) the use of past tense is restricted to the narrator's description, (2) the narrator's comment always occurs in a non-past tense, and (3) the narrator-as-a-friend comment always occurs in a non-past tense. In short, whenever the narrator offers commentary, non-past tense is chosen since such a commentary lies outside of the narrative time frame. Use of the past tense in telling what happens in the story corresponds to the temporal frame of the narrative world. However, the narrator's description within the narrative frame also appears in non-past tense. This illustrates that the narrator may describe events in the narrative world either in past or non-past tense, reminding us that storytelling involves the shifting in tense and point of view.

Authors have an array of linguistic devices through which they control how much of the narrators' perspective they wish to reveal in the story. Following Tadao Kabashima's work (1979), I list devices in terms of least to most reflecting the narrator's self-involvement with and self-exposure in the story.

1. narrator's judgment expressed through connectives.

2. use of modals that express hearsay, speculation, and impression (without mentioning the person associated with these modals), for example, *no yooni mieta* "it looked as if," *rashikatta* "it seemed that," *kamoshirenai* "may" and so on.

3. use of sentential emotional (modal) adverbs that express evaluation, interpretation, opinion, response and so on (again, without mentioning the narrator associated with these modal adverbs), for example, *okashina kotoni* "strangely," *sekkaku . . . shita noni* "despite much effort" and so on.

4. the narrator's actual appearance in the narrative world, being referred to as "I" or "we."

In Japanese narratives, partly because pronouns are often absent, other means are also used for identifying who is speaking in whose voice. These include directional verbs (e.g., *iku* versus *kuru*), donatory verbs (e.g., *ageru* versus *morau*), demonstratives (the choice between *kono* and *sono* and so on among others). These devices reveal (1) who the narrator empathizes with, (2) from whose perspective the incident is described, and (3) the relative location of participants. A variety of expressions signaling formality levels and honorifics also help identify who speaks to whom.

Some grammatical structures also signal different points of view. Active versus passive structures, use of causative sentences, incorporation of quoted sentences, presentation of information as hearsay, and so on, offer clues as to who is speaking in whose voice. Obviously, every sentence is marked in one way or another to indicate, to varying degrees, one's point of view. It is important, therefore, to pay attention to the way different perspectives manifest themselves.

As an example, study the following case taken from Jiroo Akagawa's novel (1985). At this point in the novel the narrator describes how Mayuko, waiting at a coffee shop, receives a phone call that her girl friend is not coming. Mayuko decides to order tea and cake.

(1.1)　ケーキを頼んで食べることにした。
(1.2)　ケーキと紅茶。
(1.3)　——せめて、少しは優雅にね。
(1.4)　お姉ちゃんほどでなくても、さ……。
(1.5)　ケーキをフォークで切って食べていると、
　　　　「矢吹さん」
　　　　と、またウェイトレスが呼んだ。

(1.1) Keeki o tanonde taberu koto ni shita.
(She decided to order cake.)

(1.2) Keeki to koocha.
(Cake and tea.)

(1.3) Semete, sukoshi wa yuugani ne.
(At least, with a bit of elegance.)

(1.4) Oneechan hodo denakutemo, sa . . .
(Even if I'm not as elegant as my sister . . . )

(1.5) Keeki o fooku de kitte tabeteiru to, "Yabuki-san" to, mata weitoresu ga yonda.
(When she cut into the cake with a knife and was eating it, the waitress called out again "Miss Yabuki.")

*Akagawa 1995:85, my translation*

In this segment, it is not difficult to notice a change of style from line (1.3) to the end of (1.4). For one, the tense shifts from past to non-past. All of a sudden the interactional particles *ne* and *sa* appear. Graphological marks also indicate separation from the on-going narrative discourse. These two lines are presented as direct voice; they reveal the content of Mayuko's thought. The perspective shifts from the narrator's to the character's, and this shift is marked by tense manipulation and speech style.

## Entry 10 *Danraku* as a discourse unit

Text is built of varied structural elements such as an introductory statement, topic development, citation of concrete examples, quotation from some other texts, contrast of opposing positions, and so on. Therefore, text is normally divided into smaller semantic units and is usually graphologically marked by the change of lines. These units are called *danraku* in Japanese.

*Danraku* is a unit within *bunshoo* "discourse" usually associated with a relevant sub-topic. It usually consists of more than two sentences, although a single sentence may become *danraku*. It is graphologically marked by a new line and by a one-character space indentation (or other markers such as a small upside down triangle used in newspaper columns). *Danraku* is sometimes translated as paragraph, but it is important to recognize that the internal structure of the traditional *danraku* and the English paragraph differ.

The concept of a paragraph in English rhetoric was introduced to Japan through Alexander Bain's (1886) book on rhetoric. According to Bain (1886), the paragraph is a collection of sentences with unity of purpose. Furthermore, the paragraph should possess the kind of unity that implies a definite purpose because its very definition forbids digression and irrelevant matter. (This defining concept of unity is excluded, however, in poetry, one of Bain's five kinds of composition: Description, Narrative, Exposition, Persuasion, and Poetry.)

Bain prescribes that in English, excluding the initial introductory paragraph(s), the paragraph-initial sentence is expected to specify paragraph topic. In concrete terms, the paragraph-initial sentence, i.e., the topic sentence, is expected to contain not only the topic itself but also the writer's opinion or position and to provide a clue for comprehending the entire paragraph. Thus, in English, by reading the paragraph-initial sentence, the reader should be able to grasp the gist of the paragraph and consequently anticipate what will follow. Although this prescription does not apply to all cases – and we know this from reading real-life English texts – English paragraphs possess relatively well-defined semantic consistency.

In Japanese, however, the concept of *danraku* remains less clear. The idea of a topic sentence, for example, is promoted by educators. Examining authentic Japanese discourse, however, reveals that this guideline is often ignored. One finds *danraku* only in a form (called *keishiki danraku*), which contrasts with *imi danraku*, the *danraku* as a meaning unit similar to the English paragraph. Compact Japanese writings tend to use many short *keishiki danraku*. For example, in newspaper opinion columns called "Column, my view" in *Asahi Shimbun* (from January through April, 1994 issues), the average number of sentences contained in each *danraku* turns out to be 3.18.

DS2, a brief essay, "Once Burned, Always Burned," also contains five short *danraku*, averaging two sentences per *danraku*. According to Kiyoshi Noto (1980), an ideal *danraku* length in the newspaper essay is between 140 and 170 characters. The newspaper essay column *Tensei Jingo* in *Asahi Shimbun*, with an approximate number of character spaces being 700 to 800, usually consists of 6 to 7 *danraku*. (R6, one example of *Tensei Jingo*, contains seven *danraku*, 26 sentences and 749 character spaces.)

The most significant structural difference between the Japanese *danraku* and English paragraph lies in its internal structure. The Japanese *danraku* often lacks a topic sentence. Instead, a topic is presented, most often without a concluding statement. Topic may also be preceded by a prelude involving a personal account or an example relevant to the ensuing topic. The discourse gradually flows toward the *danraku*-final segment specifying the summary-like statement, or the writer's view or opinion. Similarly to the tendency for the conclusion to appear toward the end of the entire text, on the *danraku* level the conclusive opinion is likely to appear toward the end.

A piece of discourse may contain a variety of *danraku*. We can find the following *danraku* types in Japanese (not necessarily in the following order) contributing to the overall meaning of the text; the *danraku* types listed below incorporate Takaaki Nagao's (1992) explanation.

*Types of* danraku

1. main *danraku* – discusses the main point of the discourse

2. introductory *danraku* – introduces the purpose or the topic of the discourse, or expresses the point of view or position of the writer

3. background *danraku* – provides background for points made elsewhere

4. example *danraku* – offers examples and cases related to the main point

5. concluding *danraku* – completes the discourse

6. connecting *danraku* – connects one *danraku* to another smoothly by offering transition

7. supplementary *danraku* – adds to the preceding *danraku*, or adds a slightly different angle to the preceding *danraku*

8. quotation *danraku* – contains citation and quotation from other sources

Given the relatively weak semantic consistency of the *danraku*, one may wonder how Japanese writers are expected to divide discourse into different *danraku*. The following *danraku* division bases include those suggested by Naotoshi Nishida (1992:27–28).

**Bases for *danraku* division**

1. *switching of the topics/materials described including:*
   1. information related to specific theme or topic

   2. description of the time, place, event, characters or actions

   3. persons being quoted

2. *switching of the point of view toward the topics/materials:*
   1. new issues (e.g., questions raised)

   2. new claims, points of view

   3. different positions and views (e.g., opposition, criticism)

   4. transition to a new stage of argument (e.g., evidence, supporting argument)

Another rather simple way of understanding *danraku* is to examine each in terms of what the writer intends to communicate, either "facts" (or, description of facts) or the writer's "opinions" (suggestions or proposals). Although both facts and opinions may appear within a single *danraku*, fact/description-*danraku* and opinion/proposal-*danraku* are created differently, especially by varying sentence-final forms. For example, opinions are usually expressed in non-past tense with personally qualifying expressions. Thus, different kinds of *danraku* are likely to be formed depending on whether a *danraku* is intended to present fact or the writer's opinion.

Let us return to DS4, "Color and Human Life," and identify the types of *danraku* and characterize each *danraku* in terms of (1) *danraku* types and (2) the writer's intention (fact or opinion). Table 3 summarizes the results.

**Table 3** Types and writer's intention in *danraku* of DS4

| *Danraku* | *types* | *intention: fact/opinion* |
|---|---|---|
| A: (attractive colors used in our lives): | introductory | fact/opinion |
| B: (colors in old times and now): | background | fact |
| C: (colors useful in our lives): | main | opinion |
| D: (characteristics and the use of red): | example | fact |
| E: (characteristics and the use of blue): | example | fact |
| F: (characteristics and the use of yellow): | example | fact |
| G: (characteristics and the use of color combinations): | supplementary | fact/opinion |
| H: (using colors to enrich our lives): | main and concluding | opinion |

Additional information

*Danraku* as an organizational tool is often advocated in Japanese education. When writing a report (*hookokubun*), opinion piece (*ikenbun*) or explanatory account (*setsumeibun*), Japanese students are told to use the *danraku* division and the topic sentence effectively. Typical instruction proceeds in the following manner. First, *danraku* is defined not as a formal convention (marked by a line change and a one-character-space indentation) but as a semantic one (that is, *imi danraku*). Each *danraku* should contain something relevant and important and should start with a topic sentence. The topic sentence is usually defined as a summary of, or the announcement regarding, the content of the *danraku*. The reader will find it easier to understand each *danraku* if the summary is given in the beginning.

These instructions, however, simultaneously include a warning to the students that topic sentences do not always appear within the *danraku*. The prescribed ideal *danraku* and actual real-life *danraku* we find in contemporary Japanese texts differ, sometimes vastly. We must be prepared to find *danraku* that are divided merely in form.

Regardless of whether the *danraku* is semantic or formal, noting *danraku*-initial elements, especially demonstratives and connectives, is useful since they guide our comprehension as to how *danraku* are chained in terms of cohesion and coherence. Summarizing each *danraku* also helps us grasp the gist of each *danraku*, and consequently, of the whole section, chapter, or the entire text. Again, *danraku*-final sentences are useful to that end, especially for finding summarizing and concluding remarks.

## Entry 11 **Sentence chaining**

Sentence chaining focuses on how several sentences are sequentially joined, using the metaphor of each sentence being a link that is chained to the next. Three kinds of cohesion devices for chaining are important: (1) topics, (2) types of predicates, and (3) key phrases. As a clear example of topic chaining, see DS6 given below. DS6 is a poem titled "The Deer." The entire poem develops around its single topic.

*DS6* (Murano 1975:71)

鹿
1.　　鹿は　森のはずれの
2.　　夕日の中に　じっと立っていた
3.　　彼は知っていた
4.　　小さい額が狙われているのを
5.　　けれども　彼に
6.　　どうすることが出来ただろう
7.　　彼は　すんなり立って
8.　　村の方を見ていた
9.　　生きる時間が黄金のように光る
10.　　彼の棲家である
11.　　大きい森の夜を背景にして

Vocabulary:
1.
鹿　　　　　しか　　　　　n　　　deer

| 森 | もり | n | forest |
| はずれ | | n | edge |
| 2. | | | |
| 夕日 | ゆうひ | n | evening sun |
| じっと | | adv | fixedly, still, quietly, without movement |
| 4. | | | |
| 額 | ひたい | n | forehead |
| 狙う | ねらう | v | to aim |
| 7. | | | |
| すんなり | | adv | slim, svelte |
| 8. | | | |
| 村 | むら | n | village |
| 方 | ほう | n | direction |
| 9. | | | |
| 黄金 | おうごん | n | gold |
| 光る | ひかる | v | to glitter |
| 10. | | | |
| 棲家 | すみか | n | dwelling |
| 11. | | | |
| 背景 | はいけい | n | background |

**Translation**

*The deer*

1. The deer, at the edge of the forest,

2. stood still in the evening sun.

3. He knew –

4. his forehead is being aimed at.

5. But for him,

6. what was there to do?

7. He stood slim,

8. looking toward the village.

9. The time of living glittering like gold,

10. where he lived,

11. the night of the vast forest behind him.

The topic "the deer" appears as shown below; each line (except 9) is chained to the next by the common topic. Connected sentential topics form a single discourse topic.

| Title | *Shika* | |
| --- | --- | --- |
| | ↓ | |
| Line 1 | *shika + wa* | stood |
| | ↓ | |
| Line 3 | *kare + wa* | knew |
| | ↓ | |
| Line 5 | *kare + ni* | do? |
| | ↓ | |
| Line 7 | *kare + wa* | stood |
| | ↓ | |
| Line 10 | (topic not overtly stated) | (stood) |

There are other possibilities as to how topics are chained. For example, a new piece of information may be introduced with the subject marker *ga*, and then overlaid with the topic function as it is marked with *wa*. For example: "There is a tiger (*ga*) in the jungle. The tiger (*wa*) is hungry." This chaining strategy frequently occurs in narratives in which characters are introduced first by *ga*-marked phrases and then continue to appear with *wa*. There are cases where characters already introduced continue to be marked by *ga*. These *ga*-marked characters continue to play a secondary role to the *wa*-marked central character(s) who sustain the plot development.

When a new narrative scene is introduced, the already identified characters may be introduced a second time – as if for the first time – with *ga*. In general, one can expect that the chaining of *ga*-marked subjects occurs in a text where the writer describes some new or changing phenomenon. On the other hand, the writer uses the chaining of *wa*-marked topics for maintaining a topical organization and for presenting description, opinions and arguments regarding already established topics.

In narrative discourse, sentence chaining often occurs in terms of the characters. For example, in R2, a short story titled "The Ant and the Grasshopper" by Shin'ichi Hoshi (1982), the characters are identified first with *ga* and then with *wa* (as well as the deletion of the topic phrase and the topic marker). In R2, the elderly ant is introduced first as *ojiisan ari ga* in sentence 3 and then appears the second time as *ojiisan ari wa* in sentence 11.

One can also chain sentences by the kind of predicates one chooses. Predicates are categorized into two types: facts and opinions. As an example of how fact and opinion predicates chain sentences, study the following sets of sentences taken from the first and the ninth *danraku* of a newspaper column titled *Meiro o Dasse, Arujeria* 'Algeria, Get Out of the Maze.'

**First *danraku***

(1.1)　１月末にアルジェリアの首都アルジェを訪れた。
(1.2)　カスバを見に行こうとしたら、地元の人が強く止めた。
(1.3)　入り口だけのぞいて写真を撮ったが、その数日後、無理にカスバの奥に入ったフランス人カメラマンが刺殺された。

(1.1) Ichigatsu sue ni Arujeria no shuto Aruje o otozureta.
(At the end of January I visited Algiers, the capital of Algeria.)

(1.2) Kasuba o mini ikoo to shitara, jimoto no hito ga tsuyoku tometa.
(I was going to see the *Casbah*, but locals strongly advised against it.)

(1.3) Iriguchi dake nozoite shashin o totta ga, sono suujitsugo, murini kasuba no oku ni haitta furansujin kameraman ga shisatsusareta.
(I peeked through the entrance and took a picture; several days later, a French photographer who, ignoring the warning, went deep inside the *Casbah* was stabbed to death.) (The *Casbah* refers to the eastern quarter of the city of Algiers, known for its lawlessness and anti-French sentiment.)

Asahi Shimbun, *February 23, 1994, p. 2, my translation*

**Ninth *danraku***

(2.1)  そうした迷路から抜け出すには、殺し合いを終わらせる
       ことが先決だ。
(2.2)  イスラム勢力の中心である FIS との話し合いは不可欠
       ともいえる。
(2.3)  まず手を差し伸べるべきなのは政権側だ。

(2.1) Sooshita meiro kara nukedasu niwa, koroshiai o owaraseru koto ga senketsu da. (In order to come out of such a maze, the first step is putting an end to such killings among themselves.)

(2.2) Isuramu seiryoku no chuushin dearu FIS to no hanashiai wa fukaketsu tomo ieru. (Negotiation with FIS, the central force of the Islamic movement, can be said to be indispensable.)

(2.3) Mazu te o sashinoberu bekina no wa seikengawa da. (The first who should reach out is the government side.)

Asahi Shimbun, February 23, 1994, p. 2, my translation

Sentences in the first *danraku* end with the past-tense of the verb, *otozureta* "visited," *tometa* "stopped," and *shisatsusareta* "was stabbed to death," all describing the facts. In contrast, sentences in the ninth *danraku* end with expressions corresponding to the writer's personal view and opinion, *koto ga senketsu da* "it is the first step," *tomo ieru* "it can be said," and *seikengawa da* "is the government side." Sentences in the first *danraku* are chained through consistent factual description, whereas sentences in the ninth *danraku* are chained through judgmental opinion expression.

*Danraku* presented in (1) and (2) illustrate another sentence chaining in contrast. While sentences in (1) are chained by agent topics (i.e., "I"), those in (2) are chained by non-agent topics (i.e., "coming out of such a maze," "negotiation with FIS," and "the first who should reach out").

Another chaining strategy involves important phrases. Texts usually refer to a set of key phrases (their paraphrases and other semantically related phrases) functioning as cohesive devices. By tracing these phrases one speculates what the topic (or relevant issue) of the particular text segment may be. One finds a good and somewhat extreme case in DS4, "Color and Human Life." Table 4 specifies the repeated occurrences of key phrases chaining all sentences of DS4 in one way or another.

**Table 4** Key phrases and their distribution by sentence in DS4

| | key phrases | | |
|---|---|---|---|
| sentences | (color | specific color | color combination) |
| title | shikisai | | |
| 1. | | | |
| 2. | | aka, ao, ki, midori | irodori |
| 3. | | | irodori |
| 4. | iro, chakushoku | | |
| 5. | iro | | |
| 6. | iro, chakushoku | | |
| 7. | | murasakiiro | |
| 8. | iro | | |
| 9. | nanshoku mo no iro | | |
| 10. | iro, iroai | | |
| 11. | iro, shikisai | | |
| 12. | iro | aka | |
| 13. | | akaku, akai iro | |
| 14. | iro | aka | |
| 15. | iro | ao | |
| 16. | | usuaoku | |
| 17. | | usuaoku | |
| 18. | iro | kiiro | |
| 19. | | kiiro | |
| 20. | | | iro o kumiawaseru |
| 21. | rio | | kiiro to kuro, kumiawasareru |
| 22. | | | kiiro to kuro |
| 23. | iro | | aka to midori, daidai to ao, kumiawase |
| 24. | | midori, akai | |
| 25. | shikisai | | |
| 26. | shikisai | | |

Entry 12 **The central message**

When reading, we sort out important information while slighting the peripheral in order to make sense out of what we read. The "point" of discourse, that is, the central message, may or may not appear verbatim. Furthermore, the place where such information appears may possibly be the beginning, the end, or somewhere between. However, there are some clues that we should make use of.

The most likely place to find the primary idea, issue, or point is toward the end of the discourse, both within *danraku* and within the entire text. The following guidelines should also be kept in mind when looking for the central message.

1. Note where repetition occurs. Repeated phrases are likely to be important, either as a part of the central message or as a part of the issue discussed.

2. Identify phrases marked by topic markers such as *wa, mo,* and *to ieba.* These phrases are likely to be directly associated with the central message.

3. If frequently occurring phrases are semantically connected and they form hierarchical semantic networks, the central message is likely to be associated with or represented by these words.

4. Identify sentences that contain the opinions, views and suggestions of the writer by focusing on the predicate types.

5. Distinguish the positions the writer argues for or against; the former is especially important for identifying the central message of the discourse.

6. Recognize that quotations, citations, concrete examples, evidence, and metaphors are provided merely to support the main message of the discourse.

7. Utilize organizational markers, especially those that mark conclusions – *tsumari* "in other words," *kekkyoku* "in conclusion," and *yoosuruni* "in short." What follow these markers are likely to be conclusive remarks, or, at least, remarks leading to or suggestive of the conclusion.

8. Always keep an eye on the final segment of the *danraku,* chapter, and the entire text in search of the central message.

DS4, "Color and Human Life," offers a rather simple example in which one can locate the central message. We observe sentence chaining through repeated key phrases (*iro*, and related terms). The word *iro* and *iro*-related terms are often marked by the topic marker *wa*. In fact, as we saw in Entry 4, the *iro*-related terms form hierarchically related concepts – the general concept of color, specific colors, and combinations thereof, which all point to the likelihood of "color" being the key information. This is confirmed by the title, also suggestive of the central message, "Color and Human Life." The last sentence takes the sentence-final form *ikitai mono dearu* "we should" expressing the writer's opinion. Also noteworthy is the *danraku* type; *danraku* D, E, F, G discuss concrete examples which support the writer's opinion expressed elsewhere. The central message of this essay is the sentiment expressed in *danraku* H, the very last sentence, in particular.

While the central message in DS4 is rather straightforward, the message in DS2, "Once Burned, Always Burned," is more obscure. When interpreting this essay, the reader would miss the main message if he or she simply notes repetition, topic-marked phrases, and frequently occurring phrases. Here, to identify the sentence expressing the author's opinion is key. The key sentence turns out to be the very last sentence, ending with the opinion-expressing *kamoshirenai* "may" which brings the entire essay together. The analogy of repeated burning of pans being like a person's bad habit is the key to understanding the main message.

## Entry 13 **On letters and newspapers**

Two genres in Japanese writing that follow rather strict rules of discourse organization are formal letters and newspaper news reports. In a formal personal letter, components in the initial and final segments are clearly defined. The strict structural rules are not followed, however, in casual and friendly notes and short letters.

> **Structure of formal letters**
> 1. *zenbun* (initial segment)
>      *kakidashi* (initial greeting phrase)
>      *aisatsu* (seasonal greetings)
> 2. *shubun* (main text)
> 3. *matsubun* (final segment)
>      *aisatsu* (final greetings)
>      *ketsugo* (ending phrase)
> 4. *atozuke* (date, sender's name, recipient's name)
>      And optionally,
> 5. *tsuishin* (postscript)

An example follows.

(1.1)  拝啓

(1.2)  日増しに秋が深まってまいりましたが、いかがお過ごし
        でいらっしゃいますか。

(1.3)  さて、私共、関東日本語研究会では 11 月中旬に読解指
        導についてのワークショップを開催する予定でござい
        ます。

(1.4)  つきましては、先生にぜひアメリカの大学における読解
        指導の実情についてお話しいただきたいのですが、いか
        がでしょうか。

(1.5)  後日お電話で詳しいことをお話しさせていただきたい
        と思います。

(1.6)  お忙しいこととは存じますが、どうかよろしくお願い申
        し上げます。

(1.7)  敬具

(1.8)  10 月 8 日

(1.9)  川口正樹

(1.10)  大林和雄先生

*1. zenbun:*

(1.1)  Haikei.
initial greeting phrase

(1.2)  Himashini aki ga fukamatte mairimashita ga, ikaga osugoshi deirasshaimasu ka.
(We are well into the fall season and I wonder how you are.)

*2. shubun:*

(1.3)  Sate, watakushidomo, Kantoo Nihongo Kenkyuukai dewa juuichigatsu chuujun ni dokkaishidoo nitsuite no waakushoppu o kaisaisuru yotei degozaimasu.
(Now, we, the Kantoo Japanese Language Study Association, plan to sponsor a workshop in teaching reading Japanese in mid-November.)

(1.4)  Tsukimashitewa, sensei ni zehi Amerika no daigaku ni okeru dokkaishidoo no jitsujoo nitsuite ohanash itadakitai no desu ga, ikaga deshoo ka.
(And, we would very much like you to give a talk on the current goings-on of teaching reading Japanese in the United States; would it be possible?)

*3. matsubun:*

(1.5)  Gojitsu odenwa de kuwashii koto o ohanashisasete itadakitai to omoimasu.
(I would like to discuss this with you in detail over the phone at a later date.)

(1.6)  Oisogashii koto towa zonjimasu ga, dooka yoroshiku onegai mooshiagemasu.
(I am aware that you are very busy, but we would very much appreciate your generous assistance in this matter.)

(1.7)  Keigu.
closing phrase

*4. atozuke:*

(1.8)  Juugatsu yooka.
(October 8)

(1.9)  Kawaguchi Masaki
sender's name

(1.10)  Oobayashi Kazuo Sensei
recipient's name and title

Figures 2 and 3 specify how the text of a letter appears on the writing sheet. Both vertical and horizontal writing styles are shown.

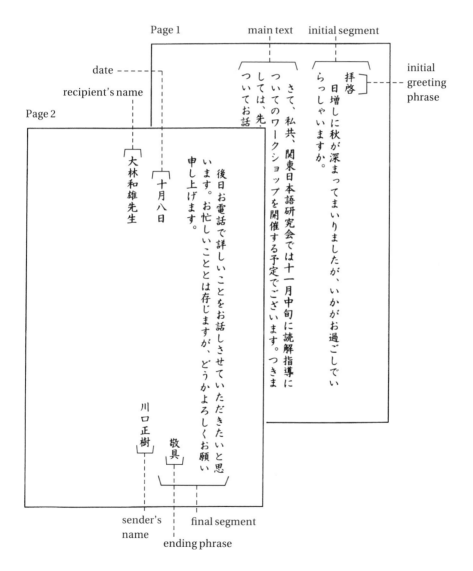

**Figure 2** Standard vertical letter format.

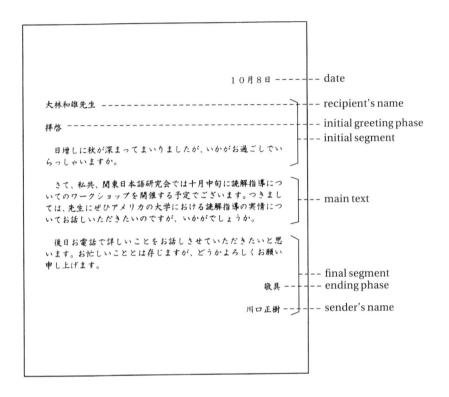

**Figure 3** Standard horizontal letter format.

Now, on the Japanese newspaper. Major daily newspapers are divided into sections often called *ichimen, nimen, sanmen,* and *yonmen,* which carry expected types of articles as listed below. The numbers reflected in these names originate in the old four-page newspaper in which the sections were divided by each page. Although today's multiple page newspapers contain many more than four pages, the names still apply.

*ichimen* (political news, important national and international news)
*nimen* (economic news, opinion columns, and editorials)
*sanmen* (social news, newsworthy events, crime reports, etc.)
*yonmen* (local news, letters to the editor, booknotes, arts and literature, television and radio programs)

The organization of most daily newspapers follow the general order of the articles listed above.

Although a typical newspaper contains many types of text including advertisements, comic strips, and announcements, one discourse organization particular to the newspaper is newswriting style. The newswriting is known to follow, as in English newswriting, the inverted pyramid, the textual organization where the critical information is spelled out in the beginning. Particularly important are the basic elements of the event – what, who, where, when, why, and how. Critical information associated with these elements is often presented in the headline, the lead, and the first few sentences in the newspaper article. The "why" is usually presented later, if known.

As an example, let me introduce a brief news item appearing in a newspaper about a visit the Crown Prince and the Princess made to Fukushima.

(2)      皇太子ご夫妻福島へ
(2.1)   皇太子ご夫妻は 27 日昼すぎ、福島駅着の JR 東北新幹線
         で福島入りした。
(2.2)   28 日からの第 31 回全国身体障害者スポーツ大会のため
         で、同日福島市での開会式に出席、各種競技を観戦して
         29 日帰京の予定。

*Headline*:  Kootaishi gofusai Fukushima e
          (Crown Prince and Princess to Fukushima)

(2.1)  Kootaishi gofusai wa nijuushichinichi hirusugi, Fukushimaekichaku no JR Toohoku Shinkansen de Fukushimairi shita.
(Shortly after noon on the 27th [← when], the Crown Prince and the Princess [← who] visited Fukushima Prefecture [← what, where] by the JR Northeast Bullet Train [← how].)

(2.2)  Nijuuhachinichi kara no dai sanjuuikkai zenkoku shintaishoogaisha supootsutaikai no tame de, doojitsu Fukushimashi de no kaikaishiki ni shusseki, kakushu kyoogi o kansenshite nijuukunichi kikyoo no yotei.
(This visit is for the occasion of the 31st national sports competition for the physically challenged starting from the 28th [← why], and they are scheduled to attend the opening ceremony held in Fukushima City, and after observing the games, are scheduled to return to Tokyo on the 29th.)

                        Asahi Shimbun, *October 22, 1995, p. 22, my translation*

The layout of Japanese newspapers differs from that of comparable English newspapers. Refer to Figure 4 illustrating a typical front page of a daily newspaper.

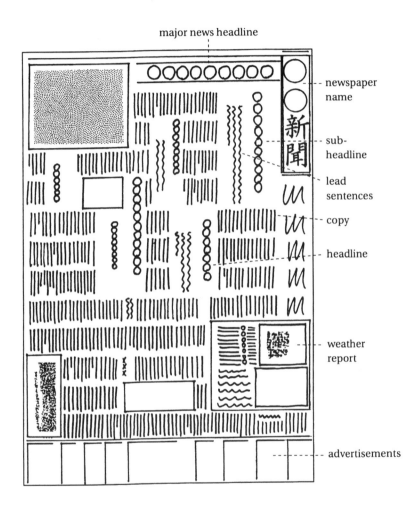

**Figure 4** Sample Japanese newspaper format, the front page.

## Prelude: co-reference and implicit cohesion

Before introducing Entries 14 to 30, let us take a moment to briefly discuss two points. First is the concept of co-reference, a key for understanding one of the mechanisms of cohesion. Second, as a cautionary measure not to ignore cases of cohesion unmarked by linguistic devices, we touch upon the issue of implicit cohesion.

Cohesion in discourse is often achieved by referring to items common across sentences and paragraphs. This leads us to the concept of "co-reference." Co-reference means referring to an identical item. For example, note the connection in terms of reference between the two sentences.

(1.1)  Otoko ga kyooshitsu ni haitte kita.
(A man came into the classroom.)

(1.2)  Otoko wa ookina kaban o motteiru.
(The man has a large bag.)

When reading these two sentences, under normal circumstances we interpret the person referred to as *otoko* in (1.1) as being identical to the person referred to in (1.2). Thus both phrases co-refer to the identical referent, a case of co-reference. Co-reference provides the most obvious clue for the semantic connection between sentences; it is a mechanism that supports the overtly marked cohesion.

One can express cohesion in many other ways, in terms of associated meanings, logical ties, through a consistent rhetorical style, and so on. Overt strategies signaling cohesion include, among others, pronouns, demonstratives, repetition, and sentence structures such as *no da* and *wake da*, all of which are presented in detail in entries to follow.

At this point we should remind ourselves of the danger of ignoring implicit cohesion, i.e., cohesion not marked by cohesive devices. After all, cohesion devices do not really "connect" sentences; rather they simply signal the writer's decision of expressing it linguistically. The interpretation of the message involves a variety of clues far beyond what overt linguistic strategies communicate. For example, a pair of utterances – "I'm not going. Too tired, really." – is interpreted in such a way that the second sentence provides the reason for the first. The two sentences are semantically connected (a case of coherence), yet unmarked by a connective. The only signal is that these sentences appear in a sequence, and we tend to interpret sequentially arranged statements as being relevant and coherent. After all, if they are not relevant, why are they arranged together in the first place? This makes our task a sort of paradox; we must know that utterances are connected without overt markers, and on the other hand, we use cohesive devices to interpret utterances as being connected.

Some frequently used cases of implicit cohesion follow. The same mechanism operates in English as well.

*1. question and answer*

    (2.1)  A:  Jaa, itsu ikimasu ka?
    (Then, when will you go?)

    (2.2)  B:  Ashita ni demo ikoo to omoimasu ga.
    (I'm thinking about going tomorrow.)

*2. quotation and narration*

    (3.1)  "Jaa mata ne."
    ("See you.")

    (3.2)  Musume wa kantanna aisatsu o shite Tookyooiki no kyuukoo ni notta.
    (My daughter gave me her simple farewell and got aboard an express train bound for Tokyo.)

*3. information presentation and commentary*

    (4.1)  Hachigatsu juugonichi.
    (The fifteenth of August.)

    (4.2)  Watashi niwa wasureru koto ga dekinai.
    (I cannot forget [it].)

These sequential connections are not signaled by overt cohesion strategies; yet one must interpret them as being connected. (2) illustrates a case of sequential cohesion in terms of human interaction; posing a question expects an answer, and an answer usually follows a question (or, more accurately, the statement following a question is often interpreted as an answer). Example (3) illustrates the kind of connection expected in linguistic behavior, the quotation followed by someone else's comment regarding the quoted person. (4) is a case where the information is connected to the commentary statement that follows. Specific cultural knowledge is often expected for an interpretation of cohesion. Here the date World War II ended (August 15, 1945) is something that many Japanese people are expected to remember, and therefore the second utterance is interpreted as being connected.

Implicit cohesion sometimes requires broad cultural knowledge. When two sentences are sequentially arranged, the reader's instinct is to connect them in some way, hoping for some semantic relevance. Without background knowledge, however, one may be unable to recognize such relevance. (5) is a clear case of that.

(5.1)  – To yuu wake de, Mayuko wa, sobani inai ane ni, yatsuatari o shiteiru no datta.
(So, Mayuko was venting her anger to her sister who wasn't even there.)

(5.2)  Mochiron, sono koro, "T Skii Rizooto" de Yuriko ga kushami o shiteita ka dooka wa, sadaka denai.
(Of course, it is not certain whether or not at that moment Yuriko, who was at T Ski Resort, sneezed.)

*Akagawa, 1995:83, my translation*

The connection between (5.1) and (5.2) depends on the understanding of a Japanese folk belief – when someone talks about you in your absence, you sneeze. Without this knowledge, (5.2) seems completely out of place. Given this cultural knowledge, (5.1) and (5.2) are connected through implicit cohesion.

## Entry 14 **Mixture of styles**

Although writers usually avoid mixing different styles, they may mix styles for specific reasons. For example, in a text written in the *da*-style, when the writer's intention is to direct the message to a particular person, the *desu/masu*-style appears. A good example illustrating such mixture is R1, a short discourse segment by Machi Tawara (1988). In R1, when the author uses expressions as if talking to "you" (sentences 10 and 12 given below) as reflected in the English translation (use of tag question, "are you?"), she chooses the *desu/masu*-style in the otherwise *da*-style essay.

*R1: Sentences 8 to 11*
   8. The sea gull, left alone without being touched by the blue of the sky, or the blue of the sea.

9. You are just like a sea gull.

10. You aren't sad, are you? (kanashikunai **desu** ka?)

11. Placing both feet on a single board, with both hands having nothing to hold on to, keeping a precarious balance, you swiftly move across my vision.

12. You aren't lonesome, are you? (sabishikunai **desu** ka?)

Another motivation for using *da* and *desu/masu* style mixture involves signaling sentences that operate just like a subordinate clause within a sentence. Study the example below, a segment taken from a mystery novel by Shizuko Natsuki (1981).

(1.1)　「多分晴江にしてみれば、自分と同年配の女が一人で洒落た家に住んで、垢抜けた身なりで通勤している。
(1.2)　時たま外車で送られて帰ってくる。
(1.3)　そういう派手な暮らしが妬ましかったということじゃないんでしょうか。」

(1.1) "Tabun, Harue ni shitemireba, jibun to doonenpai no onna ga hitoride shareta uchi ni sunde, akanuketa minari de **tsuukinshiteiru**. (*da*-style)
(Perhaps for Harue, [it was upsetting to see that] a woman about the same age as herself lives in a stylish house and goes to work wearing fashionable clothes.)

(1.2) Tokitama gaisha de okurarete **kaette kuru**. (*da*-style)
(And sometimes the woman is driven back home in a foreign-made car.)

(1.3) Sooyuu hadena kurashi ga netamashikatta to yuu koto janai n **deshoo ka**." (*desu/masu*-style)
(Isn't it that Harue was jealous of such a showy life style?)

*Natsuki 1981: 75–76, my translation*

At this point in the novel, a conversation takes place between Yazu, a secretary at a district public prosecutor's office, and Akiko, the district public prosecutor. Yazu, being subordinate to Akiko, consistently speaks in the *desu/masu*-style. Unlike other sentences, sentences (1.1) and (1.2) appear in *da*-style. It is as if (1.1) and (1.2) form a two-item list describing a kind of life style. In fact, the demonstrative expression, *sooyuu*, in (1.3) refers to the content of sentences (1.1) and (1.2). These sentences provide subordinate information incorporated into the primary information described in (1.3). By "subordinate" I mean the kind of information such as explanation or modification that feeds into primary sentences sustaining the narrative plot development in the text.

Lest the reader get the impression that the above style mixture is restricted to quoted speech, let me provide another example. The information given in sentences (2.1) through (2.3) constitutes subordinate information to be incorporated into *kooyuu jookyoo* 'these circumstances.'

(2.1)　約束を守らない。
(2.2)　ひとの悪口を言う。
(2.3)　変なうわさを流す。
(2.4)　こういう状況では人に信頼されなくなるのもあたりま
　　　　えです。

(2.1) Yakusoku o **mamoranai**. (*da*-style)
(You don't keep promises.)

(2.2) Hito no waruguchi o **yuu**. (*da*-style)
(You speak ill of people.)

(2.3) Henna uwasa o **nagasu**. (*da*-style)
(You spread strange rumors.)

(2.4) Kooyuu jookyoo dewa hito ni shinraisarenaku naru no mo atarimae **desu**.
(*desu/masu*-style)
(Under these circumstances, it is easily expected that you will not be trusted by others.)

In sum, the *da*-style within the *desu/masu*-style text is often used to signal that the information marked so is subordinate within the overall discourse organization. The dominant *desu/masu*-style is maintained, however, in sentences sustaining the primary plot or argumentation.

Another kind of style mixture occurs between *da* and *dearu*. In the *dearu*-style, if the writer uses *dearu* exclusively in writings such as essays, reports and editorials, the impression is that *dearu* is overused. In the narrative, the difference between *da* and *dearu* lies in the perspective the writer takes toward what is being described. *Da* tends to be used

when one psychologically or emotionally situates oneself closer to what is
described, while *dearu* is often used when one maintains a certain distance from what is described. The use of *da*, more than *dearu*, generally
involves a sense of immediacy. For an expression such as "Fire!" even
when appearing in written text, *Kaji da!* is the norm, *\*Kaji dearu* is inappropriate. *Dearu* often gives the discourse a recounting, and sometimes
explanatory, tone. (Note: an asterisk is used to indicate ungrammatical or
inappropriate forms.)

As an example of *da* and *dearu* mixture, compare the forms chosen in
(3), a segment taken from another mystery novel, by Seichoo Matsumoto
(1971).

(3.1)  うまいことを言うと思った。

(3.2)  重太郎が考えていたことを、娘は適切な一ことで言いえ
た。

(3.3)  食欲よりも愛情の問題か。

(3.4)  そうだ。

(3.5)  それである。

(3.1)  Umai koto o yuu to omotta.
(He thought that she used an excellent expression.)

(3.2)  Shigetaroo ga kangaeteita koto o, musume wa tekisetsuna hitokoto de iieta.
(The daughter could express in one suitable word what Shigetaroo himself was thinking
about.)

(3.3)  Shokuyoku yorimo aijoo no mondai ka.
(It's a question of love, rather than a question of appetite.)

(3.4)  Soo **da**.
(That's it.)

(3.5)  Sore **dearu**.
(That's right.)

*Matsumoto 1971:41, my translation*

Contrast *da* in (3.4) with *dearu* in (3.5). As this segment of discourse
unfolds, the narrator is psychologically closer to what is being described.

Suddenly realizing that the question at issue is of love, rather than of appetite, the narrator exclaims using *da*. (3.5) conveys the narrator's comment reached after a longer thought process; it takes *dearu*, instead.

Our R7, "Traveling to the desert," also contains *da* and *dearu* mixtures.

*R7: paragraphs C and D*

C:

7. Certainly, the world is (like) one volume of a book. (shomotsu **da**)

8. To travel is to turn the pages of that enormous book. (koto **dearu**)

9. I have traveled to many places in the world so far, but still I feel as if I haven't finished reading even the first chapter of this book named "the world."

10. At my destination, I sometimes feel dizzy because of the world – that is, this immense book of which I have absolutely no idea as to when I will ever be able to finish reading.

11. And I sometimes think that perhaps traveling means to experience this overwhelming sense of being lost.

D:

12. Why does traveling mean the same thing as reading?

13. Perhaps there is no need to elaborate.

14. It is because traveling, like reading, broadens one's small world. (kara **dearu**)

15. To travel is to come out of one's own well and to deeply feel – how vast the world is! (koto **da**)

16. The bewilderment and the perplexity; these (feelings) directly lead one to reflect on oneself. (yuku no **dearu**)

The author uses *da* to emphatically state his case (sentences 7 and 15), and chooses *dearu* for sentences that contain an explanatory and reflective tone (sentences 8, 14 and 16).

## Entry 15 **Pronouns and demonstratives**

Pronouns and demonstratives are the two most obvious strategies that mark co-reference. Although the use of pronouns is limited in Japanese, related phrases and paraphrases (often in combination with demonstrative *ko-so-a-do* phrases) function similarly to pronouns in English. DS6, "The Deer," is an example where the pronoun *kare* "he" appears repeatedly, adding to the poetic rhythm.

Pronouns and demonstratives often refer to concrete objects, but they can also refer to abstract ideas. For example, one may refer to the meaning of the preceding sentence or what is merely assumed in discourse. (1.2) illustrates a case in which the phrase *sonna* refers to the content of the previous sentence (1.1).

(1.1)  Dekiru kagiri no doryoku o shite shippaisuru no nara sore mo yokaroo.
(If I fail after having made every possible effort, that is acceptable.)

(1.2)  Watashi wa **sonna** koto o kangaeta.
(I thought so.)

The relationship between the pronouns/demonstratives and what is referred to is either "anaphoric" or "cataphoric." When one first makes a statement and then refers to it by pronouns/demonstratives, the relationship is anaphoric – as in (1). However, as shown in (2), the pronoun/demonstrative may appear first referring to what follows. Such a relationship is called cataphoric. An anaphoric relationship is the norm; a cataphoric relationship appears less frequently.

The writer uses cataphoric relationship when, by prefacing the information, he or she directs the reader's attention to the ensuing information. This strategy is particularly useful when the ensuing information takes a long sentence or an extensive stretch of text. The writer warns the reader by announcing first and placing the ensuing information in the current thread of discourse. A simple cataphoric case follows.

(2.1)  Watashi wa **konna** koto o soozooshita.
(I imagined the following.)

(2.2)  Moshi fubo ga yurushite kureru nara nihon o hanare Furansu ni ryoori no benkyoo ni ikoo to.
(If my parents allow it, I will leave Japan and go to France to study cooking.)

Now, the choice of demonstratives – among *ko-*, *so-* and *a*-references – is based not only on the situational index but also in terms of the textual context and psychological factors. The situational index operates when, for example, a speaker, while pointing to a physically existing item, utters *"Kore o mite kudasai"* "Please look at this." The textual context refers to a situation where information introduced into discourse constructs a renewed contextual framework. Such a situation occurs, for example, in the following.

(3.1)  Kinoo omoshiroi hon o yonda.
(I read an interesting book yesterday.)

(3.2)  **Kono** hon wa joohooshakai nitsuite nobeta mono de . . .
(This book is about the information society and . . . )

*Kono* refers to the book mentioned in the discourse; the item is not physically in the situation of speaking/writing but is introduced into the current discourse.

As an extension of the situational and textual indexing, psychological factors also play a role in identifying items in discourse. How a person "feels" toward items, whether close (attached, involved) or detached (distant, uninvolved), is understood analogous to the physical distance. For instance, (4) illustrates a case in which the psychological factor plays a role in the choice of the *so-* and *ko-* demonstratives.

(4.1)  大型旅客機の安全性が問われている。
(4.2)  その問題についての討論はこれから各方面でなされる
       であろう。
(4.3)  この問題は人命にかかわることだけに、真剣に討論して
       みたい。

(4.1)  Oogata ryokyakuki no anzensei ga towareteiru.
(The safety of large passenger aircraft is being questioned.)

(4.2)  **Sono** mondai nitsuite no tooron wa korekara kaku hoomen de nasareru dearoo.
(The discussion on the issue will be conducted in various sectors from now on.)

(4.3)  **Kono** mondai wa jinmei ni kakawaru koto dakeni, shinkenni tooronshite mitai.
(Since this issue involves human lives, we would like to discuss it seriously.)

Two different kinds of demonstratives – *sono* and *kono* – are used to refer to the identical item. *Sono* is used in a sentence offering objective information, whereas *kono* is chosen in a sentence involving more of the writer's personal emotion. As suggested by Chisato Kitagawa (1984), *kono* brings to discourse a sense of psychological closeness.

Another psychological factor involved in the choice of demonstratives is the sense of social belongingness. Japanese people feel close and intimate within social groups called *uchi* "inside" while they feel distant, formal and polite (and sometimes uncaring) toward members outside of one's *uchi* groups, i.e., *soto* "outside." Depending on how the writer identifies the person or item referred to in the *uchi* or *soto* relationship, different demonstratives are chosen, as if the choice of demonstratives accentuates distinct social relationships.

The following summarizes major factors influencing the choice of demonstrative/pronominal phrases.

**Basis for choosing appropriate demonstrative/pronominal phrases**

1. *situational index*

   *ko-*: items close to the writer, items close to both the writer and his or her partner(s)

   *so-*: items close to the partner, but not close to the writer

   *a-*: items far from both the writer and the partner, or when the writer and the partner consider them members of the same *uchi* group, and the writer refers to items outside of the situational context

2. *textual context*

   *ko-*: within a given textual context, items with which both the writer and the partner can readily identify

   *so-*: within a given textual context, items the writer knows but the partner may not know well – used to refer to the items the writer newly introduced in previous segments of text

   *a-*: in a given textual context, items (assumed to be) known by both the writer and the partner

3. *psychological factor*

   *ko-*: items the writer feels close to, feels attached to, particularly when the writer and the partner belong to *uchi*, and the writer wishes to emphasize their common perspective

   *so-*: items referred to in objective description

*a-*: items known by both the writer and the partner, especially when these items are called into the current discourse as a reminder of the participants' common knowledge

As an example of the choice of *sore* and *kore*, recall DS1, a passage on frustration. In DS1, the question is raised: Why do we mumble to ourselves? *Sore* (in "It is because by mumbling to ourselves, we calm our emotions down a little") refers to "mumbling to ourselves" which is an abstract concept drawn from the question. *Kore* (in "This is a compensatory act which channels anger into things other than the direct cause, and thus releases one's feelings") refers to the entire sentence "When angry, we sometimes kick at stones and calm our emotions." This statement is closer to the heart of the writer – or, at least that is how the writer wants to present it. The distinction the writer makes here is similar to the distinction made in English *the* and *this* as evidenced in the English translations of (4.2) and (4.3).

Although it is true that pronouns are often avoided in Japanese discourse – particularly when co-reference occurs sentence-internally – there are reasons for using them repeatedly. For example, in an essay the writer may shift from factual description to his or her personal view. Use of "I" in this case emphasizes that what is presented is the writer's personal opinion. In this context, "I" could function either for mitigation or emphasis. An expression such as *watashi niwa soo omoeru no da ga* "to me it seems to be" is mitigation; *watashi wa soo kakushinshiteiru* "I firmly believe so" adds emphasis.

## Entry 16 **Repetition**

Repetition occurs in discourse in three different ways involving phrases, clauses and sentences. Repetition in a narrow sense refers to cases of repetition of identical phrases, that is, reiteration. Repetition in a broad sense – and this is how we understand it – includes use of synonyms, paraphrases, related expressions or pronouns/demonstratives. In all cases, repetition offers a prime strategy for overtly signaling cohesion in discourse.

Although repetition by means of pronouns within as well as across sentences occurs frequently in English, such repetition is often considered

excessive and unnecessary in Japanese, unless the writer intends to evoke certain rhetorical effects, such as adding rhythm, emphasis, or mitigation.
    Let us contrast the repetition strategy in English and Japanese.

(1.1) A man is walking toward the station.

(1.2) The man is carrying a camera over **his** shoulder.

(1.3) It seems that **he** is not a resident of this town.

Japanese counterparts for (1.1) to (1.3), however, are best presented without repeating pronouns as shown below.

(2.1)　男が駅に向って歩いている。
(2.2)　その男は肩にカメラをかけている。
(2.3)　この町の者ではなさそうだ。

(2.1) Otoko ga eki ni mukatte aruiteiru.

(2.2) Sono otoko wa kata ni kamera o kaketeiru.

(2.3) Kono machi no mono dewanasasoo da.

In fact, a sentence such as *Sono otoko wa kare no kata ni kamera o kaketeiru* "The man is carrying a camera over his shoulder" is awkward and is normally avoided unless there is a reason to emphasize or highlight "his" shoulder. Likewise, (2.3) is a preferred form although *Kare wa kono machi no mono dewanasasoo da* "It seems that he is not a resident of this town" is not ungrammatical.
    The reader may wonder about the pronominal repetition we discussed earlier in DS6. Recall in DS6, the deer was repeatedly referred to with the pronoun *kare* "he." Here the repeated pronoun creates poetic effects of (1) highlighting the deer and treating it almost as a person, and (2) adding to the poetic rhythm. Unless special effects are intended, pronominal repetition is dispreferred.
    When establishing the discourse topic, Japanese prefer using reiteration and synonymous or related phrases as opposed to using pronouns. Through repetition, the writer can leave a strong and clear impression of

the repeated phrase, and at the same time overtly connect two items by referring back to the item given in prior discourse (a case of co-reference). Consider that in English expressions, the first mention of the "man" in (1.1) is marked with an indefinite article "a" while the second mention in (1.2) is marked with the definite article "the," thereby marking the new versus given information distinctively. Since Japanese does not possess articles, one uses the particles *ga* and *wa* (among other things) for marking the distinction between what is mentioned for the first time (new information) and what is mentioned the second time (given information). Table 5 illustrates the likely processes in which phrases are introduced, established, and maintained (partly by means of repetition of topics) in Japanese texts. (In some cases both the topic phrase and the topic-marking particle are deleted in the second and consequent occasions.)

**Table 5**  Typical process of topic introduction, establishment and maintenance in Japanese texts

| *textual context* | *status of topic* | *likely forms* |
| --- | --- | --- |
| first mention | topic introduction | *ga* following phrase |
| second mention | topic establishment | *wa* following reiteration, synonym or pronoun |
| third reference | topic maintenance | deletion |
| after an interval – such as in a new *danraku* | topic re-introduction | *wa* following reiteration, synonym or pronoun |
| focus on item – regardless of mention | focus | *ga* following reiteration, synonym or pronoun |
| contrast of items – regardless of mention | topic contrast | *wa* following reiteration, synonym or pronoun |

Now, example (3) illustrates a synonymous repetition of phrases (*wakai otoko* and *seinen*), while example (4) shows a synonymous repetition of sentences. Synonymous repetition is useful for avoiding sometimes boring text infested by reiteration while maintaining the effect of clarification and emphasis. Sentential repetitions (and repetition of identical sentence structures) may occur in order to ensure the reader's comprehension and to emphasize, as well as to create the rhythmic effect in discourse.

(3.1)　若い男がこちらに向って歩いてくる。
(3.2)　その青年は大きなかばんを肩にかけている。
(3.3)　最近の若者は何でも大きなかばんにつめこんで持ち歩くのが好きらしい。

(4.1)　我々は書くという行為を通して本当に考えることができる。
(4.2)　言語表現があってはじめて思考があるのだ。
(4.3)　さらに、筆記することによって自分のアイデアをたしかめることもできる。

(3.1) **Wakai otoko** ga kochira ni mukatte aruite kuru.
(A young man is walking in this direction.)

(3.2) **Sono seinen** wa ookina kaban o kata ni kaketeiru.
(The youth is carrying a large bag on his shoulder.)

(3.3) Saikin no wakamono wa nandemo ookina kaban ni tsumekonde mochiaruku no ga suki rashii.
(Young people nowadays seem to like stuffing things in a large bag and carrying it around.)

(4.1) Wareware wa kaku to yuu kooi o tooshite hontooni kangaeru koto ga dekiru.
(We can truly think by the act of writing.)

(4.2) Gengohyoogen ga atte hajimete shikoo ga aru no da.
(Only with linguistic expression, thinking is realized for the first time.)

(4.3) Sarani, hikkisuru koto niyotte jibun no aidea o tashikameru koto mo dekiru.
(Furthermore, by writing, one can also confirm one's idea.)

Recall that we examined earlier, in Entry 11, the repetition of key phrases appearing in DS4 used as a strategy for sentence chaining. Here we examine another sample, DS1. Phrases *hitorigoto o yuu* "say things to ourselves" (and its paraphrase) is repeated three times, and so is the phrase *kimochi ga ochitsuku* "calm our emotions" (and its paraphrase). The term *daishookooi* "compensatory act" also appears twice. Table 6 summarizes the repetition observed in DS1.

**Table 6** Repetition in DS1

| sentence | hitorigoto | kimochi | daishookooi |
|---|---|---|---|
| 1 | hitorigoto o itteshimau | | |
| 2 | hitorigoto o iu | | |
| 3 | hitorigoto o iu | kimochi ga ochitsuku | |
| 4 | | kimochi o shizumeru | |
| 5 | | kimochi o hassansaseru | daishookooi |
| 6 | | | daishookooi |

The text contains repeated phrases dispersed within and across sentences, through which the cohesion is maintained. These repeated phrases represent key concepts of DS1, leading toward the central message of *daishookooi* "compensatory act" being a wisdom given to human beings.

## Entry 17 **Deletion**

Although I use the term "deletion," the Japanese deletion does not necessarily always imply that something was once there but later deleted. In many cases "absence" may be a better term. It is a common practice in many languages not to overtly verbalize known or obvious things. But in comparison with the Japanese language, English is under stricter constraints. What one can leave unsaid in English is rather limited. In Japanese text, one expects that the known and shared information is visually absent. The topic and the grammatical subject are likely candidates to be absent in many Japanese sentences. There is a seeming contradiction here – the more one talks about a topic, the less the topic appears on the surface.

Frequent deletion – or, absence – of the topic and subject, however, does not mean that this strategy occurs randomly. When the item under discussion continues to be talked about across discourse segments, such as *danraku*, it is more likely that deletion is avoided, and instead repetition occurs. Repetition helps remind the reader that what follows still relates to the item introduced earlier. The following segment from R2, "The Ant and the Grasshopper" illustrates the mechanism of repetition/ deletion across *danraku* in the narrative text. Observe that in Japanese, *kirigirisu* "the grasshopper" appears in *danraku*-initial sentences (sentences 23 and 27), but overt reference to the grasshopper is avoided in consequent sentences (26, 28 and 29) internal to each *danraku*.

*R2: Paragraphs F and G (sentences with the "grasshopper" as an agent and topic)*

F:

23. Thus the grasshopper (**kirigirisu wa**) became the guest of the ant colony.

24. That winter turned out to be an enjoyable one for all the ants.

25. It was as if they had installed a jukebox.

26. The grasshopper (**absent**) plays on his violin whatever music the ants request.

G:

27. This grasshopper (**kono kirigirisu**), being an artist, is also brilliant.

28. As he (**absent**) took an inspection tour throughout the storage houses of the colony, he (**absent**) discovered that some of the old food stored in the back had fermented and had turned into *sake*.

29. The grasshopper (**absent**) announces to the ants.

30. "Hey, everyone, you shouldn't leave it like this.

31. Here, take a sip."

The reader may wonder about the way *kirigirisu* is presented in sentence 27, which occurs without a topic marker. At this paragraph–initial position, a mention of *kirigirisu* is necessary. A typical method is to mark the phrase with some topic marker, but presentation of the phrase itself also functions as a way of re-introducing the topic. In 27, the combination of the demonstrative *kono* and the repetition of *kirigirisu* followed by a comma all work together to re-establish *kirigirisu* as the topic.

As an example of the absence of topical phrases, let me direct your attention to paragraph B of R6, a newspaper essay, as given below. The only overt topic, the phrase *ima no kodomo niwa* "(for) today's children" appears in sentence 5. Sentences 6, 7, and 8 do not contain any mention of the topic (which is the grammatical subject), although in English the pronoun *they* appears repeatedly.

*R6: Paragraph B*

5. Speaking of that, today's children (**ima no kodomo niwa**) have no opportunity to make a fire in their daily lives.

6. They (**absent**) are probably unfamiliar with the fire in the farmhouse fire pit, and with the heat coming from the embers.

7. They (**absent**) may not have opportunities to come in contact with words that describe these conditions of fire.

8. It is regrettable if they (**absent**) cannot experience smokiness and cannot experience the pleasure of roasting sweet potatoes in the fire.

Deletion – or, absence – of linguistic expressions often produces rhetorical effects; less is more in that by not saying everything, dramatic and lingering effects are created. Observe, for example, the writing of Machi Tawara as shown in R1 in Part III. Her sentences are short (often without predicates), and reference to the subject/topic "he" is absent in sentences 5, 11, and 14. We must not consider the phenomenon of absence (or deletion) only as a means for mere convenience; we must recognize the positive literary effects it brings to discourse. For example, deletion is a strategy for the *yojoo* (lingering feeling) effect to be discussed in Entry 22.

Additional information

The Japanese preference for deletion and absence of explicit expressions may be traced to the general rhetorical characteristics of the language. According to Satoshi Ishii (1982), Japanese discourse, due to the influence it received from Buddhist teachings, follows discourse patterns different from English. Ishii points out that an American usually organizes his or her ideas explicitly and directly in a linear order as if building a bridge from points A to B. On the other hand, a Japanese often organizes his or her ideas implicitly and indirectly, as if arranging stepping stones from points A to B. Ishii attributes these differences to the Japanese "high context" culture versus American "low context" culture (adopting Edward T. Hall's terms given in Hall [1976], and explored further in Hall and Hall [1987]). The connection between points A and B is not as explicitly expressed in Japanese; interpretation depends heavily on contextual information. The tendency to depend on contextual information is likely to add to the impression that Japanese discourse is vague and hard to follow logically.

There is some truth to this. The vagueness and ambiguity often associated with Japanese rhetoric, however, are part myth. From the Japanese native's point of view, a text is not necessarily vague simply because deletion proliferates. Provided just enough overt information is given, those who share a common knowledge will comprehend the discourse fully. Contrary to the indirectness often associated with the Japanese language, it actually offers mechanisms that allow the writer to express a personal attitude more explicitly, at least in certain aspects, than does English. The notion of vagueness seems to surface when Japanese discourse is viewed from an external point of view. Likewise, the perception of illogicality is likely to result when Japanese discourse is discussed in contrast with Western rhetorical principles.

Nevertheless, reading culturally distant texts does present difficulties. This is because, although cultures share much in common, cultures also create gaps of information stemming from different world views. Understanding requires a process of incorporating new information into already known information, and therefore, what one knows both limits and expands what one can understand. To fill in the gap between these metaphorical informational stepping stones is to grasp the unsaid, the deleted, the assumed and what is shared between the writer and the reader. In this sense, reading culturally distant texts is a challenge; there is much to be learned in every aspect of culture in order to read well.

For example, in R7 we witness a case where the author refers to the Japanese people's image of the desert being too romantic and dreamlike. The author specifically states that the desert is not a fairy-tale world where a prince and princess travel across the silver sand under the moonlight. The reference for this image comes from a well-known song titled *Tsuki no Sabaku* "The Moonlit Desert." Many people with a Japanese cultural background are familiar with this song in which a prince rides a camel with a golden saddle and a silver jar across the desert, and the princess follows him riding another camel with a silver saddle and a golden jar. This scene is portrayed as occurring under the moonlight.

The reader familiar with this song will comprehend the writer's reference to the dreamy, romantic desert scene. The reader unfamiliar with this song will not comprehend fully the writer's intended criticism. Here the decision to use deletion (or absence) involves not simply linguistic forms but whether or not the specific cultural information should be explicitly stated.

## Entry 18 **Sentence-final strategies**

The Japanese language is verb-final, and verbal expressions play a critical role in defining what the sentence means. Because Japanese predicate forms (which normally include verbs, auxiliary verbs and particles) convey rich information, identification of sentence-final forms is useful for understanding not only the sentence meaning but the overall meaning of *danraku* and the entire text.

Let us recall here the two types of writer's intention discussed earlier, i.e., facts and opinions. Presenting facts requires descriptive sentence-final strategy, whereas expressing one's opinion requires more – judgmental and communicative sentence-final forms. Some representative strategies are summarized below.

**Sentence-final strategies**

1. *presenting facts: description*
    1. stating the facts

    2. reporting the facts stated elsewhere (*to yuu, to iwareteiru*)
2. *expressing opinions: judgmental and communicative*
    judgmental
    1. explanatory (*no da, wake da, kara da*)

    2. assumption and view (*daroo, dewanai ka, rashii*)

    communicative
    1. suggestion, requests and other appeals

    2. self-question often used for indirectly presenting the issue of concern (*daroo ka, no daroo ka*)

    3. rhetorical question used for presenting one's opinion

    4. emphatic appeal of personal opinion and views (*nichigainai, to shika kangaerarenai*)

DS7, taken from Kazue Shinkawa's poem, "Do Not Bundle Me," is an example in which the poet expresses a clearly different intention. Sentences that express the writer's plea (sentences 1, 4, 8, and 11) take the communicative sentence-final forms. Other sentences are descriptive. Identifying the writer's intention expressed in each sentence-final form helps interpret the overall tone of the *danraku* and the entire text.

**DS7 (Shinkawa 1985:126–128)**

わたしを束ねないで

1.   わたしを束ねないで
2.   あらせいとうの花のように
3.   白い葱のように
4.   束ねないでください
5.   わたしは稲穂
6.   秋　大地が胸を焦がす
7.   見渡すかぎりの金色の稲穂
・・・
8.   わたしを区切らないで
9.   、や　。　いくつかの段落
10.  そしておしまいに「さようなら」があったりする手紙のようには
11.  こまめにけりをつけないでください
12.  わたしは終わりのない文章
13.  川と同じに
14.  はてしなく流れていく　拡がっていく　一行の詩

<u>Vocabulary</u>:

| 束ねる | たばねる | v | to bundle together |
|---|---|---|---|
| 2. | | | |
| あらせいとう | | n | stock [flower name] |
| 3. | | | |
| 葱 | ねぎ | n | green onion |
| 5. | | | |
| 稲穂 | いなほ | n | ear of a rice plant |

6.

| 胸 | むね | n | chest |
| 焦がす | こがす | v | to burn, to char |

7.

| 見渡すかぎり | みわたすかぎり | | as far as the eye can see |
| 金色の | こんじきの | | golden |

8.

| 区切る | くぎる | v | to punctuate |

9.

| 段落 | だんらく | n | *danraku*, paragraph |

10.

| おしまいに | | | at the end |

11.

| こまめに | | adv | diligently |
| けりをつける | | v | to bring to an end, to finish, to settle |

12.

| 文章 | ぶんしょう | n | discourse |

14.

| はてしなく | | adv | endlessly |
| 流れる | ながれる | v | to flow |
| 拡がる | ひろがる | v | to broaden, to expand |
| 一行 | いちぎょう | n | one line [counter for lines of words] |
| 詩 | し | n | poem |

**Translation**

*Do Not Bundle Me*

1. Do not bundle me (**tabanenaide**)

2. like blooming stocks

3. like white green onions.

4. Please do not bundle me (**tabanenaide kudasai**).

5. I am ears of rice plants

6. that, in fall, burn the bosom of the land,

7. golden ears of rice plants as far as the eye can see.

8. Do not punctuate me (**kugiranaide**)

9. by commas, periods and so many of the *danraku*

10. like a letter that would say "good-bye" at the end.

11. Please do not bring me to an end so carefully and diligently (**tsukenaide kudasai**).

12. I am discourse without an end,

13. like a river

14. flowing endlessly, expanding, a line of a poem.

Japanese sentences are known to end on an affirmation of the writer's attitude. These include expressions such as *to omoimasu, to mo kangae-raremasu, n janai deshoo ka* and so on used to mark the writer's own statement. Rather than simply stating the fact, one's judgment and attitude are expressed by choosing a variety of sentence-final strategies. One may think of these expressions as devices wrapping the main clause with a personal attitudinal expression. Grammatically, these are modal expressions; they function similar to modal auxiliary verbs in English (such as *may, might, can, could, should*, and so on).

– *to omou* (I think that . . . )
– *no dewanai ka to omou* (I think it isn't the case that . . . )
– *yooni omowareru* (to me it seems that . . . )
– *to mo kangaerareru* (it is possible for me to think that . . . )
– *to kangaete ii daroo* (one could perhaps think that . . . )
– *to itte mo yoi* (it is permissible to say that . . . )
– *to mo ieru* (it can also be said that . . . )
– *janai daroo ka* (isn't it the case that . . . )

With these sentence-final forms in mind, let us examine some of the *danraku*-final sentences of R7, "Traveling to the Desert."

*R7:* Danraku-*final sentence-final strategies*

| | |
|---|---|
| Q (sentence 75) | – *miushinawarete shimau* **no dewanai ka** . . . |
| R (sentence 80) | – *hiteisuru koto ni nari wa* **shimai ka** . . . |
| S (sentence 84) | – *ari wa* **shimai ka** . . . |
| T (sentence 91) | – *hansei dake ga aru* **no da**. |
| U (sentence 92) | – *mi ni yuku* **no dearu**. |
| V (sentence 97) | – *kite shimatta* **no ka**! |
| W (sentence 99) | – *utsutte iku. Ikiru koto no kiboo e.* |
| X (sentence 103) | – *tabi* **dewanai ka**. |
| Y (sentence 105) | – *jikkansuru koto da* **to omou**. |
| Z (sentence 106) | – *ataisuru* **no dearu**. |

Indeed, sentences rarely end without expressions of the writer's attitude. Sentences 75, 91, 92, 97, and 106 all take nominal predicates (to be explained in Entry 19). Sentences 75, 80, 84, 97, and 103 all take the question marker *ka*. The expression *shimaika* is a formal written version of *shinai daroo ka* "wouldn't it be?" Sentence 97 is an exclamatory expression; 103 is a rhetorical question emphatically expressing the writer's view. We observe that toward the end of each *danraku*, the writer uses judgmental and communicative sentence-final forms which help create a conclusive tone to the *danraku*.

A similar observation can be made regarding the last seven sentences of R7.

*R7: Last seven sentences, sentence-final strategies*

100.  – *watashi wa* **omou**.

101.  – *omowareru* **kara da**.

102.  – **koto dearu**.

103.  – **dewanai ka**.

104.  – **kangaerareyoo**.

105.  – *koto da to* **omou**.

106.  – *ataisuru* **no dearu**.

Toward the end of an essay, one can expect that the writer will reveal his or her own, often emotionally involved, conclusion. Paying attention to the way in which the last few sentences end helps understand the writer's feelings, views and opinions. In the last seven sentences of R7, mixed strategies are used. Some take the *omou* ending (sentences 100 and 105), some take the nominal predicate form (101, 102, and 106), and others employ question (103) and potential (104) forms. Clearly, all of these express the writer's view. We can readily expect that this segment would show sharp contrast with a discourse segment which presents the facts straightforwardly.

For example, compare the segment we just discussed with another segment taken from R7.

*R7: Sentences 37 to 40, sentence-final strategies*

37. – *shitagatteita*.

38. – *gyooshishita*.

39. – *niranda*.

40. – *koo oshieta*.

Here the sentences end in descriptive predicates – the past tense of informal verb endings without extensive layering of sentence-final strategies. The reader of these expressions knows that they represent (or, more accurately, in the writer's view they represent) facts, and not the writer's views or opinions. The reader may recall a similar discussion earlier in Entry 11 where we examined two different paragraphs from a newspaper column.

## Entry 19 **Nominal and commentary predicate**

Another important feature in the Japanese predicate strategy is the grammatical distinction among nominal, adjectival and verbal predicates. Nominal predicates in Japanese are sentences that take *da* and its variants. For example,

(1) Kawaisan wa gakusei **da**. (nominal predicate)
(Ms. Kawai is a student.)

This sentence contrasts with two other kinds of Japanese predicates, adjectival and verbal.

(2) Kawaisan wa **wakai**. (adjectival predicates, which include *na*-adjectives)
(Ms. Kawai is young.)

(3) Kawaisan wa yoku **benkyoosuru**. (verbal predicate)
(Ms. Kawai studies hard.)

By adding what is usually called a "nominalizer" in Japanese, clauses become like nouns. For example, the nominalization of *benkyoosuru* results in *benkyoosuru koto* and *benkyoosuru n(o)*. These phrases may construct nominal predicates as shown in sentences (4) and (5).

(4) Taisetsuna no wa yoku **benkyoosuru koto** da.
(What is important is to study hard.)

(5) Kawaisan wa hontooni yoku **benkyoosuru n** desu yo.
([literally] It is that Ms. Kawai studies really hard.)

When the verbal phrase transforms itself into a noun, the rhetorical effect changes. According to Robert Langacker (1987:90) the English verb "explode" imposes a "processual construal on the profiled event, while 'explosion' portrays it as an abstract region." The distinction Langacker draws between the process (of what happens) and an abstract region (of a conceptual unit) is useful for understanding the phenomenon of nominalization of clauses as well, which Japanese *n(o)* and *koto* perform.

Nouns cluster about concrete concepts while verbs cluster about concepts of activity. Another way to look at the difference is to distinguish nouns and verbs in terms of time. Nouns are associated with "things" or "objects" not involving the time span, whereas verbs describe prototypically "action" or "events" requiring the duration of time.

Prominent in the Japanese language are a number of sentence types ending with [clause + nominalizer + *da/dearu*]. Let us call these sentences "commentary predicate" because they offer the writer's commentary toward the nominalized concept. The most frequently occurring type is *n(o) da* and its variants (such as *n(o) desu, no, n(o) desu ka* and *no?*). Although the *n(o) da* expression occurs more frequently in spoken Japanese, its use in written discourse is also substantial. It should be added that commentary predicate includes *kara da*, although *kara* is not strictly a nominalizer.

The commentary predicate shares the following features.

1. It takes the grammatical structure of [clause + nominalizer + *da/dearu* (and variants)], that is, the nominalized unit followed by the *be*-predicate; nominalizers include *no, koto, mono, wake*, as well as *kara*.

2. It expresses an interpretive, evaluative, and sometimes emotional commentary of the writer regarding the nominalized unit.

In Japanese texts, making a sentence into a nominal clause and using it in the commentary predicate is a preferred strategy. Preference for this commentary mode of communication is statistically evident. Sentences ending with *n(o) da* (and its variants) occur in approximately 20% to 25% of predicates in casual conversations as well as published *taidan* "dialogue" conversations. Some texts adopting spoken style also feature frequent use of commentary predicate. For example, we find the frequent occurrence of the nominal predicate, often in its shortened version, in R4, Pro-Keds shoes advertising taken from a young men's magazine. This advertising copy takes the tone of a friendly writer talking to the reader and contains, out of a total ten sentences, five commentary predicates.

In paragraph D of R7, "Traveling to the Desert," commentary predicates occur frequently as shown below.

*R7: Paragraph D*

D:

12. Why does traveling mean the same thing as reading? (motsu **no** ka)

13. Perhaps there is no need to elaborate.

14. It is because traveling, like reading, broadens one's small world. (**kara dearu**)

15. To travel is to come out of one's own well and to deeply feel – how vast the world is! (jikkan suru **koto da**)

16. The bewilderment and the perplexity; these (feelings) directly lead one to reflect on oneself. (yuku **no dearu**)

Commentary predicates offer the author's commentary (and sometimes explanatory) attitude. One should pay attention to the frequent occurrence of *n(o) da, wake da* and *kara da* because they offer explanation, cause, reason, or evaluative attitudes of the writer toward the nominalized units. The nominalized conceptual units normally represent something already given, expected, or something the writer presents as known, and because of this, commentary predicates mark cohesion in discourse, further assisting our text comprehension.

### Additional information

Although it is true that nominalization and commentary predicate appear in different frequency depending on the type of discourse segments and genres, the difference also exists across languages. Japanese discourse shows preference toward nominalization in general, and commentary predicate in particular. Such preference is evident when we compare Japanese and English novelistic discourse. I compared Kobo Abe's (1968) *Tanin no Kao* and Saul Bellow's (1944) *Dangling Man* along with E. Dale Saunders' (1966) English translation, *The Face of Another* and Minoru Oota's (1971) Japanese translation *Chuuburarin no Otoko*. Japanese sentences ending with *no da* often appear without comparable nominal construction in English (sentence with *be* and clauses marked by *that, if, to* and verb gerund forms). Furthermore, when sentences without nominal construction in English are translated into Japanese, they often take on nominal predicates. Statistically, in the initial 500 sentences of these novels, nominal predicate appeared in 32.60% of sentences in *Tanin no Kao*, while it appeared in only 3.53% of sentences in English translation. Although *Dangling Man* contained only 2.60% of sentences with nominal predicate, 15.12% of sentences in its Japanese translation contained nominal predicates.

## Entry 20 **Ordering and post-posing**

Although word order within the Japanese sentence is relatively free, various elements within a sentence have preferred positions. Table 7 offers a guide. (Numbers under II show the preferred order of elements within that column.)

**Table 7** Order of elements in Japanese sentence

| I | II | III | IV |
|---|---|---|---|
| topic | 1. temporal | verbal/adjectival predicate | interactional particles |
| | 2. locative | | |
| | 3. subject | | |
| | 4. joint action (*to*) | | |
| | 5. method (*de*) | | |
| | 6. starting point (*kara*) | | |
| | 7. direction (*ni, e*) | | |
| | 8. object (*o*) | | |

Although most sentences follow this order with the verbal elements at the end, sometimes sentences are divided into two parts – the first part ending with a verbal phrase, and the second part consisting of sentence elements appearing as a separate unit. See examples taken from DS5 "Noisy Departure" and R1, an excerpt from Machi Tawara's essay on her *tanka*.

*DS5: Sentences 16 and 17*

16.  Basu wa hitasura hashiri tsuzuketeiru.
(The bus is moving steadily.)

17.  Haneda Kuukoo e to mukatte.
(Heading for Haneda Airport.)

*R1: Sentences 4 and 5*

4.  Futatsu no ao ga sessuru tokoro o saafuboodo no kare ga yuku.
(Where the two bluenesses meet, he moves on the surfboard.)

5.  Marude ichiwa no kamome no yooni.
(As if he were a sea gull.)

Sentences 16 and 17 can be a single sentence if 17 is placed immediately after *basu wa* "the bus" in 16. Likewise, one can combine 4 and 5 into a single sentence by adding 5 immediately after *tokoro o* "place" in 4. We call cases where sentences are divided into two separate (sub-)sentences and then ordered as described above as post-posing. Although post-posing occurs more frequently in spoken style, it occurs in written style as well.

Why do writers use post-posing? To attract attention to the phrase. The post-posed sentence is unusual, dividing the expected sentence into two parts and repositioning one. The post-posed element occupies the independent sentence-initial position in a new context, and this surprises the reader. Moreover, being independent of, and at the same time a part of, the preceding sentence, the post-posed sentence encourages the reader to pause and re-trace its meaning. The incompleteness of the post-posed sentence has an effect similar to deletion – the less said, the more interpretation is required on the part of the reader, thereby often providing a place for contemplation and dramatic appreciation.

In example (1), *Haneda Kuukoo e to mukatte* "To Haneda Airport" is isolated and placed in a separate clause. Likewise in (2), the author adds her expression, *Marude ichiwa no kamome no yooni* "As if he were a sea gull" with prominence, thereby adding to the poetic effect. Moreover, since post-posed elements lack usual sentence-final predicates, they create a lingering feeling that the thought is unfinished. This lingering effect sometimes contributes to the *yojoo* effect (to be discussed in Entry 22).

## Entry 21 **Tense marking**

It is probably a good idea to quickly review the Japanese tense system before we study how tense marking operates in discourse. We understand Japanese tense in terms of two forms, past and non-past; I use the term non-past because the same form marks both present and future tenses. The non-past tense (-*ru* and -*u* forms) is used for (1) description of the present state (for stative verbs), (2) description of definite future (for active verbs), (3) personal will (for active verbs when the subject is "I"), (4) pointing out principles or the nature of things, (5) description of regulations and habits, and (6) description of procedures. In contrast, past tense (-*ta* and -*da* forms) is used for (1) description of past events, (2) commentary on fulfillment of a wish or desire, (3) reaffirmation of an assumption, and (4) expressions that urge someone to act or to perform (abrupt form only).

The non-past Japanese tense is used differently from English in that it does not require grammatical tense agreement. For example, in (1) the subordinate clause does not have to take phrases such as "that day" or the auxiliary verb "would" as is the case in English.

(1)  Tanaka-san wa sono toki ashita wa hareru daroo to itta.
([literally] Tanaka said then that tomorrow it will clear up.)
(Tanaka said then that the next day it would clear up.)

Japanese writers, however, do use the tense shift in text for various literary effects. By focusing on DS4, "Color and Human Life, " let us study how tense is used in discourse.

*DS4: Paragraph B*

5. In old times, it was not possible to manufacture colors as freely as (we do) today. (**dekinakatta**)

6. They used natural colors as they came, by using such things as plant extract and crushed minerals, which they used for dying other things. (chakushoku**shiteita**)

7. But in the mid-nineteenth century in England, the color purple was manufactured from coal tar. (**tsukurareta**)

8. Since then it has become possible to manufacture colors. (dekiru yooni **natta**)

9. Today, it is possible to manufacture tens of thousands of colors. (yooni **natteiru**)

Paragraph B of DS4 presents information distinct in temporal reference: what happened in the past (sentences 5 to 8) and what is happening today (sentence 9). When the writer describes the history of color manufacturing, he chooses the past tense. When the writer discusses what is happening at present (the time of his writing) or when the writer expresses his personal views and thoughts, the tense shifts to non-past.

While the tense shift above is simple, in DS6, "The Deer," we find interesting cases. DS6 is a poem in which the deer is described in the past tense, *tatteita*, *shitteita*, and *miteita*. Line 6 ends with the expression *dekita daroo*: the verb takes the past tense followed by *daroo* which expresses the writer's speculation and doubt. (*Daroo* itself cannot take the past tense; it marks the writer's attitude at the time of the language use.)

Unexplained cases are lines 9 and 10.

**DS6: Lines 9 to 11**

9.　生きる時間が黄金のように光る
10.　彼の棲家である
11.　大きい森の夜を背景にして

9. Ikiru jikan ga oogon no yooni **hikaru**
(The time of living glittering like gold,)

10. Kare no sumika **dearu**
(where he lived,)

11. Ookii mori no yoru o haikei ni shite
(the night of the vast forest behind him.)

Here the poet's perspective is not the mere description of the deer (in the past) any longer. He expresses his thought as depicted in 9 as if he were there and as if he himself witnessed the precious moment of life. The non-past tense offers the rhetorical effect of as-if-being-there, adding significance and drama to the expression. Through this dramatic effect, the reader also senses that the statement in 9 transcends the time constraint. Line 10 modifies *ookii mori* appearing in 11; this post-posed adverbial phrase in turn modifies the main verb *hikaru* in 9, further adding the lingering effect.

Let us study another example taken from R2, "The Ant and the Grasshopper." Here the writer mixes tenses when describing the past event.

*R2:* Danraku *C, D and F*
　　　C:
11. The elderly ant is unsympathetic. (**sokkenai**)

12. But the grasshopper is not too disappointed. (rakutan mo **shinai**)

13. "Oh, well, that's OK.

14. Maybe I should stop by another ant's place . . .''

D:

15. As the grasshopper is about to leave, a young ant calls out. (**yobitomeru**)

16. "Please, please wait for a moment."

F:

23. Thus the grasshopper became the guest of the ant colony. (kyaku to **natta**)

24. That winter turned out to be an enjoyable one for all the ants. (mono to **natta**)

25. It was as if they had installed a jukebox. (mono na **no da**)

26. The grasshopper plays on his violin whatever music the ants request. (hiite **kureru**)

*Danraku* C and D contain non-past tense only and F contains both past and non-past tenses. In the narrative world, events "took" place in the past, and therefore they are reasonably expressed in the past tense. By using non-past tense, however, the writer creates this illusion that the event is now, rather than occurring in the narrative past, thus pulling the reader in, so to speak. When the action is described in non-past tense in the context of the narrative past, such expression de-emphasizes the temporal aspect of the verb. Instead, these non-past expressions describe events as if happening then, as if changing and transforming before the narrator's (and therefore the reader's) very eyes. When the event is described in the past tense, however, the action is conceived as something that already happened and is later recollected and described. The past tense gives the impression that things have happened, have transformed themselves and have changed through time, and are no longer the same.

Compare *danraku* C and D with F which contain past-tense expressions. In F, sentences 23 and 24 refer to past events within the temporal framework of the narrative. These events happened and things have changed. The tense shifts at sentence 25, which offers the writer's explanation. Whenever the writer takes the position of "talking" or "explaining" directly to the reader, the writer is outside the narrative time, and therefore non-past tense appears. Sentence 26 describes a factual statement that is true and that will hold true through time – at least during the grasshopper's stay.

A Japanese text known for an effective tense shift is a short story titled *Torokko* "A Trolley" by Ryuunosuke Akutagawa (1969). In this short story, the narrator describes how a boy named Ryoohei was attracted to the construction trolley going up the mountain side. One day he helps push the trolley and rides it with the workers up into the mountain. Although he is delighted in the beginning, he soon realizes that he came too far. In the relevant *danraku*, Ryoohei's experience is described completely in the past tense except for two sentences given below.

(2) Many yellow fruits are shining in the sunlight, in the orange grove lined along both sides [of the tracks] (kiiroi mi ga ikutsumo hi o **uketeiru**).

*Akutagawa 1969:8, my translation*

(3) In front of the tea house, the evening sun begins to fade shedding its waning light on the plum blossoms in bloom (nishibi no hikari ga **kiekakatteiru**).

*Akutagawa 1969:10, my translation*

Eventually, with nightfall, Ryoohei had to run back home alone along the trolley line. The two above-mentioned sentences appearing in two different *danraku* highlight the mood in which Ryoohei takes in the scenes; one with happiness in (2), and the other with fear in (3). Through the tense shifting, Akutagawa successfully brings into focus Ryoohei's contrasting feelings embedded within the past-tense narrative text.

As a final note, let me discuss the progressive tense in Japanese. In addition to the known characteristic of the progressive tense of Japanese non-stative verbs marking the continuation of action, progressive forms, especially past-tense progressive forms (i.e., -*teita*) index the writer's involving point of view (this explanation is attributed to Hiroko Fujishiro [1996]). Progressive tense describes the event as something being perceived by someone from outside, and the very manner of perception defines the ways in which the writer or the characters interact with the event. Study the sentences taken from Fujishiro (1996).

(4.1)看護婦A　　　田中さん、今日はちゃんとごはん食べた？

(4.2)看護婦B　　　ええ、きれいに食べました/食べていましたよ。

(4.3)田中　　　　　ええ、きれいに食べました/*食べていましたよ。

| (4.1) Nurse A: | Tanaka-san, kyoo wa chanto gohan tabeta? |
| | (Did Mr. Tanaka eat his meals well today?) |
| (4.2) Nurse B: | Ee, kireini tabemashita/tabeteimashita yo. |
| | (Yes, he ate/was eating them completely.) |
| (4.3) Mr. Tanaka | Ee, kireini tabemashita/*tabeteimashita yo. |
| | (Yes I ate/*was eating them completely.) |

(Note: an asterisk is used to indicate ungrammatical or inappropriate forms.) In (4.3) it is inappropriate to answer in the progressive tense – eating meals described as facts, not as a continuing action by the patient. In (4.2), however, it is possible to describe Mr. Tanaka's eating with the progressive tense, *tabeteimashita*. The progressive tense introduces into discourse the situation where the nurse B reportedly witnessed (or perceived) the event, rather than merely stating that Tanaka ate. Conveying this narrator's perceptual observation point of view is an important function of the progressive tense in Japanese.

## Entry 22 *Yojoo* in literary discourse

*Yojoo* is a kind of rhetorical effect often acknowledged and discussed in literature. Although the *yojoo* effect is usually limited to writings aiming for literary effects, its importance in Japanese discourse cannot be denied. This entry explores this literary notion based on the discussion by Akira Nakamura (1984, 1991). *Yojoo* ([literally] remaining, lingering or sustained feeling) is perhaps best translated as the reader's emotional experience triggered by (images created through) reading certain kinds of indirect, often implicit, writing. More concretely, *yojoo* may take the following forms.

1. yojoo *experienced after reading*
    1. sustained visual image

    2. empathy toward the world created by the writing

    3. image associated with characters and their feelings

    4. empathy toward the writer's philosophy expressed by the writing

2. yojoo *experienced while reading*

    5. response toward the unsaid, toward what the reader assumes the writer wants to convey

    6. sentiment toward personal memories recalled by things mentioned

    7. experience of the reader's imagined life transposed in the fictional world

    8. psychological and emotional response, such as sadness, emptiness, loss, surprise, and so on

Given these forms of *yojoo*, where in the text do Japanese readers find them? *Yojoo* is said to be experienced first when emotion is suggested, often in its association with scenes from nature, especially when calm, sad and lonely scenes are described without directly using these descriptive words. Second, topics close to the reader's personal life or in reference to common experiences offer favorable contexts for *yojoo*. Third, one finds the *yojoo* effect mostly at the end of the text, especially when the writer describes human emotions indirectly and suggestively, leaving things unsaid.

In actual texts, the writer may use an array of rhetorical strategies to bring about the *yojoo* effect, including the following.

**Strategies for *yojoo***

1. *post-posing*

    Post-posing gives the impression that the predicate for the post-posed element is missing. This encourages the reader to mentally fill in the gap and to supply the missing element.

2. *use of graphological marks such as dotted lines or the dash*

    The use of these deletion marks encourages the reader to read into the text what has been left out.

3. *past tense*

    Past tense, rather than non-past tense, gives the impression that something really happened; the certainty of reality encourages the reader to think about the consequences.

4. *similes and metaphors*

    The reader is given two images, one associated with the literal meaning and one worked through similes and metaphors. This double interpretation encourages appreciation of the text beyond overt description.

5. *simple and appropriately short sentences*

    Along the lines of less is more in that what is left out prompts a response, short (but not excessively short) sentences encourage *yojoo*.

6. *detached writing*

   Writings in which emotions are apparent but the writer does not directly specify
   them prompt the reader to fill in the reader's own emotions.

7. *unsaid text*

   Avoiding the impression of being complete encourages the reader to supply the
   rest, encouraging lingering *yojoo* feelings.

According to Nakamura (1984, 1991), some writings are rich in *yojoo*
expression. Nakamura cites as an example, the literary text *Tabi no Owari*
"The End of the Travel" by Kunio Tsuji (1986). In this story a middle-aged
Japanese couple travel to Italy and come to know an Italian family, the
Guzeppes. One day the couple encounter a double suicide of young lovers
who were staying at a house across from their hotel. Faced with these sudden deaths, the narrator "I" muses that ironically in death the lovers
might find their spiritual comfort. That night – in which it happened to
rain throughout – "I" thinks about what his wife had mentioned earlier.
His wife had expressed that it might not be a bad idea to live in a quiet
place like this town without anyone knowing about them, without any
social concerns, and without even any personal ambitions. "I" wonders
about the possibility of living in this Italian town – perhaps staying there
offers the desired respite from a hectic life itself. The *danraku* given in the
following in English translation ends the story.

(1.1)  I went on thinking as I watched the rain constantly falling in the dark
deserted street.

(1.2)  Perhaps we will leave this town behind when we take the train tomorrow
afternoon, without any regret . . .

(1.3)  And in five years, memories of the Guzeppe family will also fade.

(1.4)  Including, perhaps, this small incident . . .

(1.5)  Despite that, I felt a strong and desperate desire surging inside me; I want to
stay here in this town.

(1.6)  This is, I felt, something that life encounters once, and yet something one is
destined to part with forever.

(1.7)  "Dionysus, the Lord of Syracuse . . ." I uttered.

(1.8)  And for a long time I gazed at the splash of rain hitting the street as it shone
in the light from the street lamps.

*Tsuji 1986:12, my translation*

First, in this final *danraku*, the image of rain effectively creates a lonesome and sad scene, a likely context for *yojoo*. Second, the writer connects the scene to his internal feelings; the rain adds to the atmosphere for keenly sensing the transient nature of travel, which resonates with the transient nature of life itself. The writer uses uncertain – almost speculative – expressions often; for example *osoraku . . . daroo* in (1.2), *daroo* in (1.3), and *osoraku* in (1.4), through which the reader is encouraged to continue wondering. The use of dotted lines in (1.2), (1.4), and (1.7) are examples of ellipsis which encourages the reader to fill in the *yojoo* feelings on the reader's own terms. To be noted also is the use of the term *watashi* and the tense of the final sentence; . . . *watashi wa . . . gaitoo no hikari no naka ni shibuku amaashi o, nagai koto mitsumeteita. Mitsumeteita* suggests that "I" is not really there; rather "I" observes "I" in a scene that happened in the past. Recall the rhetorical effect of perceptual observation point of view that the progressive past tense brings to discourse (discussed regarding *tabeteimashita* in Entry 21). This detached description of "I" leaves room for the reader to fill in his or her own feelings regarding the incident – perhaps by overlapping himself or herself with "I." The last sentence describes "I" observing nature – without directly stating how "I" felt, further enhancing the *yojoo* effect. When creating *yojoo*, various linguistic, symbolic and cultural factors come into play; *yojoo* depends on overall combined effects of literary strategies.

Another well-known example is the ending of a fiction by Shootaroo Yasuoka titled *Umibe no Kookei* "The Scene of the Sea Side." The narrator tells a story of Shintaroo's mother passing away – as he returns to his home and goes through nine days of social and emotional agony. The last paragraph describes how Shintaroo, after his mother's death, finally steps outside the old house and walks toward the sea. He is hoping that the bright sun will wash away his sad gloomy experience. He is struck by the scene of the sea that suddenly comes into his view – hundreds of black sticks protruding out from the sea. Here are the last two sentences.

(5.1)　風は落ちて、潮の香りは消え失せ、あらゆるものが、いま海底から浮かび上がった異様な光景のまえに、一挙に干上がって見えた。

(5.2)　歯を立てた櫛のような、墓標のような、杭の列をながめながら彼は、たしかに一つの"死"が自分の手の中に捉えられたのをみた。

(5.1)  Kaze wa ochite, shio no kaori wa kieuse, arayuru mono ga, ima kaitei kara ukabiagatta iyoona kookei no mae ni, ikkyoni hiagatte mieta.
(The wind died down and the smell of the ocean disappeared; everything looked suddenly bone-dry in front of the strange scene which has just emerged from the ocean floor.)

(5.2)  Ha o tateta kushi no yoona, bohyoo no yoona, kui no retsu o nagamenagara kare wa, tashikani hitotsu no "shi" ga jibun no te no naka ni toraerareta no o mita.
(Looking at the lines of sticks in the sea – resembling something like the raised teeth of a comb, or tombstones – he undoubtedly saw one "death" captured in the palm of his hand.)
*Yasuoka 1972:231, my translation*

Again in these sentences the narrator describes human emotion symbolized in nature in a detached, almost distant way. In its simplicity, unsaidness and indirectness, the reader senses *yojoo*. In the last sentence we find a death indirectly expressed through a metaphor – black sticks like tombstones. And this final sentence, detached and almost void of feelings further enhances the sense of *yojoo*.

Although *yojoo* is a nebulous and elusive concept whose effect is sometimes difficult to pinpoint, it offers an important literary effect. Especially when reading a literary text, and particularly when the reader senses that toward its conclusion much is left unsaid, it is important to appreciate *yojoo*, or at least to look for such an effect.

## Entry 23 **Quotation and related expressions**

Quotation in Japanese is marked with quotation marks called *kagikakko*. Although many direct quotes appear within quotation marks (and often a line change occurs on the printed page), a direct quote is not always clearly marked. Expressions otherwise considered direct quotations and those marked by the quotative *to* and verbs related to saying, may appear without any graphological marks. Furthermore, the quotative *to* is frequently used not for quotation in a strict sense, but for a variety of expressions related to quotation.

While in English the distinction between direct and indirect quotation is generally clear, in Japanese this distinction is somewhat blurred. However, linguistic features and contextual cues help identify whether a clause

is a direct or indirect quotation, or whether or not it is a quotation at all.
A guideline follows.

**Grammatical features associated with quotation**

1. *direct quotation may contain*
    1. psychological or perception verbs in non-past tense
    2. imperative endings and expressions
    3. polite forms such as *masu* and *desu*
    4. modal expressions such as *daroo, no da, yoo da*, and sentence particles such as *ka, na, ne, no, yo*, and so on
2. *indirect quotation is characterized by*
    1. absence of items 2, 3, and 4 listed above
    2. informal (or abrupt) verb forms (before the quotative marker *to*)

Although these features serve as guidelines for identifying the types of quotation, some cases are difficult to determine. Understanding the types of quotation is important, however, since quotation is a strategy which allows for a mixture of voices. Different voices echo in direct quotations (predominantly the voice of the quoted person) and in indirect quotations (voice of the quoting person). Paying attention to distinct voices in quotation and quotation-like expressions helps us understand textual points of view.

For instance, how should we interpret the following quotations?

(1)  Ototoi atta toki "Kyoo wa tsugoo ga warukute, warui kedo ikarenai no yo" tte itta.
(The day before yesterday she said, "I have other plans today; sorry, I can't go.")

(2)  Tsugoo ga warui kara ikenai tte itteta yo.
(She said that she had other plans and couldn't go.)

(3)  Kyoo wa tsugoo ga warukute ikenai tte itteta yo.
(She said, "I have other plans today and cannot go.")
(She said that she had other plans today [that day] and couldn't go.)
(She said that she had other plans today [that day] and cannot go.)

Let us assume that (1) contains a direct quotation of someone's words reproduced verbatim. (2) does not quote verbatim what was said (absence of *kyoo*, and *yo*, etc.) – a case of indirect quotation. English translation reflects this difference. (3), however, can be interpreted as direct or indirect quotation as shown in the English translation. One must be aware that in Japanese quotation voices may be mixed without overt markings along with mixed tenses, and consequently, the point of view may be shifted. For example, in the third reading of (3), one must interpret the time reference of *kyoo* from the point of view of the quotee.

Given the unclear distinction between direct and indirect quotation, along with the frequent absence of overt markings of who said what in Japanese, one must use other clues to decide whose voice a quotation represents. Here stylistic features such as male versus female speech, level of politeness and honorifics and the age-specific speech style can serve as clues. Because the Japanese language overtly expresses varied speech styles, it is often possible to find out indirectly who speaks in the quotation. Various expressions marking the narrative points of view also give clues as to who the speaker might be.

Quotation is normally followed by the quotative particle *to* (or its colloquial variant *tte*) followed by a verb of "saying" (such as *yuu* "to say," *noberu* "to state," *sakebu* "to scream," *tsubuyaku* "to mumble"). But quotative *to* appears in a broader context than the strict case of "saying" something. It appears with the verbs of "hearing" and "reporting" such as *kiku* "to hear" and *uwasasareru* "to be rumored." Critically important in Japanese is the quotation strategy frequently used with the verbs of "thinking" and "feeling." For example, observe the following segment taken from DS5, "Noisy Departure."

**DS5: Sentences 20 and 21**

20. この辺で「あれ？」と思われる読者もおられるかもしれない。

21. 矢吹由利子、桑田旭子に加えて、もう一人、甚だユニークな仲間、弘野香子がいるんじゃないの、と。

20. Kono hen de "are?" **to omowareru** dokusha mo orareru kamoshirenai.
(At this point some of the readers may think "Wait!")

21. Yabuki Yuriko, Kuwata Akiko ni kuwaete, moo hitori, hanahada yuniikuna nakama, Hirono Kyooko ga iru n janai no, **to**.
("In addition to Yuriko Yabuki and Akiko Kuwata isn't there another rather unusual (clique) member, Kyooko Hirono?")

The direct quotation in sentence 20 is an expression of what the writer thinks some of the readers may think. In fact, all of sentence 21 is understood to be the thought the readers are assumed to have. Of course this is not a direct quotation in a strict sense; no one actually said the quoted passage. But quotative expressions of this type occur frequently in Japanese, often adding dialogue-like effect to Japanese written discourse.

We can find other similar examples from R7, "Traveling to the Desert."

*R7: Sentences 15 and 76*

15.  Tabi to wa, jibun no sumu ido kara nukedete, sekai wa hiroi n da naa, **to jikkansuru** koto da.
(To travel is to come out of one's own well and to deeply feel – how vast the world is!)

76. Shikashi, mate yo, **to** watashi wa **kangaeru.**
(But, wait – I think.)

Notice direct-quotation-like expressions used for presenting thought in sentences 15 and 76. The expression *sekai wa hiroi n da naa* and *mate yo* both contain interactional particles (*naa* and *yo*). These are expressions a person utters in conversation, a style clearly distinct from other parts of the sentence. Because these are features of actual speech, we, as readers, get the impression of having direct access to how the writer thinks – almost to the extent that we are able to listen in on his thinking.

Compare these two direct representations of thought with sentence 100 of R7.

100.  Kono imi de, sabaku koso mottomo romanchikkuna basho deari, meruhen no sekai da **to** watashi wa **omou.**
(In this sense, I think the desert is the most romantic place, a world of fairy tales.)

In 100, the thought is expressed in indirect quotation. Using quotation which contains direct speech features in a broad context – as shown in sentence 20 of DS4 and sentences 15 and 76 of R7 – makes it possible to mix different worlds, the world where the quoted person says (or, thinks) something and another world where what is reportedly and presumably said (or, thought) appears in quotation.

Writers use quotation and related expressions for the following rhetorical effects.

1. Direct quotation increases drama by adding excitement and change to otherwise reportive narrative discourse.

2. The spoken language appearing in the direct quotation expresses abundantly and directly the speaker's feelings, thoughts and other reactions to the context in which the utterance is made.

3. The speech style in direct quotation signals the socio-cultural background of the speaker (for example, occupation, social status, gender, age, region [through dialect and speech pattern], and so on).

4. The speech style in direct quotation can reveal interpersonal relationships among quoted people (for example, intimacy level, relative social status, the type of relationship, and so on).

One additional point should be briefly mentioned regarding quotation and related expressions. We must remind ourselves that quotations, including those graphologically marked direct quotations, do not guarantee that those utterances were actually made. In fact, as Deborah Tannen (1989) points out, reportive speech in language is actually constructed by the quoter. Constructed speech is a literary and conversational tool for mixing different voices. One can think of various expressions that may be quoted – summary of what was said, what one says to oneself, what the listener thought the speaker said; even an animal's feelings can be expressed by human speech-like quotation. Moreover, the writer may make one of the characters say, "*Watashi ga yatta to yuu n desu ka? Masaka!*" "Are you saying that I did it? No way!" although no one actually said "*Omae ga yatta n da*" "You did it."

Some clear cases of constructed dialogue follow. First, the segment taken from R7, "Traveling to the Desert."

**R7: Sentences 87 to 91**

87.　私は砂漠に身を置くたびに、ある探検家がしみじみ洩らしたつぎのことばをかみしめる。

88.　「砂漠とは、そこへ入りこむさきには心配で、そこから出て行くときにはなんの名残もない。

89.　そういう地域である。

90.　砂漠には何もない。

91.　ただ、その人自身の反省だけがあるのだ。」

87.  Watashi wa sabaku ni mi o oku tabini, aru tankenka ga shimijimi morashita
tsugi no kotoba o kamishimeru.
(Whenever I place myself in the desert, I ponder upon the following words that an explorer
spoke with deep-felt emotion.)

88.  "Sabaku towa, soko e hairikomu saki niwa shinpai de, soko kara dete iku toki
niwa nanno nagori mo nai.
("The desert is a place where one worries before entering, and one never feels reluctant
when departing.)

89.  Sooyuu chiiki dearu.
(Such a place, it is.)

90.  Sabaku ni wa nanimo nai.
(There is nothing in the desert.)

91.  Tada, sono hito jishin no hansei dake ga aru no da.''
(Nothing except a person's self-reflection.'')

In the above segment, the writer states that he recalls the words of his
explorer friend (sentences 88 to 91). But it is uncertain (in fact unlikely)
that his friend actually said what was quoted verbatim. More likely,
although the writer does not recall the words verbatim, he put the expression in the direct quotation simply because this is an effective way to
make his point.

Quoting others is useful particularly when one writes to persuade.
For example, in newspaper opinion columns, graphologically marked
quotations appear frequently. Quotations highlight the known concepts
and ideas, report someone else's opinions, report hearsay, and appear
as noun modifiers. In persuasive discourse, incorporating others' voices
reinforces one's position since support from others in society adds credi-
bility to one's view. The study of thirty-eight newspaper opinion columns
(*Asahi Shimbun*'s "Column, my view" appearing in January to April of
1994) showed that graphologically marked quotations touch 32.8% of all
sentences; either the *kagikakko* markers appear within the sentence or
the sentences appear within the *kagikakko* markers.

Quotation – whether direct or indirect – involves more than who said what in what words. Quotation generates rhetorical effects such as those mentioned here. Examining quotation from the perspective of discourse principles such as the mixing of different narrative voices as well as the repeated shifting of points of view also helps in placing "others' speech" in context.

In scanning a Japanese text, the reader might notice the high frequency of quotative *to* and *to yuu* (and related forms). *To yuu* is used in many ways: (1) a quotation marker – direct or indirect, (2) a constructed dialogue – representing thoughts, imagination, summary, and all other possible things that are presented in a quotation, (3) for the presentation of proper names – *Tanaka to yuu hito* (the person called Tanaka), and (4) in idiomatic ways such as *hito to yuu hito* (every possible person).

One may use the optional *to yuu* for expressing general concepts or to indicate indirectness as well. For example, *tabi o suru to yuu koto* "the fact of traveling," instead of *tabi o suru koto* "traveling" and *shinu to yuu koto* "the fact of dying" instead of *shinu koto* "dying" (appearing in R7). *To yuu* also more closely connects direct speech with noun phrases. For example, *toosoosuru zo to yuu osore* "the fear that he will run away" instead of *toosoosuru osore* "fear of running away." In general, the insertion of *to yuu* in the clause-noun structure evokes the sense of quotation, that someone is voicing the content of the clause.

Beyond these cases, *to yuu* and related expressions of saying are idiomatically used. These idiomatic markers reveal how the writer "says" or "talks" in the text. They qualify the degree of the writer's commitment to the statement. Examples follow.

(4)    新宿といえば誰でもあの高層ビル群を思い浮かべるでしょう。

(5)    はっきり言ってそんな規則はナンセンスだと思います。

(6)    言いかえればそれはもう無効であるということですね。

(7)    今改革と述べましたが、それについて少し説明する必要があるものと思われます。

(8)    木村さんは木曜日の朝いつものように 8 時に家を出たという。

*1. topic marking*

    *to yuu no wa* (what is said is), *to ieba* (as for, speaking of), *ni kanshite yuu to* (regarding)

    (4) Shinjuku **to ieba** dare demo ano koosoo birugun o omoiukaberu deshoo.

    (Speaking of Shinjuku, everyone perhaps thinks of those high-rise buildings.)

*2. qualification – commenting on what one says*

    *kara yuu to* (speaking from), *gutaitekini yuu to* (in concrete terms), *kantanni ieba* (put simply), *hakkiri itte* (frankly), *yuu made mo nai koto desu ga* (needless to mention/elaborate but), *hitokuchi de yuu to* (in a word)

    (5) **Hakkiri itte** sonna kisoku wa nansensu da to omoimasu.

    (Frankly, I think such regulations don't make sense.)

*3. paraphrasing*

    *iikaereba* (in other words, put differently)

    (6) **Iikaereba** sore wa moo mukoo dearu to yuu koto desu ne.

    (In other words, those are no longer effective, right?)

*4. discourse organization markers*

    *ima . . . to nobemashita ga* (I just mentioned . . . but), *tsugini nobemashoo* (let me state next)

    (7) Ima kaikaku **to nobemashita ga**, sore nitsuite sukoshi setsumeisuru hitsuyoo ga aru mono to omowaremasu.

    (I just mentioned "renovation," but perhaps a bit of explanation is necessary.)

*5. utterance-final qualification*

    *to ieru* (can be said), *to yuu koto ga dekiru* (can be said that), *tomo ieru no dewanai daroo ka* (isn't it that one can say that), *to yuu* (reportedly, they say, I heard)

    (8) Kimura-san wa mokuyoobi no asa itsumo no yooni hachiji ni uchi o deta **to yuu**.

    (Kimura reportedly left home as usual at 8:00 a.m. on Thursday.)

A couple of examples from R7, "Traveling to the Desert," follow where the author uses an idiomatic expression through which he describes his attitude toward his own writing.

*R7: Sentences 12–14, and 79*

    12. Why does traveling mean the same thing as reading?

    13. **Yuu** made mo aru mai.

    (Perhaps there is no need to elaborate.)

14. It is because traveling, like reading, broadens one's small world.

79. Bunka towa **ittemireba**, yokeina mono no shuuseki na no dewanai no ka.
([literally] As for culture, if I say so, isn't it something of an accumulation of unnecessary things?)

Whether it is a quotation, thought representation or idiomatic expression, paying special attention to *to yuu* (and related phrases) assists in our understanding of the text. This special attention enables the reader to follow the writer's line of thought, especially how the writer incorporates others' views as well as how the writer weaves his or her act of writing and manner of thinking into the text.

## Entry 24 **Modification grouping**

Understanding Japanese discourse depends not only on a grasp of discourse principles but also on a knowledge of how to interpret accurately the meaning of long complex sentences. Since written Japanese sentences are often structured with multiple layers of clauses, we must understand the inner workings of these sentences.

One basic clue for handling complex sentence structure is to divide the elements into modification units. Incorporating the work of Seiichi Makino and Michio Tsutsui (1995), let me explore this idea of modification grouping further. A modification unit consists of modifying phrases / clauses with the items modified, and constitutes a closely related group in terms of both grammar and meaning. There are two major groupings of modification; (1) those that modify nouns and nominalizers, and (2) others that modify other items such as verbs, adjectives and particles. Some sample groupings follow.

Types of modification grouping

| Modifying elements | Items modified | meaning |
|---|---|---|
| Group (1): Modification of nouns | | |
| A: Phrasal | | |
| **adjective** | **noun** | |
| muzukashii | hon | (difficult book) |
| atarashii | koto/no | (the fact that is new) |
| **nominal modification phrase** | | |
| nihongo no | hon | (Japanese book) |
| B: Clausal | | |
| **clausal modifier** | | |
| kesa yonda | shinbun | (the newspaper I read this morning) |
| rainen nihon e iku | koto/no | ([literally, the fact that I go to Japan] my going to Japan next year) |
| nihon ni itta | toki | (the time [when] I went to Japan) |
| Group (2): Modification of elements other than nouns | | |
| A: Phrasal | | |
| **adverb** | **adjective** | |
| hontooni | utsukushii | (really beautiful) |
| **clausal modifier** | **adjective** | |
| warai ga tomaranaku naru kurai | omoshiroi | (funny to the point that one cannot stop laughing) |
| **adverb** | **verb** | |
| asa hayaku | okiru | ([I] get up early in the morning.) |
| **attitudinal adverb** | | |
| doose | aenai daroo | ([I] won't be able to see [him] anyway.) |
| B: Clausal | | |
| **clausal modifier** | **particle** | |
| mado o akeru | to | (when I open the window) |
| **clausal modifier** | **connective** | |
| densha ga okureta | kara | (because the train was late) |

| <u>Modifying Elements</u> | <u>Items Modified</u> |
|---|---|
| 1.A | |
| むずかしい | 本 |
| 新しい | こと／の |
| にほんごの | 本 |

1.B

| 今朝読んだ | 新聞 |
| 来年日本へ行く | こと／の |
| 日本に行った | 時 |

2.A

| 本当に | 美しい |
| 笑いがとまらなくなるくらい | おもしろい |
| 朝早く | 起きる |
| どうせ | 会えないだろう |

2.B

| 窓を開ける | と |
| 電車が遅れた | から |


Grouping these items together helps identify larger chunks within a sentence. As a sample case, we now examine the first two paragraphs of R6, a newspaper essay column *Tensei Jingo*. In the presentation to follow, the modifiers are in brackets followed by the modified elements (in bold letters and double-underlined). Paragraph presentation (1) shows the noun modification, while paragraph presentation (2) illustrates modification groups other than those of nouns.


Paragraph Presentation (1)

1. 　【はらはらと葉の散る】**季節**である。
2. 　【熊手やほうきで集めた】**落ち葉**を、昔はよく焼いた。
3. 　一般に焚き火が珍しくなかった。
4. 　人々は尻などをあぶりながら雑談をし、
   子どもたちは【火の】**おこし方**や
   【始末の】**仕方**を覚えた。

5. 　そういえば、【いまの】**子ども**には、
   【日常的に火をおこす】**機会**がない。

6.　　　【囲炉裏の】ほたびや
　　　　【おきの】<u>熱気</u>などにも、
　　　　なじみが薄いだろう。
7.　　　そういう、
　　　　【【【火の】<u>様子</u>を示す】<u>言葉</u>に接する】<u>こと</u>もないか
　　　　も知れない。
8.　　　煙たさも経験できず、
　　　　【焚き火で焼きいもをつくる】<u>楽しみ</u>も
　　　　知らぬとすると、残念だ。

Paragraph Presentation (2)

1.　　　【はらはらと】葉の<u>散る</u>季節である。
2.　　　【熊手やほうきで】<u>集めた</u>落ち葉を、
　　　　昔は【よく】<u>焼いた</u>。
3.　　　【一般に】焚き火が<u>珍し</u>くなかった。
4.　　　人々は尻などをあぶりながら雑談をし、
　　　　子どもたちは火のおこし方や始末の仕方を覚えた。

5.　　　そういえば、いまの子どもには、
　　　　【日常的に】火を<u>おこす</u>機会がない。
6.　　　囲炉裏のほたびやおきの熱気などにも、
　　　　なじみが薄いだろう。
7.　　　そういう、
　　　　火の様子を示す言葉に接することもないかも知れない。
8.　　　煙たさも経験できず、
　　　　【【焚き火で】焼きいもをつくる楽しみ<u>も</u>
　　　　知らぬとする】<u>と</u>、残念だ。

Among noun modification groups, sentence 7 in paragraph presentation (1) shows multiple layers of modification groupings embedded within: *hi no* modifies *yoosu*, *hi no yoosu o shimesu* modifies *kotoba*, and *hi no yoosu o shimesu kotoba ni sessuru* modifies *koto*. Sentence 8 of paragraph presentation (2) is also a case of multiple modification groupings: *takibi de* is an adverbial modifier modifying the verb *tsukuru*, and the clause, *takibi de yakiimo o tsukuru* modifies *tanoshimi* and the entire clause *takibi de yakiimo o tsukuru tanoshimai mo sniranu to suru*, modifies the particle *to*. When reading long sentences, it is useful to re-write them as shown in (2) so that multiple modification groupings can be assigned. To avoid potential confusion in the markings, investigate noun modifications and others separately as shown in (1) and (2).

Here are some ideas for reading sentences with multiple modification clauses.

1. Find adjectives and nominal modification phrases that modify nouns and noun phrases. Identify them as modification groups. (e.g., *utsukushii kisetsu, hi no okoshikata*)

2. Find adjectives and nominal modification phrases that precede nominalizers such as *koto* and *no*. Identify them as modification groups. (e.g., *mezurashii koto*)

3. Find adverbs that modify adjectives and verbs, and identify them as modification groups. (e.g., *haraharato ha no chiru, yoku yaita*)

4. Find informal (abrupt) verb endings that do not appear in the sentence-final position, especially paying attention to those cases where the verbs are immediately followed by nouns and noun phrases. Identify them as clausal modification groups. (e.g., *haraharato ha no chiru kisetsu, hi no yoosu o shimesu kotoba*)

5. Find informal (abrupt) verb endings that precede nominalizers such as *koto* and *no*. Identify them as clausal modification groups. (e.g., *yoosu o shimesu kotoba ni sessuru koto*)

6. Find informal (abrupt) verb endings that precede particles, connectives and so on, and identify them as clausal modification groups. (e.g., *shiranu to suru to*)

7. Recognize all modification groupings and understand the meaning accordingly.

8. When multiple modification applies to a single modified element, sort out the relationship among them, while recognizing multiple layers of modification groups embedded within.

9. Use the chunks of modification groups when identifying their functions in relation to the subject, predicate, topic, and comment of the entire sentence.

10. Understand the meaning of the entire sentence as you integrate modification groups according to their grammatical relations.

## Entry 25 **Complex sentences**

Besides the modification groupings, two other guidelines are useful for the accurate interpretation of sentential meaning in discourse. The first is the predicate search and the second, the topic-comment search. Assuming that modification units are already determined, the next task involves realizing the grammatical relationship among these chunks. The first is to identify the main predicate. The main predicate is most likely to be found at the very end of the sentence. If the sentence contains coordinate clauses, those clause-final predicates should be noted as well. Modifying predicates are ignored in this task; for example, *chiru* in *haraharato ha no chiru kisetsu dearu* is a verb, but since it modifies a noun, it is irrelevant for our present task.

Using the identical text segment examined in Entry 24, we first underline predicates. See the Japanese text presented below. The sentences are broken down into smaller units in order to show the main predicates clearly.

|   | predicate | corresponding overt subject and topic |
|---|---|---|
| 1. | はらはらと葉の<br>散る季節<br><u>である</u>。 | |
| 2. | 熊手やほうきで集めた落ち葉を、<br>昔はよく**<u>焼いた</u>**。 | 昔は |
| 3. | 一般に焚き火が<br><u>珍しくなかった</u>。 | 焚き火が |
| 4. | 人々は<br>尻などを**<u>あぶり</u>**ながら<br>雑談を<u>し</u>、<br>子どもたちは<br>火のおこし方や始末の仕方を<u>覚えた</u>。 | 人々は<br><br>子どもたちは |
| 5. | そういえば、<br>いまの子どもには、<br>日常的に火をおこす機会が<br><u>ない</u>。 | 機会が |
| 6. | 囲炉裏のほたびやおきの熱気などにも、<br>なじみが<br><u>薄いだろう</u>。 | なじみが |

7.　そういう、
　　火の様子を示す言葉に
　　接することも
　　<u>ないかも知れない</u>。　　　　　　　　　ことも
8.　煙たさも
　　経験で<u>きず</u>、
　　焚き火で焼きいもをつくる楽しみも
　　知らぬとすると、
　　<u>残念だ</u>。

Sentence 4 contains multiple coordinate clauses, and it is necessary to identify three different predicates. Sentence 8 also has multiple clauses and contains two predicates. Once the predicate is identified, one should undertake the search for the corresponding subject or topic. As shown in the presentation of the Japanese text, it is possible to extract overt subjects and topics from the text. We must interpret covert ones based on available discourse knowledge. For this purpose it is useful to construct a table like the one below.

**Table 8** Predicate-subject/topic relations of R6, paragraphs A and B

| Sentence number | predicate | subject | topic (covert subjects and topics in parentheses) |
|---|---|---|---|
| 1 | dearu | | (ima wa) |
| 2 | yaita | (hitobito ga) | mukashi wa |
| 3 | mezurashikunakatta | takibi ga | |
| 4 | aburi | | hitobito wa |
| | shi | | (hitobito wa) |
| | oboeta | | kodomotachi wa |
| 5 | nai | kikai ga | |
| 6 | usui daroo | najimi ga | |
| 7 | nai kamoshirenai | | koto mo |
| 8 | dekizu | | (kodomotachi wa) |
| | zannen da | | (sore wa) |

Here are some guidelines for reading complex sentences, after identifying modification clauses.

1. Identify the main predicate and the predicate in the coordinate clause.

2. Identify the sentence-final predicate, and find the corresponding subject and topic. Do the same for predicates in coordinate clauses.

3. If no overt subject or topic is found, search for a relevant topic in the immediate context.

4. Recognize subject-predicate and topic-comment relations within the sentence, by noting that under normal circumstances the topic appears first and comment appears last.

5. Incorporate modification groups into appropriate grammatical and semantic relationships in correspondence with the overall subject-predicate and topic-comment structure of the sentence.

6. Identify and interpret discourse strategies such as connectives, demonstratives, repetition and so on when forming the meaning.

7. Understand the meaning of the entire sentence as you confirm how it fits in the overall discourse organization.

8. When facing difficulties, ignore the order of the suggestions made above. Do the kind of task that seems relatively easy at the time, and use that knowledge to compensate for the lack of knowledge elsewhere.


## Entry 26 **Viewing position and focus of attention**

In Entry 9 we discussed the narrative point of view, with special attention given to how the narrator reveals himself or herself in the narrative world when talking to the reader. This entry addresses two additional aspects involving the writer's point of view, with closer attention given to linguistic forms associated with them, namely, (1) viewing position and (2) focus of attention.

Incorporating the work of Masae Matsuki (1992), we concentrate on how viewing positions and foci of attention are marked in Japanese sentences. First, let us examine sentences (1) to (3), all similar except that they take different particles associated with the adjectival predicate *chikai* "near."

(1)    神戸は大阪から近い。
(2)    神戸は大阪に近い。
(3)    神戸は大阪と近い。
(4)    神戸と大阪は近い。

(1) Koobe wa Oosaka kara chikai.
([literally] Kobe is near from Osaka.)

(2) Koobe wa Oosaka ni chikai.
([literally] Kobe is near to Osaka.)

(3) Koobe wa Oosaka to chikai.
([literally] Kobe is near with Osaka.)

(4) Koobe to Oosaka wa chikai.
(Kobe and Osaka are close [to each other].)

In sentences (1) to (3) the focus of attention is placed on the topic phrase, Kobe. The writer's viewing positions, however, differ in that (1) is viewed from somewhere near Osaka as reflected in the expression *Oosaka kara* "from Osaka," (2) is viewed from somewhere near Kobe as suggested by the expression *Oosaka ni* "to Osaka," and (3) is viewed somewhere in-between in a more or less neutral manner – the two locations are viewed from a position apart from both – while focusing on Kobe.

Sentence (4) represents a sentence structure similar yet different. (4) is an example where the viewing position is apart from both Kobe and Osaka and both locations are in focus. This phenomenon is summarized in Table 9.

**Table 9**  Assignment of viewing position and focus of attention for sentences

|  | *viewing position* | *focus of attention* |
| --- | --- | --- |
| *Koobe wa Oosaka kara chikai.* | near Osaka | Kobe |
| *Koobe wa Oosaka ni chikai.* | near Kobe | Kobe |
| *Koobe wa Oosaka to chikai.* | (neutral) | Kobe |
| *Koobe to Oosaka wa chikai.* | (neutral) | Kobe and Osaka |

We find another Japanese device marking viewing position and focus of attention in the verbs of giving and receiving. The verb *kureru* "to give to me/someone close to me" is a good example where the viewing position is close to the receiver and yet the focus of attention is on the giver. Although these effects are subtle, they are nonetheless important for accurately interpreting the writer's position.

In addition to the use of these particles to mark the viewing position, several phrases are useful for expressing from what or whose viewing positions the statement is made. The following idiomatic phrases mark viewing positions and indicate the degree the writer thinks the statements are valid.

(5)    日本語の動詞は使い方から見て、大きく４つに分けることができる。

(6)    彼にとって幸せとは自分が出世することであった。

(7)    インド人にとって、死ぬということは母なるガンジスへ帰ってゆくことなのだ。

(8)    あの青年は日本人にしては自分の意見をはっきり言う。

(9)    ニューヨークへ行ってきた友人によると、五番街は日本人の観光客であふれているそうだ。

(10)    インドの友人の話によると、女の人はつい涙をこぼしてしまうので遠慮するのだ、とのことであった。

*. . . kara mite* (viewed from . . . )
(5)  Nihongo no dooshi wa tsukaikata **kara mite**, ookiku yottsu ni wakeru koto ga dekiru.
(Japanese verbs, when viewed from their use, can be divided into four groups.)

*. . . ni totte* (for . . . )
(6)  Kare **ni totte** shiawase towa jibun ga shussesuru koto deatta.
(For him success meant his getting ahead in society.)

(7)  Indojin **ni totte**, shinu to yuu koto wa hahanaru Ganjisu e kaette yuku koto na no da. (Similar to R7, sentence 36)
(I understand that for the people in India, to die is to return to the mother Ganges.)

*. . . ni shitewa* (given that . . . )

(8) Ano seinen wa nihonjin **ni shitewa** jibun no iken o hakkiri yuu.

(That young man, given that he is a Japanese, expresses his opinion clearly.)


*. . . ni yoruto* (according to . . . )

(9) Nyuu Yooku e itte kita yuujin **ni yoruto**, Gobangai wa nihonjin no kankookyaku de afureteiru soo da.

(According to my friend who came back from New York, Fifth Avenue is mobbed by Japanese tourists.)


(10) Indo no yuujin no hansahi **ni yoruto**, onna no hito wa tsui namida o koboshiteshimau node enryosuru no da, to no koto deatta. (Similar to R7, sentence 34)

(According to my Indian friend, women sometimes cannot hold back tears and therefore they decline attending.)


Marking the viewing position sometimes requires a corresponding predicate style. Among those listed above, especially to be noted is the use of *ni yoruto*. As shown by examples (9) and (10), the sentence with the *ni yoruto* phrase must end with an expression conveying hearsay such as *soo da* and *to no koto deatta*, although the English version does not require literal translation of these phrases.


## Entry 27 **Experiential impressionism**

The writer expresses his or her own voice and attitude through various strategies, some of which are critically important in Japanese. First, let me start with a well-known beginning of a novel *Yukiguni* by Yasunari Kawabata (1996:7) and its English translation, "Snow Country" by Edward Seidensticker (1964:11).


(1.1)  国境の長いトンネルを抜けると雪国であった。

(1.2)  夜の底が白くなった。

(1.3)  信号所に汽車が止まった。

(1.1)  Kunizakai no nagai tonneru o nukeru to yukiguni deatta.

(1.2)  Yoru no soko ga shiroku natta.

(1.3)  Shingoojo ni kisha ga tomatta.

(2.1)  The train came out of the long tunnel into the snow country.

(2.2)  The earth lay white under the night sky.

(2.3)  The train pulled up at a signal stop.

At issue is the sentence structure of (1.1). The Japanese original contains no indication of the agent. Who, or what, did *tonneru o nukeru*? Contrast this sentence with its English translation in which "the train" is the agent. Although sentence (1.1) is taken from a literary text, this type of sentence construction is by no means limited to literary work. Study examples (3), (4), and (5).

(3)    あした晴れればいいんですけど。

(4)    私の気持ちなどわかってもらえないだろう。

(5)    まもなく、神宮前、神宮前でございます。

(3) Ashita harereba ii n desu kedo.
([literally] Tomorrow, if it clears up, it would be nice.)
(I hope it will clear up tomorrow.)

(4) Watashi no kimochi nado wakatte moraenai daroo.
([literally] Anyway, my feelings, [they] won't understand [for me].)
(I don't think [they] will understand my feelings.)

(5) Mamonaku Jinguu Mae, Jinguu Mae degozaimasu.
([literally] Soon, Jinguu Mae Station, Jinguu Mae Station, it is.)
(Soon we will be arriving at the Jinguu Mae Station.)

Here again, the agent is missing. Although it is possible to create an agentless English sentence, the penchant in English is to describe events in terms of who-does-what-to-whom. Reading all Japanese sentences with this expectation will only increase one's frustration. One way to understand sentences such as (1.1), (3), (4), and (5) is to vicariously experience the writer's involvement with the world described.

Think of the writer "I," as being in the middle of the experience described by these sentences. Accordingly, sentence (1) might be read – I was there experiencing this train ride that went through the tunnel. My view opened at the end of the tunnel, and there I was in snow country. (3) may read – For me, if it clears up tomorrow, it would be nice; this is what I experience now. One may interpret (4) – To me the most pressing issue is my feelings, and these feelings, they would not be able to understand; that's what I feel now. (5) may be read – We will soon experience the stop, Jinguu Mae; coming to the Jinguu Mae Station is the most immediate and important thing at the moment. The person involved in communication takes precedence over the description of the event. The writer experiences (or imagines to experience) the event, responds to it, and creates the sentence as an immediate personal response to it. The sentences are impressionistic in that they describe the writer's immediate impressions on the events and matters.

Other Japanese sentence structures functioning in similar ways follow.

(6)    海が見える。

(7)    お金が欲しい。

(8)    ふるさとがなつかしい。

(6) Umi ga mieru.
(The ocean is in view.)

(7) Okane ga hoshii.
(Money is what I want.)

(8) Furusato ga natsukashii.
(Hometown is something I miss.)

Sentences (6), (7), and (8) express the way in which the writer responds to the relevant things happening to him or her. The passive nature of these sentences makes sense when the whole event becomes the experience the writer reacts to and expresses the self's feelings in an impressionistic way.

Recall our DS2, "Once Burned, Always Burned." This essay contains sentences with no overt subjects, among which is sentence 5 whose interpretation requires some care.

5. Mottainai ga, korekara saki nannen mo osewani naru daidokoro no kataude o shiagete yuku no dakara, kono kurai wa oome ni mite morawanakutewa naranai. (Although it is a bit wasteful, since I am rearing my right-hand assistant in the kitchen from whom I will receive assistance for some years to come, I suppose this extent of waste should be tolerated.)

Nowhere in this sentence do we find an overt agent. Moreover, verbs are associated with different elements of description. The entire sentence, however, makes sense when one reads it as an experience-based impression of the writer. First, the writer's feeling of wastefulness surfaces; then she feels that her situation is an exception since she is investing in something that will help her for many years. *Mite morau* "have someone regard" is used because the writer expects receiving someone else's tolerance and good will. This self-centered description of the event is prevalent in Japanese discourse. To view Japanese sentence construction and discourse from the writer's personal perspective is useful, particularly when we find it difficult to comprehend who is doing what in the described event and to understand to whom the event is meaningful. Such problems are likely to arise when the agent and its relevant predicate are not clearly presented in the text.

Additional information

Yoshihiko Ikegami (1981, 1988, 1991) convincingly points out the non-agent preference of the Japanese language. Ikegami identified Japanese as "Become-language" versus English "Do-language." In Become-language, the agent becomes less prominent and more diffused, and the context in which the agent appears assumes greater significance. Think of sentences such as *Kodomo ga sannin aru* "([literally] There are three children) He has three children" and *Kono tabi kekkonsuru koto ni narimashita* "([literally] It has become that) we will be getting married soon." The Japanese language tends to frame the event as something existing (rather than someone-possessing-something), and as something becoming (rather than happening). The event occurs often beyond the agent's control. The Japanese language provides a means to interpret an event as a situation that becomes and comes to be on its own, while English provides a means to perceive an event resulting from an agent doing something and thus causing things to happen.

This structural preference of the Japanese sentence influences how discourse is formed. The agent-free sentence structure allows the writer to construct a piece of text based on the writer's experiential impression.

### Entry 28 **Adverb–predicate correspondence**

Some Japanese adverbs require corresponding types of predicate. Knowing the adverb–predicate correspondence is useful particularly because sometimes once an adverb is recognized, one can predict the consequent predicate, and thus predict the meaning of the entire sentence. The adverb–predicate combination directly marks the writer's attitude toward the statement. Adverbs appearing in combination with predicates are not manner adverbs (such as "slowly" in a sentence "I walked slowly," where the adverb describes the manner in which the action takes place). Rather, they are adverbs that express the degrees and types of the writer's attitude and judgment.

The most frequently occurring adverb–predicate correspondence is the kind where the predicate takes negation. Other cases of adverb–predicate correspondence include (1) adverbs often followed by conditionals, and (2) adverbs accompanying similes. There are also several adverbs that offer distinct meanings depending on whether they appear with affirmative or negative predicates.

The adverb–predicate combination signals the writer's personal attitude, and it identifies the writer's position toward the statement. These attitude-indicating adverbs and their corresponding predicates personalize the discourse in that the tone of voice is made manifest. Identifying them and appropriately integrating their attitudinal information can guide the reader in correctly interpreting the writer's intention.

(1)     イタリア語はぜんぜんわからない。

(2)     千里の旅ならいまはジェット機の時代だから、けっして
        むずかしくはない。

(3)     毎朝練習しているのに、テニスはちっとも上手にならな
        い。

(4)     あの人にもう一度会えるとは夢にも思わなかった。

(5)  朝五時に起きてジョギングにいくなど私にはとうてい
     できない。

(6)  このごろの若者はろくに働きもしない。

(7)  たいして仕事をしたわけでもないのに、疲れてしまった。

(8)  しかし、キリギリス、さほど落胆もしない。

(9)  たくさん本を読んでも必ずしも全部理解しているとは
     かぎらない。

(10) もし空港であの人に会えなかったら、この番号に電話し
     なさい。

(11) 万一飛行機に間に合わなかったらどうしましょうか。

(12) たとえどんなに高くてもあの本は買います。

(13) 夕暮れの空はまるで（あたかも）あかい絵の具を塗った
     ような色をしていた。

(14) まるで一羽のかもめのように。

(15) その子はうそをついているのに、さも本当のように話し
     ている。

(16) あんまりおいしかったので食べ過ぎてしまった。

(17) その映画はあんまりおもしろくなかった。

(18) どうもありがとうございました。

(19) あの人の言ってることはどうもよくわからない。

(20) この写真はなかなかよくとれている。

(21) いろいろ計画をたててもなかなか実行できないのが残
     念だ。

(22) もう終わりましたよ。

(23) もう二度とあんなまずいものは食べさせないでくださ
     い。

## 1. with negative predicate

*zenzen* (not at all)

(1)  Itariago wa **zenzen** wakara**nai**.

(I don't understand Italian at all.)

*kesshite* (not ever, never)

(2)  . . . senri no tabi nara ima wa jettoki no jidai dakara, **kesshite**
muzukashikuwa**nai**. (R7, sentence 4)

( . . . traveling one thousand miles, since this is the era of jet travel, is not difficult at all.)

*chittomo* (not even a bit)

(3) Maiasa renshuushiteiru noni, tenisu wa **chittomo** joozuni nara**nai**.

(Although I practice every morning, my tennis doesn't improve even a bit.)

*yume nimo* (not even in the dream [I thought])

(4) Ano hito ni mooichido aeru towa **yume nimo** omowa**nakatta**.

(I didn't even dream that I would be able to see him again.)

*tootei* (not possibly [can])

(5) Asa goji ni okite jogingu ni iku nado watashi ni wa **tootei** deki**nai**.

(I cannot possibly do such a thing as getting up at five in the morning and going out to jog.)

*rokuni* (not much [used when criticizing the insufficiency])

(6) Konogoro no wakamono wa **rokuni** hatarakimo **shinai**.

(Young people today don't work enough.)

*taishite* (not much [used for expressing a surprisingly small amount to effect a certain result])

(7) **Taishite** shigoto o shita wake demo**nai** noni, tsukareteshimatta.

(I haven't worked much, but I got tired.)

*sahodo, sorehodo* (not that much [used to express less than expected])

(8) Shikashi, kirigirisu, **sahodo** rakutan mo shi**nai**. (R2, sentence 12)

(But the grasshopper is not too disappointed.)

*kanarazushimo* (not necessarily)

(9) Takusan hon o yondemo **kanarazushimo** zenbu rikaishiteiru towa kagira**nai**.

(Even though one may read many books, it does not necessarily mean that one understands them.)

## 2. with conditionals

*moshi*

(10) **Moshi** kuukoo de ano hito ni aenakat**tara**, kono bangoo ni denwashinasai.

(If you can't find him at the airport, give a call to this number.)

*man'ichi* (in case something happens [although it is not likely to happen])

(11) **Man'ichi** hikooki ni maniawanakat**tara** doo shimashoo ka.

(If I can't make the flight, what should I do?)

*tatoe* (even if [occurs with *temo*])

(12) **Tatoe** donnani takaku**temo** ano hon wa kaimasu.

(However expensive that book is, I will buy it.)

## 3. with similes

*marude, atakamo, samo* (as if [*atakamo* is normally limited to written style])

(13) Yuugure no sora wa **marude (atakamo)** akai enogu o nutta**yoona** iro o shiteita.

(The evening sky was colored as if painted with a red paint.)

(14) **Marude** ichiwa no kamome no **yooni**. (R1, sentence 5)
(As if he were a sea gull.)

(15) Sono ko wa uso o tsuiteiru noni, **samo** hontoono **yooni** hanashiteiru.
(The child, although lying, is speaking as if he is telling the truth.)

*4. different meanings in affirmative/negative predicates*
    *anmari*
    (16) **Anmari** oishikatta node tabesugishite shimatta.
    (It was so delicious, I ended up eating too much.)

    (17) Sono eiga wa **anmari** omoshiroku**nakatta**.
    (That movie was not so entertaining.)

    *doomo*
    (18) **Doomo** arigatoo gozaimashita.
    (Thank you very much.)

    (19) Ano hito no itteru koto wa **doomo** yoku wakara**nai**.
    (I cannot quite understand what she is saying.)

    *nakanaka*
    (20) Kono shashin wa **nakanaka** yoku toreteiru.
    (This photograph is shot surprisingly well.)

    (21) Iroiro keikaku o tatetemo **nakanaka** jikkoo deki**nai** no ga zannen da.
    (Although I make many plans, it is regrettable that I have a hard time making them happen.)

    *moo*
    (22) **Moo** owarimashita yo.
    (It's already over.)

    (23) **Moo** nidoto anna mazui mono wa tabesase**naide** kudasai.
    (Please don't make me eat such terrible-tasting food ever again.)

## Entry 29 **Homonyms and puns**

Like other languages, Japanese writings use puns for enhancing the effect of humor. Since puns are often based on homonyms, a brief discussion on the Japanese homonym is perhaps in order. The Japanese language contains a limited number of syllables which promotes extensive homonyms (same pronunciation, different meanings), and writers take advantage of them when creating puns. In reality, because of the context in which the words appear, surprisingly few misunderstandings result. Here are some examples of homonyms.

(1.1)　美談に感心する。
(1.2)　政治に関心を持つ。
(2.1)　身元を照会する。
(2.2)　誰かにいい人を紹介する。
(3.1)　日本の習慣
(3.2)　週刊誌
(4.1)　身長180センチ
(4.2)　慎重にことを運ぶ。
(4.3)　スーツを新調する。
(5.1)　平衡感覚
(5.2)　平行してすすめる。

(1.1) bidan ni **kanshin**suru (*kanshin* "admiration")
(to be moved by a good and moral story)

(1.2) seiji ni **kanshin** o motsu (*kanshin* "interest")
(to have interest in politics)

(2.1) mimoto o **shookai**suru (*shookai* "inquiry")
(to make an inquiry regarding a person's background)

(2.2) dareka ni ii hito o **shookai**suru (*shookai* "introduction")
(to introduce a nice person to someone)

(3.1) nihon no **shuukan** (*shuukan* "custom, practice")
(Japanese custom)

(3.2) **shuukan**shi (*shuukan* "weekly")
(weekly magazine)

(4.1) **shinchoo** 180 senchi (*shinchoo* "height")
(height of 180 centimeters)

(4.2) **shinchoo**ni koto o hakobu (*shinchoo* "prudence")
(to carry on matters prudently)

(4.3) suutsu o **shinchoo**suru (*shinchoo* "newly made")
(to have a new suit made)

(5.1) **heikoo** kankaku (*heikoo* "balance")
(sense of balance)

(5.2) **heikoo**shite susumeru (*heikoo* "side by side")
(to go ahead with things side by side)

Examples of puns using homonyms appear in R4 and R7, which will be
discussed later in Part III. To show how puns work in Japanese, here are
three of the commonly known Japanese two-line jokes using sound-
based puns.

(6.1)　おい空き地にへえができたね。
(6.2)　へえ。
(7.1)　このぼうしどいつんだ。
(7.2)　おらんだ。
(8.1)　富士山に登ったかい？
(8.2)　いいやまだねえ。

(6.1) Oi akichi ni **hee** ga dekita ne.
(You know, I heard that the *hee* [wall] was built at the empty lot.)

(6.2) **Hee!**
(*Hee* [I see].)

(7.1) Kono booshi **doitsu** n da. (*Doitsu* is a pun between *doitsu*, an abrupt version
of *dare* "who" and the country name *doitsu* "Germany.")
(Whose hat is this?)

(7.2) **Oran-da.** (Here *oran-da* is a colloquial and dialect-bearing version of
*watashino da. Oranda* is also a country name referring to Holland, the
Netherlands.)
(It's mine.)

(8.1) Fujisan ni nobotta kai?
(Have you climbed Mt. Fuji?)

(8.2) **Iiyamada** nee. (This answer can be interpreted in two ways as shown below)
a. **Ii yama da** nee.
(It's a great mountain.)
b. **Iiya, mada** nee.
(No, not yet.)

Beyond these overt puns used in two-line jokes, ordinary discourse is occasionally spiced with puns. Puns are especially common in advertising copy which often makes use of verbal play, humor, and cleverness. Understanding language-based puns is difficult for foreign language learners. Appreciating humor in a foreign language and culture is difficult because in order to "get" the joke, one must know more than the surface meanings of words. A keen knowledge of homonyms offers some clues.

## Entry 30 Similes, metaphors, and proverbs

Using linguistic expressions analogically is a common practice in communication. Similes, metaphors and proverbs are rhetorical devices referring to things in a conventionally expected, often formula-like manner. These strategies are mostly culture-specific although some are common across cultures. Ordinary everyday Japanese texts often contain these expressions, and, therefore, knowing how they are integrated into Japanese discourse should be included in one's study.

Figurative language is a deviation where a speaker chooses a term to refer not to objects ordinarily referred to but to something else through comparison or analogy (as in the phrase "in the evening of life"). Specifically, we recognize two different kinds of figurative language, that is, simile and metaphor. In English, a simile contains the expression *as* or *like* – "white as snow," for example. A metaphor does not contain *as* or *like*. Likewise in Japanese, a simile (*chokuyu*) contains *yooni* or *yoona*, while a metaphor (*in'yu*) does not. The English examples cited above can find their counterparts in Japanese: *bannen*, and *yuki no yooni shiroi*. There are many English similes and metaphors that work in Japanese, but there are many others that do not.

An example appears in R1, an excerpt from Machi Tawara's book on *tanka*, where the author uses the expression *kamome no yoona anata* "You (are) just like a sea gull." What one imagines about a sea gull may differ from one person to another and from one culture to another. The author uses the metaphor based on a well-known Japanese *tanka* written by Bokusui Wakayama. This *tanka* depicts the sea gull as an unattached lonesome creature, and therefore, when the author uses the expression *kamome no yoona anata*, that image serves as an analogical bridge. (More about this in Part III.)

What follow are some contemporary and creative examples of simile taken from novels by (1) Sooji Shimada (1991) and (2) Shoogo Utano (1992).

(1)    そうして自分という存在が角砂糖のようにこの雨に溶
       け、アスファルトに流れていけるなら、悲しみもどこか
       へ消えていくだろうと思った。

(2)    死体が...雪深い地面へ横たわっていく様子が、頭の中
       でアニメーションのように流れていく。

(1)  Sooshite jibun to yuu sonzai ga **kakuzatoo no yooni** kono ame ni toke, asufaruto ni nagarete ikeru nara, kanashimi mo dokoka e kiete iku daroo to omotta.
(And he thought – if his existence, like a cube of sugar, melts into this rain and flows over the asphalt, the sadness will also disappear somewhere.)

*Shimada 1991:282, my translation*

(2)  Shitai ga . . . yukifukai jimen e yokotawatte iku yoosu ga, atama no naka de **animeeshon no yooni** nagareteiku.
(The scene of the corpse being laid down in deep snow passes by in his mind as in an animated cartoon.)

*Utano 1992:310, my translation*

In modern literature, Japanese similes are sometimes translated straight into English. As pointed out by Kan'ichi Hanzawa (1995), Haruki Murakami's (1983) novel *Senkyuuhyaku Nanajuusannen no Pinbooru* and its English translation, "Pinball, 1973," by Alfred Birnbaum (1985) contain parallel similes.

(3)    そういった街を、僕は冬眠前の熊のように幾つも貯めこ
       んでいる。

(5)    小学校の廊下みたいなフェアウェイがまっすぐに続い
       ているだけだった。

(3) Sooitta machi o, boku wa **toomin mae no kuma no yooni** ikutsumo
tamekondeiru. (Murakami 1983:8)

(4) I had stocked up a whole store of these places, **like a bear getting ready for
hibernation**. (Birnbaum 1985:8)

(5) **Shoogakkoo no rooka mitaina** feawei ga massuguni tsuzuiteiru dake datta.
(Murakami 1983:107)

(6) Only straight fairway **like the corridor of an elementary school**. (Birnbaum
1985:110)

Although culturally bound, similes and metaphors find much commonality in contemporary global culture. Parallel translation is frequently
interpretable across languages and cultures.

DS7, "Do Not Bundle Me," uses extensive and creative similes and
metaphors as summarized in Table 10.

**Table 10** Similes and metaphors in DS7

| line | expression | translation | simile/metaphor |
|---|---|---|---|
| 2 | *araseitoo no hana no yooni* | (like blooming stocks) | simile |
| 3 | *shiroi negi no yooni* | (like white green onions) | simile |
| 5 | *inaho* | (ears of rice plants) | metaphor |
| 6 | *konjiki no inaho* | (golden ears of rice plants) | metaphor |
| 9 | *konma ya piriodo* | ([like] commas and periods) | simile |
|  | *ikutsuka no danraku* | ([like] so many of the *danraku*) | simile |
| 10 | *tegami no yooni* | (like a letter) | simile |
| 12 | *bunshoo* | (discourse) | metaphor |
| 14 | *shi* | (a poem) | metaphor |

Phrases appearing in 9 continue on to line 10 which contains *yooni*.

Now, proverbs, mostly culturally specific, are frequently used for rhetorical purposes. Between Japanese and English proverbs, some are common, some share different interpretations, and others are non-existent in the other culture. Japanese texts incorporate proverbs frequently, more frequently when compared with English counterparts. We find an example in R7, "Traveling to the Desert."

**R7: Paragraph E**

17. 日本人は井のなかの蛙のようなものだ。
18. たしかに日本は小さな島国だから、世間知らずになりやすい。
19. けれど、人間というのは、どこに住んでいようと、じつは例外なく井のなかの蛙なのである。
20. いや、そもそも、ひとつところに住むということが、すなわち井のなかの蛙になるということである。

17. Nihonjin wa **i no naka no kawazu** no yoona mono da.
(Japanese are like frogs in a well.)

18. Tashikani nihon wa chiisana shimaguni dakara, seken shirazu ni nariyasui.
(True, because Japan is a small island country, the Japanese are likely to be ignorant of the world.)

19. Keredo, ningen to yuu no wa, doko ni sundeiyoo to, jitsuwa reigai naku **i no naka no kawazu** na no dearu.
(The truth of the matter is that human beings are, no matter where they live, without exception, frogs in a well.)

20. Iya, somosomo, hitotsu tokoro ni sumu to yuu koto ga, sunawachi **i no naka no kawazu** ni naru to yuu koto dearu.
(Or, rather, the very fact that human beings live in one location means that they turn into frogs in a well.)

The expression "frogs in a well" may not make immediate sense to English readers although because of the context, the meaning – a provincial person, one who has never seen the world – may come through. This expression originates in a Japanese proverb "*I no naka no kawazu taikai o shirazu*" ([literally] A frog in the well doesn't know the sea). Japanese are aware that being in a small island country may make them less aware of what is happening in the world. Often used to self-criticize, this warns people not to be narrow-minded. In R7, the writer uses the phrase "*i no naka no kawazu*" (simile in sentence 17, metaphor in sentences 19 and 20) to refer to such a person as described by this well-known Japanese proverb.

Many idiomatic expressions also appear in Japanese texts. Although sometimes one can guess the meaning of these phrases, they often require conventional and cultural interpretation. The phrase "*hachi no su o tsutsuita*" appearing in R7, sentence 26, is one such example. It literally means "poking a beehive." This expression, which refers to the pandemonium that might break out as a result of poking a beehive, describes uncontrollable frenzied bedlam. Again such idiomatic expressions add a certain colorfulness to texts, and knowing these idiomatic expressions will help the reader enjoy the Japanese text more.

*Part III*
## Selected readings

# Prelude: on reading different genres of contemporary Japanese texts

When discussing rhetoric as it applies to the English language, four kinds of discourse are commonly recognized: (1) exposition, (2) argument (and persuasion), (3) description, and (4) narration. Exposition informs about something, for example, to make an idea clear to the reader, to give directions, to define concepts, and so on. Argument and persuasion aim to convince someone. Argument uses logic as a means to bring about a change of thought, while in persuasion one appeals to emotion emphasizing a common ground. Description tells how a thing looks, sounds or feels. Description attempts to re-create for the reader as vivid as possible an impression of what the writer has perceived. Or, the writer may vividly describe what is imagined. Through description, the writer hopes the reader will share the experience with him or her. Narration reports what happened. In narration, the reader finds an event chronologically ordered; the reader experiences the sense of witnessing an event as it unfolds from beginning to end.

In reality, the distinction between these different types is somewhat blurred. For example, a magazine article on the trade imbalance may be primarily expository, but may, after all, aim to convince the reader of the need for a certain policy – and thus its primary thrust may be categorized as argument. Although blending different discourse types occurs frequently, it is still possible to identify the primary intention of a particular text, and therefore one can usually assign an overall type to any discourse.

Summarizing Egon Werlich's (1982) work, Jan Renkema (1993:91) presents a typology of English discourse as shown in Table 11. Adding the "instructive" category to the four discussed above, Werlich adds text categories depending on whether the method of presentation is either subjective (based on the writer's perception) or objective (being independently verifiable).

**Table 11** Werlich's discourse typology as summarized by Renkema

| *Basic Forms* | *Subjective* | *Objective* |
|---|---|---|
| descriptive | impressionistic description | technical description |
| narrative | report | news story |
| explanatory | essay | explication |
| argumentative | comment | argumentation |
| instructive | instructions | directions, rules, regulations and statutes |

Among the variety of methods available for structuring a typology of contemporary Japanese texts, I find the categorization scheme based on intentional communication most practical. Accordingly, the three categories are (1) information, (2) persuasion, and (3) emotion. In general, texts primarily intended to convey information correspond with the English descriptive, explanatory and instructive text types. Texts intended to persuade correspond with argumentative (and persuasive) texts, and texts intended to stir emotions, with English narrative and persuasive discourse. More specifically, Japanese writings of various sorts are categorized into these three groups as listed below.

### 1. conveying information

| | |
|---|---|
| *kijibun* or *hoodoobun* | newspaper articles, magazine articles, reports |
| *kirokubun* | report based on observations, for example, of experiments, natural phenomena or disaster |
| *nikkibun* | diary, a record of a person's life – *nikkibun* may fall into the literary genre when it takes the form of an essay or novel |
| *kikoobun* | travelogue, travel diary, writings of travel experience – may be considered a literary work |
| *annaibun* or *kokuchibun* | invitation, announcement and bulletin |
| *tsuushinbun, shokanbun* or *tegamibun* | correspondence, letter, fax or electronic mail |
| *hookokubun* | report of (field) research, or of observation |
| *kooyoobun* | official document, forms, letters and documents used for official purposes by the government |

### 2. persuading someone

| | |
|---|---|
| (*gakujutsu*) *ronbun* | academic thesis, academic article |
| *hyooronbun* | criticism |
| *shohyoo* | book review |
| *kaisetsubun* | commentary, analysis |
| *setsumeibun* | explanation, commentary |
| *ikenbun* | opinion piece |
| *kookokubun* | advertising |
| *ronsetsubun* | editorial |

**3. stirring emotion**

| | |
|---|---|
| *shiika* | includes *shi*, *waka* (or *tanka*), *haiku* – verse, poetry |
| *zuihitsu* | essay |
| *gikyoku* or *shinario* | play, drama |
| *manga* | comic |
| *doowa* | nursery story, fairy tale |
| *minwa* and *mukashibanashi* | folktale and old tale |
| *tanpen (shoosetsu)* | short story |
| *shoosetsu* | novel |
| *bijinesu shoosetsu* | business novel |
| *suiri shoosetsu* | mystery novel |

As I touched upon at various points in Part II, organizational principles and discourse strategies apply to different types in varying degrees. Furthermore, discourse types are not mutually exclusive; narratives may and often do contain description and exposition. It is also the case that Japanese writings in general incorporate the essay-like style in genres other than the essay. Therefore, in order to understand Japanese texts, we must not only possess knowledge of discourse principles but also nurture the understanding of discourse types, and accordingly, an understanding of when and when not to apply them.

I should also remind the reader that the Japanese publishing industry categorizes books in many specific groups. Some of them are listed below.

| | | |
|---|---|---|
| Fiction: | *junbungaku* | literary works |
| | *rekishi, jidai shoosetsu* | period and historical novels |
| | *kigyoo, keizai shoosetsu* | industry, economics, business novels |
| | *taishuu shoosetsu* | mass-consumption popular novels |
| | *poruno shoosetsu* | pornographic novels |
| | *kaigai noberuzu* | overseas novels |
| | *jidoo bungaku* | children's literature |
| | *yangu adaruto bungaku* | teens' literature |
| | *SF/fantajii* | science fiction/fantasy |
| Non-fiction: | *ippan kyooyoo* | general knowledge |
| | *shumi no hon* | hobby-related publications |
| | *jitsuyoosho* | how-to books |
| | *taidanshuu* | dialogue and interview collection |

Other topic-based non-fiction publications include: sports, out-door activities, arts and crafts, knitting, cooking, movies, music, photography, child rearing, health, dieting, celebrity authors, pets, personal computer, foreign languages, travel, letter writing, speech making, fortune telling, interior design, license examination, and so on.

When we read, we read for a purpose. Through reading we obtain knowledge necessary for achieving a particular goal. We may read for pleasure, but even then we read for a purpose. We choose what we read based on these goals. When reading in a foreign language, especially in the early stages of learning, students read not so much for content but rather as a part of language training. For a Japanese language student choosing what to read requires some prior knowledge. Your instructors are the best source from whom you can obtain suggested readings suitable to your interest and comprehension level.

For those who might be interested in finding material to read in Japanese on your own, here are some suggestions. As a general rule, choose texts that cover topics personally interesting to you. What you already know about a topic will serve as background knowledge when reading the Japanese text. Also your prior knowledge of the topic in English will sustain your interest as you read through the Japanese text.

If you have access to libraries whose collections include Japanese language materials, that would be a good place to browse. Look through collections of modern literature published by major publishers; most libraries have at least a few shelves full of these hardcover collections of representative literary works (for example, *Gendai Nihon Bungaku Taikei* by Chikuma Shoboo). You will no doubt recognize the names of some authors. Choose short texts with relatively short sentences with simple sentence structures. If the library subscribes to Japanese newspapers, you might find something interesting to read – news, editorials, newspaper essays, sports articles, popular culture items, interviews, special features, four-frame comic strips, and so on.

For readers who may have access to Japanese bookstores overseas, or have opportunities to be in Japan, look for magazines and books specializing in current publication news and related information. For example, a monthly magazine, *Da Vinchi*, published by Recruit in Tokyo offers excerpts of contemporary and new publications categorized into various genres (information available through the internet as well). It offers a good resource for what is currently being read in Japan. Major publishers also publish their own monthly magazines releasing publication news, essays by authors, interviews, and so on.

The magazine industry in Japan produces an array of weekly and monthly magazines for specific readers – adolescent women, young men, housewives, career-seeking women, businessmen, intellectuals and so on. Magazines for youth carry articles in colloquial language style (often gender-specific) with current vocabulary, useful for learning the most current spoken style. Magazines carry short, concrete, and instructional texts that might interest the readers.

Major publishing houses regularly publish new titles in established series of non-fiction paperbacks. For example, Koodansha publishes the *Koodansha Gendai Shinsho* series covering everything from philosophy and religion to economics and history. Each book written by an expert in the field provides relevant information in plain non-technical language. In the literary market, you will find many reasonably priced paperbacks of contemporary authors' works.

Particularly suitable for language students are collections of short essays, short stories and interview dialogues. These are compact and easier to handle than long novels, for example. Although lengthy, mystery novels may also interest language students; the text contains contemporary vocabulary, vivid descriptions, and realistic dialogue within the entertaining who-done-it format. Some of the novels and comics targeted to adolescent Japanese contain *yomigana* (*hiragana* readings attached next to *kanji*) for some or most of the *kanji*, making it easier to read. Stories for children are not necessarily suitable; they contain vocabulary unfamiliar to and often not so useful for adult Japanese language learners. Magazines and newspapers targeted specifically to Japanese language students are also available (for example, *The Nihongo Journal* published by Aruku in Tokyo). Given that material available to Japanese language students in the publishing market will change over time, it is wise to keep abreast with changes in order to learn about and find reading materials appropriate for your level of comprehension.

In Part III to follow, we apply our knowledge of principles of Japanese discourse to the interpretation of several genres of contemporary Japanese readings. These readings include a poetic essay, narrative, newspaper column and essay, print advertising, a comic, and a philosophical essay.

# 8 Reading Japanese texts

## Reminder to the reader

Each of the Readings contains no grammar explanation. Although students with knowledge of basic Japanese grammar should not face serious difficulty, occasionally, some additional explication may be required. Refer to Seiichi Makino and Michio Tsutsui (1986, 1995) and Maynard (1990) for additional grammatical information.

Discourse notes should be clearly understood by those readers who have studied Parts I and II. Depending on your proficiency level, tasks and activities suggested for each reading may require revision, assistance, and guidance. Use as much Japanese as possible when performing these tasks and activities. If you are using this book as a part of a language course, share the results of tasks and activities with other students, thereby increasing the opportunities to interact in Japanese.

## 1. Introduction

This brief portion of an essay is taken from a 1988 book titled *Yotsuba no Essei* "The Four-leaf Essay" by Machi Tawara. The book features essays commenting on some of her *tanka* which had become popular earlier in her *tanka* collection *Sarada Kinenbi* "The Salad Anniversary" (1987). For *Sarada Kinenbi* she received the 32nd Modern *Tanka* Poets Association Award in 1988. Formerly a high school teacher, she is a celebrated *tanka* poet/essayist/critic in the Japanese literary world. The excerpt to follow contains her comment on her *tanka*, given in line 1.

A few words about *tanka* (and *waka*) are in order here. Traditional Japanese verses are based on the mora-count; moras refer to consonant-followed-by-vowel syllables and the sound of "n" counted as one syllable. Different types of poetry are usually distinguished by the number of moras they contain. The *tanka* is a poem with 31 moras, arranged in lines of 5, 7, 5, 7, and 7 moras. (The *haiku* contains 17 moras in three lines of 5, 7, and 5 moras.) The earliest collection of *waka*, *Man'yooshuu*, was compiled in the late eighth century. In Japan today, many people, especially when they reach a mature age, enjoy composing *tanka* and *haiku*. Newspapers regularly print *tanka* and *haiku* sent in by readers and selected by leading poets and critics. Many *tanka* and *haiku* lovers organize groups which often publish their members' works in monthly journals.

## 2. Pre-reading tasks

1. What images and memories do you have about the sea? Think of the times you went to the beach for the first time, for example. What do you think of when you hear the words such as ocean, sea and beach? Write a few Japanese sentences about those memories and images.

2. If you were to write a love poem, what words would you use? Jot down a few Japanese words expressing your feelings.

### 3. Text and vocabulary: R1 (Tawara 1988:154)

1.  空の青海のあおさのその間
    サーフボードの君を見つめる

2.  夏の空。
3.  夏の海。
4.  二つの青が接するところを、サーフボードの彼
    がゆく。
5.  まるで一羽のカモメのように。
6.  ＜白鳥はかなしからずや空の青
    海のあをにも染まずただよふ＞
7.  ――若山牧水のこの一首を私は自然に思い出す。
8.  空の青からも、海の青からも、染め残されたカ
    モメ。
9.  カモメのようなあなた。
10. あなたはかなしくないですか。
11. 一枚の板に両足をのせ、両手にはつかまる何も
    のもなく、危ういバランスを保ちながら、私の
    視界を横切ってゆく。
12. あなたは寂しくないですか。
13. サーフボードの下は波。
14. 気まぐれでとらえどころのない、そのゆらゆら
    に身をまかせ、私の視界を横切ってゆく。
15. サーフボード。
16. それはあなたの生き方そのもののようで。

Vocabulary:

1.

| 空 | そら | n | sky |
| 青 | あお | n | blue |

| 海 | うみ | n | ocean, sea |
|---|---|---|---|
| あおさ | | n | blueness |
| 間 | あわい | n | [poetic] in between |
| サーフボード | | n | surfboard |
| 見つめる | | v | to stare at, to gaze at |

4.

| 接する | せっする | v | to touch |
|---|---|---|---|
| ゆく | | v | [same as *iku*] to go |

5.

| 一羽 | いちわ | n | one bird [counter for birds] |
|---|---|---|---|
| カモメ | | n | sea gull |

6.

| 白鳥 | しらとり | n | white bird (sea gull) |
|---|---|---|---|
| かなしからずや | | | [old style] *kanashikunai no daroo ka* 'isn't it sad?' |
| 染まず | そまず | | [old style] *somaranai de* 'without being dyed' |
| ただよふ | | v | to drift, to float |

7.

| 若山牧水 | わかやまぼくすい | | Wakayama Bokusui [*tanka* poet, 1885–1928] |
|---|---|---|---|
| 一首 | いっしゅ | n | one *tanka* [counter for *waka* and *tanka*] |
| 思い出す | おもいだす | v | to recollect |

8.

| 染め残す | そめのこす | v | to leave undyed |
|---|---|---|---|

11.

| 板 | いた | n | board |
|---|---|---|---|
| 両足 | りょうあし | n | both feet |
| 両手 | りょうて | n | both hands |

| | | | |
|---|---|---|---|
| つかまる | | v | to grasp, to hold |
| 危うい | あやうい | adj | dangerous, precarious |
| バランス | | n | balance |
| 保つ | たもつ | v | to maintain, to keep |
| 視界 | しかい | n | vision |
| 横切る | よこぎる | v | to cross, to go across |
| 13. | | | |
| 波 | なみ | n | wave |
| 14. | | | |
| 気まぐれ | きまぐれ | adj | whimsical |
| とらえどころのない | | | difficult to hold on to |
| ゆらゆら | | adv | swaying, wobbling |
| 身 | み | n | body |
| まかす | | v | to let something else take over |
| 16. | | | |
| 生き方 | いきかた | n | way of life |
| そのもの | | | itself; *ikikata sonomono* 'the way of life itself' |

## 4. Discourse notes

1. In this reading, note the briefness of some of the sentences. Particularly interesting are lines 2, 3, 9, and 15 where phrases are presented as sentences. As in English, these presentations of ideas (without specific predicates) leave the reader to interpret them in his or her ways, encouraging the feeling of *yojoo*.

2. Another noteworthy effect of this poetic writing is the experiential impressionism. These short sentences and phrases report the author's views and feelings unmediated. The author is in the center of her emotional experience; she offers fragments of her personal impression rich with her feelings.

3. Different styles appear in this text. The sentence-final form in lines 10 and 12 is a question addressed to "you" in the *desu/masu*-style. A stylistic change such as this signals the shifting of the writer's communicative intention. Being aware of such a shift is critical for comprehending the text correctly.

4. Although we studied that, in general, pronouns are absent in Japanese discourse, in this text we find six occurrences of the personal pronoun in reference to "him/you" – *kimi*, *kare*, and four cases of *anata*. *Kimi* is used in the *tanka* presented in line 1 when calling out for "you," *kare* when describing "him," and *anata* when the writer "talks" directly to "you" in the essay. The pronominal use is important in this text because it shows how the writer's point of view shifts as she reaches out for *kare*.

5. Note the simile appearing in lines 5 and 9 in which "you" and the sea gull are poetically connected.

6. When reading, we sometimes witness another text introduced into the current text: in R1 a *tanka* by Bokusui Wakayama (1885–1928) is introduced into Machi Tawara's essay. This intertextual manipulation mixing multiple (literary) worlds creates a rich interpretive context.

## 5. Discourse activities

1. Identify items the author introduces into the scene in R1. Describe the author's feelings toward them.

2. Find the repeated phrase "surfboard" and describe how each occurrence (including its paraphrase in line 11) helps develop the *bunmyaku* of R1.

3. Tell a story in Japanese that reports your experience with sea gulls and other marine creatures. Tell your story by chronologically ordering related events and by using appropriate connectives. Incorporate in your story direct and indirect quotations.

## 6. Post-reading tasks

1. What are the facts that the author reports in R1? And, what are the implied feelings that the author expresses?

2. What is the stylistic characteristic of this writing? Explain what you like or dislike about the writing style of R1.

3. Did the author's description of the sea and surfboard resemble in any way the image of the sea you described in your pre-reading task? How do they differ?

## 1. Introduction

Aesop's fables are well-read by Japanese children. Shin'ichi Hoshi, one of the most celebrated short story writers in Japan, wrote a series of short stories titled *Mirai Isoppu* "Future Aesop's Fables." This 1982 collection contains several up-dated versions of well-known Aesop's fables, one of which is *Ari to Kirigirisu* "The Ant and the Grasshopper." In this "new" version of the story, Hoshi presents a critical view of some contemporary societies where the abundance of food challenges the traditional work ethic and social values.

## 2. Pre-reading tasks

1. Do you know any fables, old tales, fairy tales of Japan? Do you recall fables and stories you read in your childhood in your own culture? Can you recite any one of Aesop's fables? If you answered positively to any of the questions, summarize one of the stories you know in Japanese.

2. Recalling Entry 8 on narratives, think of an expected beginning, middle, and end along with a likely plot development of a typical Japanese story. Would such a plot coincide with that of the Aesop's fable? With other stories do you know?

3. If you are not familiar with the original version of "The Ant and the Grasshopper," here is the story taken from a collection of *Aesop's Fables* (1960:137). In this story a cicada appears instead of a grasshopper.

> **The Ant and the Cicada**
> In winter time an ant was dragging
> The food he'd stored, across the flagging,
> And cooling what he'd heaped and had
> In summer. A cicada bade
> The ant (for he was starved) to give
> Some food to him that he might live.
> "What did you do," the other cried,
> "Last summer?" "I have nought to hide.
> I hadn't time to work; I passed
> The time in singing." Shutting fast
> His store of wheat, the other laughed,

And launched at him this parting shaft:
"Dance in the winter, if you please
To sing in summer at your ease."

4. Based on this Aesop's fable, can you think of a way to "update" it to today's world? Or, is this story applicable as it is to most contemporary societies?

## 3. Text and vocabulary: R2 (Hoshi 1982:9–11)

アリとキリギリス

A:
1.    秋の終りのある日、アリたちが冬ごもりの準備をしていると、そこへバイオリンをかかえたキリギリスがやってきて言った。
2.    「食べ物をわけてくれませんかね」
B:
3.    おじいさんアリが、その応対をした。
4.    「あなたはなぜ、夏のあいだに食料あつめをしておかなかったんだね」
5.    「わたしは芸術家なんですよ。
6.    音楽をかなでるという、崇高なことをやっていた。
7.    食料あつめなどしているひまなんか、なかったというわけです」
8.    「とんでもない怠け者だ。
9.    ふん、なにが芸術だ。
10.   お好きなように歌いつづけたらどうです、雪の上ででも......」
C:
11.   おじいさんアリはそっけない。

12.    しかし、キリギリス、さほど落胆もしない。
13.    「だめなら、しようがない。
14.    じゃあ、よそのアリさんのとこへ行ってみる
       か.....」

D:

15.    帰りかけるのを、若いアリが呼びとめる。
16.    「ま、まって下さい.....」

E:

17.    その一方、おじいさんアリに説明する。
18.    「.....おじいさん、考えてみて下さいよ。
19.    われわれ先祖代々の勤労愛好の性格によって、
       巣のなかはすでに食料でいっぱい。
20.    毎年のように巣を拡張し、貯蔵に貯蔵を重ねて
       きたわけですが、それも限界にきた。
21.    さっきも貯蔵のために巣をひろげたら、壁が崩
       れ、むこうから古い食料がどっと出てきて、そ
       れにつぶされて三匹ほど負傷しました。
22.    キリギリスさんに入ってもらって少し食べてい
       ただかないと、もう住む空間もないほどなんで
       す」

F:

23.    かくして、キリギリスはアリの巣の客となった。
24.    その冬はアリたちにとっても楽しいものとなっ
       た。
25.    ジュークボックスがそなえつけられたようなも
       のなのだ。
26.    曲目さえ注文すれば、なんでもバイオリンでひ
       いてくれる。

G:

27.    このキリギリス、芸術家だけあって、頭のひら
       めきもある。

28.  アリの巣の貯蔵庫を見て回っているうちに、奥
     の古い食料が発酵し酒となっているのを発見し
     た。
29.  アリたちに言う。
30.  「あんたがた、これをほっぽっとくことはない
     ぜ。
31.  飲んでみな」
H:
32.  アリたち、おそるおそるなめ、いい気持ちとな
     り、酒の味をおぼえる。
33.  酒と歌とくれば、踊りだって自然と身につく。
34.  どうくらべてみても、勤労よりこのほうがはる
     かに面白い。
35.  この冬ごもりの期間中に、このアリ一族の伝統
     精神は完全に崩壊した。
I:
36.  つぎの春からこのアリたちは、地上に出ても働
     こうとせず、キリギリスのバイオリンにあわせ
     て踊りまわるだけだった。
37.  ただ、おじいさんアリだけが慨嘆する。
38.  「なんたることだ、この堕落。
39.  このままだと遠からず......」
J:
40.  そして、若いアリたちを理論で説得すべく、食
     料の在庫を調べ、あとどれくらいでそれが底を
     つくか計算しようとした。
41.  だが、あまりに貯蔵量が多すぎ、どうにも手に
     おえない。
42.  あと数十年を踊り暮したって、なくなりそうに
     はないのだ。
43.  そこでつぶやく。

44.　「世の中が変ったというべきなのか。

45.　わしにはわけがわからなくなった......」

K:

46.　おじいさんアリは信念と現実との矛盾に悩み、その悩みを忘れようと、酒を飲み、若い連中といっしょに踊りはじめるのだった。

L:

47.　教訓。

48.　繁栄によりいかに社会が変ったからといって、古典的な物語をこのように改作すること、はたして許されるべきであろうか。


Vocabulary:

| アリ | | n | ant |
|---|---|---|---|
| キリギリス | | n | grasshopper |
| 1. | | | |
| 冬ごもり | | n | wintering, hibernation |
| バイオリン | | n | violin |
| 準備 | じゅんび | n | preparation |
| かかえる | | v | to carry, to hold in one's arms |
| 2. | | | |
| わける | | v | to share |
| 3. | | | |
| おじいさんアリ | | n | elderly ant |
| 応対する | おうたいする | v | to receive visitors |
| 4. | | | |
| 食料 | しょくりょう | n | food |
| あつめ | | n | collection |
| 5. | | | |
| 芸術家 | げいじゅつか | n | artist |

6.

| かなでる | | v | to play (music) |
| 崇高な | すうこうな | adj | lofty, noble |

7.

*Nanka* in *hima nanka nakatta* is a colloquial (and emotional) version of *nado* – 'I didn't have time to do such (silly) things as...'

8.

| とんでもない | | adj | outrageously bad, terrible |
| 怠け者 | なまけもの | n | lazy person, sloth |

9.

| ふん | | exc | hum! humph! |
| 芸術 | げいじゅつ | n | art |

*Nani ga geijutsu da* is a rhetorical question used for exclamatory expression – 'What's artistic about it!', 'So what if it is art!'

10.

| 雪 | ゆき | n | snow |

*Utaitsuzuketara doo desu* is a sarcastic suggestion – 'How about continuing in your singing? (that's what you deserve!)'

11.

| そっけない | | adj | unsympathetic |

12.

*Sahodo* is used in negative sentences – '(not) too,' '(not) overtly,' [a case of adverb-predicate correspondence]

| 落胆する | らくたんする | v | to be disappointed |

13.

| しょうがない | | | there is no other way, cannot be helped |

14.

| よその | | | elsewhere, other |

15.

| 帰りかける | | | to be about to leave |

| 呼びとめる | よびとめる | | to call out, to stop by calling |
|---|---|---|---|

17.

| その一方 | そのいっぽう | | meanwhile, on the other hand |
|---|---|---|---|
| 説明する | せつめいする | v | to explain |

19.

| 先祖代々 | せんぞだいだい | n | (generations of) ancestors |
|---|---|---|---|
| 勤労愛好 | きんろうあいこう | n | love for work, work-loving |
| 性格 | せいかく | n | character, personality |
| 巣 | す | n | colony, nest |
| いっぱいだ | | | to be filled with |

20.

| 拡張する | かくちょうする | v | to expand |
|---|---|---|---|
| 貯蔵 | ちょぞう | n | storage |
| 重ねる | かさねる | v | to pile up, to repeat |
| 限界 | げんかい | n | limitation |

21.

| 壁 | かべ | n | wall |
|---|---|---|---|
| 崩れる | くずれる | v | to collapse |
| どっと | | adv | all at once |
| つぶす | | v | to crash |
| 負傷する | ふしょうする | v | to be wounded, to be injured |

22.

| 空間 | くうかん | n | space |
|---|---|---|---|

23.

| かくして | | conn | in this way |
| 客 | きゃく | n | guest |

25.

| ジュークボックス | | n | jukebox |
| そなえつける | | v | to install |

26.

| 曲目 | きょくもく | n | name of the song |
| 注文する | ちゅうもんする | | |
| | | v | to place an order |

27.

| 頭のひらめき | | | brilliance of mind |

28.

| 貯蔵庫 | ちょぞうこ | n | storage house |
| 見て回る | みてまわる | | to make an inspection tour |
| 奥の | おくの | | in the back |
| 発酵する | はっこうする | v | to ferment |
| 発見する | はっけんする | v | to discover |

30.

| ほっぽっとく | | | [colloquial] *hotteoku* 'to leave as is' |

32.

| おそるおそる | | adv | hesitantly |
| 味 | あじ | n | taste |
| おぼえる | | v | to learn |

*Sake no aji o oboeru* means 'to develop an acquired taste for *sake*.'

33.

| 踊り | おどり | n | dancing |
| 自然と | しぜんと | adv | naturally, easily |
| 身につく | みにつく | | to master, to learn |

34.

| | | | |
|---|---|---|---|
| くらべる | | v | to compare |
| 勤労 | きんろう | n | labor, work |
| はるかに | | adv | exceedingly |

35.

| | | | |
|---|---|---|---|
| 期間中 | きかんちゅう | n | duration of the period |
| 一族 | いちぞく | n | tribe |
| 伝統精神 | でんとうせいしん | | |
| | | n | traditional spirit, traditional value |
| 完全に | かんぜんに | adv | completely |
| 崩壊する | ほうかいする | v | to collapse, to break down |

36.

| | | | |
|---|---|---|---|
| 地上 | ちじょう | n | land |
| あわせる | | v | to match with |

*Baiorin ni awasete odoru* means 'to dance to the tune of the violin.'

37.

| | | | |
|---|---|---|---|
| 慨嘆する | がいたんする | v | to lament, to regret |

38.

| | | | |
|---|---|---|---|
| なんたることだ | | | [lamenting] What is this! |
| 堕落 | だらく | n | decadence |

39.

| | | | |
|---|---|---|---|
| 遠からず | とおからず | adv | soon |

40.

| | | | |
|---|---|---|---|
| 理論 | りろん | n | theory, logical thinking |
| 説得する | せっとくする | v | to persuade |
| 在庫 | ざいこ | n | stored goods, stock |
| 調べる | しらべる | v | to appraise |
| 底をつく | そこをつく | | to run out |
| 計算する | けいさんする | v | to calculate |

41.

| | | | |
|---|---|---|---|
| 貯蔵量 | ちょぞうりょう | | amount of storage |
| 手におえない | | | too difficult to handle |

42.

*The use of *suu* in *suujuu-nen* is 'several', *suu-nen* 'several years,' *suujuu-nen* 'lit. several tens of years,' *suuhyaku-nen* 'lit. several hundred years.'

| | | | |
|---|---|---|---|
| 踊り暮す | おどりくらす | | to spend time dancing |

43.

| | | | |
|---|---|---|---|
| つぶやく | | v | to mutter, to mumble |

44.

| | | | |
|---|---|---|---|
| 世の中 | よのなか | n | society, world |

45.

| | | | |
|---|---|---|---|
| わけ | | n | reason |

46.

| | | | |
|---|---|---|---|
| 信念 | しんねん | n | belief |
| 現実 | げんじつ | n | reality |
| 矛盾 | むじゅん | n | incongruity, contradiction |
| 悩む | なやむ | v | to suffer, to agonize |
| 忘れる | わすれる | v | to forget |
| 連中 | れんちゅう | n | others, other members |

47.

| | | | |
|---|---|---|---|
| 教訓 | きょうくん | n | moral |

48.

| | | | |
|---|---|---|---|
| 繁栄 | はんえい | n | prosperity |
| 社会 | しゃかい | n | society |
| 古典的 | こてんてき | adj | classic |
| 物語 | ものがたり | n | story, narrative |
| 改作する | かいさくする | v | to modify, to re-make |
| はたして | | adv | really, ever |
| 許す | ゆるす | v | to permit, to allow |

## 4. Discourse Notes

1. Pay attention to the narrative-initial sentence which defines items required for the narrative setting.

> *Aki no owari no aru hi* (← time)
> *aritachi ga* (← character)
> *fuyugomori no junbi o shiteiru to, soko e* (← place/situation)
> *baiorin o kakaeta kirigirisu ga yatte kite itta.* (← character)

2. The narrative structure of R2 may be analyzed in terms of narrative elements as shown in Table 12.

**Table 12**  Narrative structural elements assigned for R2.

| *danraku* | *narrative elements* | |
|---|---|---|
| A | Setting | |
| A | Episode | Conflict 1 |
| B, C, D, E | Event 1 | |
| F, G, H | Event 2 | Resolution of Conflict 1 |
| I, J, K | Event 3 | Conflict 2 |
| K, L | Ending Remarks | Resolution of Conflict 2 |

3. The main *bunmyaku* thread of R2 is the situational thread – the temporal thread, in particular. In fact, one can divide the story into three different temporal spaces chronologically ordered. These segments also correspond to the three-part organizational scheme as illustrated in Table 13.

**Table 13**  The situational thread and the three-part organization of R2

| *danraku* | *time/events* | *three-part organization* |
|---|---|---|
| A–E | late fall<br>the grasshopper's visit and<br>the response of the ants | Initial |
| F–H | winter<br>the grasshopper's stay in the<br>colony, changes taking place | Middle |
| I–K | spring<br>ants not working, the<br>elderly ant's dilemma | Final |

4.  Let us focus on the connectives in R2. We find seven connectives and organizational markers at the sentence-initial position: *shikashi* at 12, *jaa* at 14, *sono ippoo* at 17, *kakushite* at 23, *soshite* at 40, *daga* at 41, and *sokode* at 43. Three of them (*sono ippoo*, *kakushite* and *soshite*) appear also at the *danraku*-initial position. Take these connectives into consideration when you follow the plot.

5.  Examining the predicate types excluding the quoted portion, we find four nominal predicates: *mono na no da* in sentence 25, *dake datta* in 36, *nai no da* in 42, and *hajimeru no datta* in 46. By finding these commentary predicates and understanding them as expressions of the narrator's explanation and commentary, we can interpret the text as the author intended.

6.  Study the manner in which the author presents the elderly ant in the text: *ojiisan ari ga* in 3; *ojiisan ari wa* in 11; *ojiisan ari ni* in 17; *ojiisan ari dake ga* in 37; absent in 40; absent in 43; *ojiisan ari wa* in 46. The *ga*-marked phrase introduces the elderly ant in sentence 3, followed by the same phrase marked with *wa* in sentence 11. The elderly ant appears as an indirect object in 17. It is re-introduced in 37 with *ga*, and then *ojiisan ari* is deleted in the consequent two sentences. Finally, *wa* marks the elderly ant again in 46. Other participants are introduced in a similar manner. See Entry 17 where we studied the identification of the grasshopper.

## 5. Discourse activities

1.  Create a vocabulary list in Japanese by collecting vocabulary items related to the condition of the ant colony and the information surrounding the grasshopper. (This can be used for a vocabulary review as well as a tool for understanding, through contrast, the world of the ant colony and the world view represented by the grasshopper.) By referring to the items in the list, write a report that describes what happened in the ant colony. In your report use appropriate connectives.

2.  Assume that you are the grasshopper, the artist type. Tell a story in Japanese about the ant colony you visited. Describe the kind of life style you witnessed and how you helped change it. Mention also the elderly ant who has failed to understand you. Incorporate direct or indirect quotations in your answer. Use commentary predicates when including your opinions and views.

3.  Are you more like an ant or a grasshopper (or a cicada)? Which do you like better? Why? Write a short opinion piece using one of the logical *bunmyaku* or using the three-part or *ki-shoo-ten-ketsu* organization principle.

4. Think of some other fables or fairy tales that can be made relevant to today's world. Write a short summary of the original story in Japanese. Write a modern (or future) version of the story again in Japanese paying particular attention to the narrative structure and the chronological order of events.

## 6. Post-reading tasks

1. Summarize in Japanese the author's view toward contemporary Japan. Comment in Japanese whether or not you agree with his view.

2. Which societies can be described in the way the author does? What other countries cannot be described as such?

3. Did reading this story change the way you view Japan? The way you view your own and other countries? How and why?

## 1. Introduction

As one of the opinion pieces in a newspaper, *Asahi Shimbun*'s *Mado* "window" offers a relatively compact persuasive and expository text. The *Mado* column written by staff members (only initials are given; the writer's name is not revealed) appears regularly with a variety of headlines. Some columns argue for the writer's position on issues; others are essay-like and offer information and commentary. R3 consists of nine *danraku*, 16 sentences and 728 character spaces. It discusses issues related to automobile safety, what the writer calls the *sofuto* "soft-ware" side of the traffic accident problems, in particular.

## 2. Pre-reading tasks

1. Do you own a car? Do you drive a lot? What safety precautions do you take when you drive? If you were to answer these questions in Japanese, what vocabulary would you need? List words related to these topics.

2. What do you think of the automobile industry's policies toward the safety of the general public? What are the safety features available in automobiles? Write down your thoughts in Japanese in a memo format.

3. If you were asked to write a brief opinion piece about motorists' safety, what kind of things would you write? List items in Japanese.

## 3. Text and vocabulary: R3 (*Asahi Shimbun*, October 31, 1995, p. 3)

「窓」
論説委員室から
交通安全ソフト

A:
1.  千葉県の幕張メッセで第 31 回東京モーターショーが始まった。

B:

2. 今年は新車のお披露目も多く、例年にも増して華やかだが、デザインや性能とならんで、エアバッグなど、「安全」が一つのキーワードになっている。

C:

3. 交通事故による死者は、日本だけで毎年一万人を超える。

4. 考えてみると、毎年必ず一万人が死ぬような工業製品の使用が社会で許されているのは、不思議なことだ。

D:

5. それだけに、「安全」がセールスポイントになり、テレビのコマーシャルにも衝突実験の画像が登場してきたのだろう。

6. 安全のための技術開発はむしろ遅すぎたくらいだ。

E:

7. 日本の交通事故死は、1960年代後半から急速に増え、70年に一万六千余人に達した。

8. 官民一体の事故撲滅運動の結果、70年代はぐんぐん減り、79年には八千人台にまで下がった。

9. けれども80年代には再び増加に転じ、88年からはずっと一万人を超えている。

F:

10. 交通安全白書によれば、日本の事故死者数を車の走行キロ数当たりに直して欧米諸国と比べると、米国やドイツとはほとんど変わらない。

11. ところが英国だけは大違いで、ざっと半数なのだ。

G:

12. 英国の車が特別に安全というわけではないし、英国人の運転が特にうまいとも聞かない。

13.　恐らく、車とか道路とかの「ハード」の問題で
　　はなく、総合的な交通政策といった「ソフト」
　　の成果なのであろう。

H:

14.　日本の交通安全政策の所管は総理府だが、総合
　　的な「ソフト」の研究を十分にしているとは思
　　えない。

15.　たとえば、英国のケースを徹底的に研究するこ
　　とによって、毎年五千人の命を救えるのかもし
　　れないのだ。

I:

16.　車などハード面だけでなく、ソフトの研究にも
　　力を結集したいものである。

Vocabulary:

| 窓 | まど | n | window |
| 論説 | ろんせつ | n | editorial |
| 委員 | いいん | n | committee member |
| 交通 | こうつう | n | traffic |
| 安全 | あんぜん | n | safety |
| ソフト | | n | software |
| 1. | | | |
| 幕張 | まくはり | prop | Makuhari (place name) |
| メッセ | | | [German] Messe, fair, trade show |
| モーターショー | | n | auto show |
| 始まる | はじまる | v | to begin |
| 2. | | | |
| 新車 | しんしゃ | n | new car |
| お披露目 | おひろめ | n | introduction (with celebration) |
| 例年 | れいねん | n | normal year, average year |
| 増して | まして | | more than |

| 華やか | はなやか | adj | colorful |
|---|---|---|---|
| デザイン | | n | design |
| 性能 | せいのう | n | capacity, performance |
| エアバッグ | | n | air bag |
| キーワード | | n | key word, important concept |

3.

| 事故 | じこ | n | accident |
|---|---|---|---|
| 死者 | ししゃ | n | death, dead person |
| 超える | こえる | v | to surpass |

4.

| 必ず | かならず | adv | without fail |
|---|---|---|---|
| 死ぬ | しぬ | v | to die |
| 工業製品 | こうぎょうせいひん | n | industrial goods, products |
| 使用 | しよう | n | use, usage |
| 許す | ゆるす | v | to permit, to allow |
| 不思議な | ふしぎな | adj | strange, curious |

5.

| それだけに | | | because of that |
|---|---|---|---|
| セールスポイント | | n | selling point |
| テレビ | | n | television |
| コマーシャル | | n | commercial, radio and television ads |
| 衝突 | しょうとつ | n | collision |
| 実験 | じっけん | n | experiment |
| 画像 | がぞう | n | visuals on the screen |
| 登場する | とうじょうする | v | to appear |

6.

| 技術 | ぎじゅつ | n | technology |
|---|---|---|---|
| 開発 | かいはつ | n | development |
| むしろ | | adv | rather |

| | | | |
|---|---|---|---|
| 遅すぎる | おそすぎる | | to be too late |

7.

| | | | |
|---|---|---|---|
| 事故死 | じこし | n | death due to accident |
| 後半 | こうはん | n | latter half |
| 急速に | きゅうそくに | adv | rapidly |
| 増える | ふえる | v | to increase |
| 余人 | よにん | | additional number of people |

*Yo* is an affix to convey quantity over a certain level; for example, *sanjuu yonin* 'more than thirty people, thirty some people.'

| | | | |
|---|---|---|---|
| 達する | たっする | v | to reach |

8.

| | | | |
|---|---|---|---|
| 官民 | かんみん | n | government and people |
| 一体 | いったい | n | one body, unification |
| 撲滅 | ぼくめつ | n | eradication, extermination |
| 運動 | うんどう | n | movement, crusade |
| 結果 | けっか | n | result |
| ぐんぐん | | adv | increasingly |
| 減る | へる | v | to decrease |
| 台 | だい | n | level |

*Quantity words followed by *dai* means the level of that unit; for example, *hassennin dai* 'the level of eight thousand people.'

9.

| | | | |
|---|---|---|---|
| 再び | ふたたび | adv | again |
| 増加 | ぞうか | n | increase |
| 転じる | てんじる | v | to shift, to turn |
| ずっと | | adv | all the time, ever since |

10.

| | | | |
|---|---|---|---|
| 白書 | はくしょ | n | white paper |
| 死者数 | ししゃすう | n | (the number of) deaths |
| 走行 | そうこう | n | traveling, covering [by car, train, etc.] |

| キロ数 | | | (the number of) kilometers |
|---|---|---|---|
| 当たり | あたり | n | per |
| 直す | なおす | v | to convert, to turn into |
| 欧米 | おうべい | n | Europe and U.S.A. |
| 諸国 | しょこく | n | countries |
| 比べる | くらべる | v | to compare |
| ほとんど | | adv | [in negative sentences] hardly |

11.

| 大違い | おおちがい | n | big difference |
|---|---|---|---|
| ざっと | | adv | roughly, approximately |
| 半数 | はんすう | n | half (in number) |

12.

| 特別に | とくべつに | adv | especially |
|---|---|---|---|
| 特に | とくに | adv | specially |
| うまい | | adj | skillful |

13.

| 恐らく | おそらく | adv | perhaps |
|---|---|---|---|
| 車 | くるま | n | car |
| 道路 | どうろ | n | road |
| ハード | | | hardware, machine-related |
| 問題 | もんだい | n | problem |
| 総合的 | そうごうてき | adj | integrated, synthesized |
| 政策 | せいさく | n | policy |
| 成果 | せいか | n | result, fruit of one's effort |

14.

| 所管 | しょかん | n | jurisdiction |
|---|---|---|---|
| 総理府 | そうりふ | n | the Prime Minister's Office |
| 研究 | けんきゅう | n | research, study |
| 十分に | じゅうぶんに | adv | sufficiently |

15.

| ケース | | n | case |
|---|---|---|---|
| 徹底的に | てっていてきに | | |
| | | adv | thoroughly |
| 命 | いのち | n | life |
| 救う | すくう | v | to save, to rescue |

16.

| 面 | めん | n | aspect |
|---|---|---|---|
| 力 | ちから | n | power, resource |
| 結集する | けっしゅうする | | |
| | | v | to concentrate, to collect in a mass |

*Mono de aru* is a nominal predicate adding the meaning of "ought to" or "should," especially the way the things ideally should be. *Kesshuushitai mono dearu* expresses the writer's wish, 'we should gather all resources.'

## 4. Discourse notes

1. The organization of R3 follows the rule of *ki-shoo-ten-ketsu*, as summarized in Table 14. (Table 14 also includes predicate forms of sentences in R3.)

**Table 14** The *Ki-shoo-ten-ketsu* organization of R3 and sentence-final predicate forms

| organizational label | danraku | sentence-final predicate forms |
|---|---|---|
| *Ki* | A | *hajimatta* |
| | B | *natteiru* |
| *Shoo* | C | *koeru, koto da* |
| | D | *no daroo, kurai da* |
| | E | *tasshita, sagatta, koeteiru* |
| *Ten* | F | *kawaranai, na no da* |
| | G | *kikanai, na no dearoo* |
| *Ketsu* | H | *omoenai, kamoshirenai no da* |
| | I | *mono dearu* |

The main points of four parts may be summarized as below.

*Ki*:      This year's Tokyo Motor Show opened with its focus on safety.
*Shoo*:    The number of traffic accidents in Japan, once decreased, is on the rise
           again; more effort needed.
*Ten*:     Comparing Japan with other countries, England boasts better record.
*Ketsu*:   Japan must learn from British attention to "soft" human factors in traffic
           safety.

2. Study predicate forms of sentences in R3 as listed in Table 14. Commentary
predicate sentences include: *no daroo* in 5, *na no da* in 11, *na no dearoo* in 13,
*kamoshirenai no da* in 15, and *mono dearu* in 16. Additionally predicates
conveying personal opinion include *kurai da* and *omoenai*. Noting these forms
is helpful for understanding whether the writer informs the reader with fact or
expresses his or her opinion.

3. We find a few cases of graphologically marked quotation for labeling purposes.
The concepts of *anzen* "safety," *sofuto*, and *haado*. By marking with *kagikakko*,
the writer successfully highlights the importance of these concepts.

4. English loan words *sofuto* and *haado* in R3 apply in broader contexts in
Japanese: these are examples where the original English meaning is transformed
within the Japanese vocabulary system.

5. R3 is written mostly in non-past tense. We find two situations involving past
tense sentences. Line 1 reporting that the motor show started appears in the past
tense. Lines 7 and 8 report in the past tense the historical change that occurred in
the traffic accident deaths. These two situations emphasize the events that took
place in the past.

6. R3, being a column in a major newspaper, contains proportionately more
*kango* written in *kanji* compounds. Many of these *kanji* compounds consist of
more than two *kanji*. When faced with multiple *kanji*, the following strategy is
often useful, although in some cases it fails to work. Divide multiple *kanji* by two
from the beginning, leaving the last character as one unit. Interpret two-*kanji*
words and combine them to obtain the meaning of multiple *kanji* compounds.
For example, *koo-tsuu* plus *ji-ko*, *koo-gyoo* plus *sei-hin*, *shoo-totsu* plus *jik-ken*,
*boku-metsu* plus *un-doo*, and so on. Also study five-character words – *koo-tsuu*
plus *ji-ko* plus *shi*, and *ji-ko* plus *shi-sha* plus *suu*.

7. Note the connectives appearing in R3; *keredomo* in 9, *tokoroga* in 11, and
*tatoeba* in 15.

## 5. Discourse activities

1. List Japanese vocabulary related to cars and driving. Using these phrases, create sentences and arrange them following the *bunmyaku* of R3.

2. In Japanese provide summaries for all the *danraku* in R3. Choose key phrases from your summaries to come up with phrasal summaries as well.

3. Based on the article, explain the numbers listed below. Arrange them so that the organizational steps adopted in the article are recreated in your explanation.

　　1988, 1960s, 1970s, 1980s, 1979

　　10000, 5000, 16000, 8000

　　31st

4. What is the central message of this column? How do you know? Is there a sentence summarizing the writer's conclusion? Identify the central message of R3; explain it in your own words.

## 6. Post-reading tasks

1. What new information did you obtain by reading this column?

2. Do you agree with the article's central message?

3. Do you think the international contrast the writer makes is accurate? What is the situation of automobile accidents in your state or country?

## 1. Introduction

R4 contains the headline and body copy of a magazine advertisement for an American product, Pro-Keds shoes. This advertisement appeared in the May 25th, 1995 issue of a young men's magazine *Popeye*. *Popeye* is a fashion-information magazine published twice a month targeted to young men in their late teens to early twenties. Circulation in 1995 is estimated to be 650,000 (*Zasshi Shinbun Sookatarogu* 1995).

Advertisements featuring American products for young men often emphasize the product's American-ness, for instance, by introducing the historical background of the company to build the image of an authentic and genuine American product. You will note many English words transcribed in *katakana*, which further add authenticity to the product.

## 2. Pre-reading tasks

1. What do you know about Japanese advertising? Have you seen any Japanese print, television or internet advertising? When marketing American products, what kind of advertising do you think will sell in Japan? Write in a memo format some of your thoughts in Japanese.

2. Have you seen advertisements of Japanese products outside Japan, in the United States or elsewhere? What kind of cultural images are portrayed in those advertisements? Do you think Japanese images will sell in the global market?

## 3. Text and vocabulary: R4 (*Popeye* 1994:65)

愛すべき故郷。
≪プロケッズ≫は永遠のアメリカン・ストーリー・テラーです。

1.    みんなが知らないケッズの功績を話してあげよう。
2.    アメリカ中には、それまで確か 19 のメーカーがあって
      それぞれが、"スニーカ" という無限の可能性を持った

この新しい商品で何とかひと儲けしようと他人のやらない色々な工夫を凝らしていたわけさ。

3.    でも、ある時誰かがこう言ったんだ。

4.    「こんな高価な靴を買ってくれる金持ちがアメリカ中にいったい何人居るって言うんだい。

5.    誰でも買えるくらいに安くする方法を考えよう」...と。

6.    19のゴム底シューズ・メーカーの16社が賛同しこうして生まれたのが、ケッズ、プロケッズの母胎となった"ナショナル・インディアンラバー・カンパニー"。

7.    おかげで、それまでペッグ＆スナイダーのカタログにも6ドル50セント（！）で載ってたようなクロケット・サンダルが1897年のシアーズのカタログでは60セントで売られるほどに身近になったってわけ。

8.    あれからもう100年もたつけれどだからアメリカ人にとってケッズは今も特別なのさ。

9.    誰だって、まるで空気を呼吸するようにケッズをはいている。

10.    日本で売られているよりもっと沢山の中から選んで...。

Vocabulary:

| 愛す | あいす | v | to love |
|------|--------|---|---------|
| 故郷 | こきょう | n | hometown |
| 永遠 | えいえん | n | eternity |
| 1. | | | |
| 功績 | こうせき | n | achievement, success |
| 2. | | | |
| それまで | | | up until that time |
| 確か | たしか | adv | if I remember right |
| メーカー | | n | maker, manufacturer |
| それぞれ | | n | each |
| 無限の | むげんの | | limitless |

| 可能性 | かのうせい | n | possibility |
| 商品 | しょうひん | n | product |
| 何とか | なんとか | adv | somehow |
| ひと儲け | ひともうけ | n | a big profit |
| 他人 | ひと | n | others, other people |
| 工夫を凝らす | くふうをこらす | | to devise, to invent |

3.

| 誰か | だれか | | someone |

4.

| 高価な | こうかな | adj | expensive |
| 靴 | くつ | n | shoes |
| 金持ち | かねもち | n | wealthy person |

5.

| 誰でも | だれでも | | anyone |
| 安くする | やすくする | | to lower the price |
| 方法 | ほうほう | n | ways, methods |

6.

| ゴム底 | ゴムぞこ | n | rubber sole |
| 16社 | じゅうろくしゃ | | sixteen companies |
| 賛同する | さんどうする | v | to agree upon |
| 母胎 | ぼたい | n | (mother's) womb, source |

7.

| おかげで | | | thanks to |
| 載る | のる | v | to be printed on, to appear in print |
| カタログ | | n | catalogue |
| ドル | | n | dollar |
| セント | | n | cent |
| 身近に | みぢかに | adv | familiar, easily accessible |

8.

| たつ | | v | to pass |
| 特別な | とくべつな | adj | special |

9.

| | | | |
|---|---|---|---|
| 空気 | くうき | n | air |
| 呼吸する | こきゅうする | v | to breathe |
| はく | | v | to wear [items on the lower torso] |

10.

| | | | |
|---|---|---|---|
| 沢山 | たくさん | adv | many |
| 選ぶ | えらぶ | v | to choose |

## 4. Discourse notes

1. The reader of this advertising copy immediately notices one stylistic feature, i.e., its colloquial tone. Except the headline which takes the *desu/masu*-style, the main body of the copy consistently follows the *da*-style, often accompanied with nominal predicates and particles. Nominal predicates occur frequently: *shite ita wake sa* in sentence 2, *koo itta n da* in 3, *yuu n dai* in 4, *natta tte wake* in 7, and *tokubetsu na no sa* in 8. All these commentary predicates mark the writer's commentary and explanatory intention, adding to the tone of a friendly expert introducing and explaining about the product.

2. R4 contains a few pronominal and demonstrative expressions. The mixture of *ko-*, *so-* and *a-*references illustrates the writer's psychological distance toward the items mentioned. While the product's history is initially described with the *so*-reference (*sore made* and *sorezore*) in sentence 2, soon the present tense takes over and the *ko*-reference appears (*kono* in 2, *konna* in 4 and *kooshite* in 6). The *a*-reference (*are kara* in 8) also reflects the writer's position. It appeals to the *uchi* feeling enjoyed by the writer and the reader based on the shared knowledge the pronoun *are* evokes.

3. Study the case of cataphora in sentence 3, where the quotation in 4 is referred to by *koo* prior to its appearance.

4. The language of mass media (the popular culture, in particular) is rife with foreign words (mostly American English). This text contains words that are now part of Japanese vocabulary (e.g., *katarogu* "catalogue") as well as proper nouns (e.g., *shiaazu* "Sears"). Sometimes the English words do not have the original English meaning, which can cause confusion. For example, the word *meekaa* comes from the English word "maker," literally meaning "one who makes," but in

Japanese English *meekaa* exclusively refers to the manufacturing company and not the person who makes things. Some *katakana* words in mass media may not be considered a part of Japanese vocabulary, for example, *Amerikan sutoorii teraa* "American story teller" in R4.

5. A case of post-posing appears in 9 and 10, where the adverbial clause, *nihon de urareteiru yori motto takusanno naka kara erande* is post-posed.

6. The advertising copy, when it takes a colloquial tone, uses fewer *kango* and more *katakana* words, enhancing the fashionable effect. The print advertising copy also makes use of a variety of graphological marks. Note the English double quotation marks in R4, for example.

7. The simile appearing in 9 is interpretable when literally translated into English; *marude kuuki o kokyuusuru yooni kezzu o haiteiru* "wearing Keds just like we breathe air."

## 5. Discourse activities

1. Re-write the text of R4 in the non-spoken, standard written style. How does the stylistic change affect the overall tone and the voice of the body copy?

2. Create Japanese advertising copy (with a headline) for another American product. Follow the structural organization of the Pro-Keds advertisement. Divide the text into *danraku*, including a *danraku* on the product history.

## 6. Post-reading tasks

1. What do you think of this advertisement? How is American culture portrayed?

2. Did reading this text change your view about how goods are internationally marketed? How? Explain.

3. How did you like the style of this text? What features of this advertising copy do you think appeal to Japanese youths?

## 1. Introduction

R5 is taken from a comic book series titled "Crayon Shinchan," also produced as a television cartoon series and a movie. Shinchan, the protagonist, is a wild kindergartener who is known for his straightforward, rude
and often offensive speech habits. Shinchan constantly says things that
upset adults. For example, the comic book writer, Yoshito Usui, has
Shinchan yell out to his mother, *"Deta na, kaijuu shiwakuchan"* "Here
comes the monster, the wrinkled" in one of his comic strips (1994:20).

The language of this rude little kid is said to influence four- to twelve-
year-olds in Japan in the 1990s. Whether such straightforward and often
offensive talk will continue into these children's maturity is unknown.
However, it is in our interest to be aware of impolite Japanese. Although
the reader may not have opportunities to use offensive Japanese, it is
useful to know what it is like.

## 2. Pre-reading tasks

1. Have you seen Japanese animation films or read comic books? What
impression do you have about them? What do you like or dislike about them?

Reminder: When reading this material, make sure to look at the original
comic strip by Usui reproduced in Appendix 1.

## 3. Text and vocabulary: R5 (Usui 1994:98–100)

ひまわり組 VS バラ組の熱戦開始だぞ編、その４

1.
母：　　　　キャッ　海だわ
　　　キイーッ
父：　　　　さあ　ついたぞ
　　　ザザーン　ザザーン

2.

しんちゃん：　これから何やるの？
　　　　　　　このまま海にとびこむの？
父：　　　　　んなことするか!!

3.

母：　　　　　もっと子供らしい発想しなさい
　　　　　　　海でやること他にもあるでしょ
しんちゃん：　ん —— 水死体ごっこ
父：　　　　　釣りだよ!!
　　　　　　　釣りに来たの!!

4.

しんちゃん：　おおっ　つり　つり
　　　　　　　オラくじらさんとペンギンさんつる!!
母：　　　　　ふふ　子供ね
　　　　　　　考えることがむじゃき ♡

5.

母：　　　　　じゃあママは人魚さんでも釣っちゃおうかな
　　　　　　　ァ!!
　　　　　　　キャピ

6.

しんちゃん：　人魚はくうそうの生き物だからいないの!!
　　　　　　　いい年して子供っぽいこと言うなよ　みさえ〜
母：　　　　　ムカッ
父：　　　　　まあ　まあ　まあ

7.

　　　　　　船をチャーターすることにした
　　　　　　玄海丸
船主Ａ：　　　半日で３万円だよ
父：　　　　　高いなァ

8.

船主Ｂ：　　　ウチは半日で９千円
父：　　　　　おじさんとこに決めた!!

9.
船主B:　　　　さあのってくれ
　　　　限界丸
母:　　　　　ピッタリな船名ね...ハハ...
父:　　　　　浮きわ持ってくればよかった
しんちゃん:　わーい　ゆうれいせん

10.
　　　ポン　ポン　ポン　ザザーン　ザザーン

11.
母:　　　　　けっこう波が荒い〜
　　　　　　　だいじょうぶかなァ
しんちゃん:　オラこわーい
父:　　　　　なんだなんだ　だらしないなァ君たち
　　　　　　　ワッハッハ

12.
　　　　数分後
父:　　　　　へえええー
　　　　船酔い
母:　　　　　はん　だっらしないの
しんちゃん:　へん　足くっさいの

13.
船主B:　　　エサはこうやってつけるだよ
母:　　　　　へえ
しんちゃん:　ほう

14.
しんちゃん:　教えてくれてありがとございますぅ
船主B:　　　えらいな　ぼうや　ちゃんとお礼言えて
母:　　　　　しつけがいいもんで　ホホホ

15.
しんちゃん:　お返しにこの人が「すね毛を早くそる方法」教
　　　　　　　えます!!

母：　　　　　肌に対し直角にカミソリをあてすべるように
　　　　　　　そるべし!!
　　　　　　　そるべし!!
16.
母：　　　　　何やらせんのよ
船主Ｂ：　　　教えてくれてありがとございまーす　ハハ...
17.
母：　　　　　それっ
　　　　しゅっ　しゅっ
しんちゃん：　とおっ
父：　　　　　へえええ　まだ気持ちわり～
18.
父：　　　　　いえええ
しんちゃん：　おっ　父ちゃん　お元気になってあんなにはし
　　　　　　　ゃいでる
　　　　　　　つれてきてよかったウンウン
母：　　　　　あんたの釣り針がひっかかってんのよ!!
19.
母：　　　　　きゃっ　かかった!!
父：　　　　　お
20.
　　　　ピチチ
母：　　　　　や～ん　気持ちわる～い　触れな～い
21.
母：　　　　　もっかいもどしちゃお
　　　　ちゃぼっ
22.
　　　　ぐいっ
しんちゃん：　うお～っ　だれかがひっぱってるぅ
父：　　　　　しんのすけもかかったな!!
23.
しんちゃん：　負けるもんか!!　う～っ
父：　　　　　切ってどーする!!

24.

ピチ　ピチ

母：　　　　　　やったァ

25.

船主Ｂ：　　　すぐさしみにしてやるだよ

父：　　　　　お　いいね!!　ビールある？

しんちゃん：　お魚さんかわいそう...

母：　　　　　やさしいのね　しんちゃん...

　　　　　　　キュン

26.

父：　　　　　んまい

しんちゃん：　か〜〜っ!!　舌にとろけるねい!!

母：　　　　　どーゆー性格しとんのじゃ...


<u>Vocabulary</u>:

| ひまわり組 | ひまわりぐみ | n | sunflower class |
|---|---|---|---|
| バラ組 | | n | rose class |
| 熱戦 | ねっせん | n | heated competition |
| 開始 | かいし | n | start, beginning |
| 編 | へん | n | section, volume |

*Numbers correspond to the sequence of frames.

1.

| つく | | v | to arrive |
|---|---|---|---|

2.

| このまま | | | as is, as they are |
|---|---|---|---|
| とびこむ | | v | to jump into |
| んな | | dem | [colloquial] *sonna* 'such' |

*Nna koto suru ka* is a rhetorical question – 'There's no way that we'd do such a thing!'

3.

| 発想する | はっそうする | v | to think of, to imagine |
|---|---|---|---|
| 水死体 | すいしたい | n | drowned body |

| ごっこ | | n | [suffix used for] game or play |
| 釣り | つり | n | fishing |
| 4. | | | |
| オラ | | pn | [male blunt dialect style] I |
| くじら | | n | whale |
| ペンギン | | n | penguin |
| むじゃき | | adj | innocent |
| 5. | | | |
| ママ | | n | mom |
| 人魚 | にんぎょ | n | mermaid |
| 6. | | | |
| くうそうの | | | imaginary |
| 生き物 | いきもの | n | creature |
| いい年して | | | [sarcastically] despite the mature age |
| 子供っぽい | こどもっぽい | adj | childish |

*Misae is Shinchan's mother.　Referring to one's mother by her first name is outrageous, yet this is routine for Shinchan.

| 7. | | | |
| 船 | ふね | n | boat, ship |
| チャーターする | | v | to charter |
| 玄海丸 | げんかいまる | prop | "Deep Sea" [name of a ship] |
| 半日 | はんにち | n | half a day |
| 8. | | | |
| ウチ | | n | my side, our side |
| とこ | | n | [colloquial] *tokoro* 'place' |
| 決める | きめる | v | to decide |
| 9. | | | |
| 限界丸 | げんかいまる | prop | "The Limited" [name of a ship] |

| ピッタリな | | adj | perfectly matching |
| 船名 | せんめい | n | name of a boat or ship |
| 浮きわ | うきわ | n | inner tube float |
| ゆうれいせん | | n | ghost boat |
| 11. | | | |
| けっこう | | adv | quite, to a surprising degree |
| 波 | なみ | n | wave |
| 荒い | あらい | adj | rough |
| だいじょうぶ | | adj | all right, safe, O.K. |

*The expression *nan da nan da* is an exclamatory utterance used to show a critical attitude – 'What's the matter! What's with you!'

| だらしない | | adj | helpless |
| 12. | | | |
| 数分後 | すうふんあと | | after several minutes |
| 船酔い | ふなよい | n | seasick |
| くさい | | adj | smelly |
| 13. | | | |
| エサ | | n | bait |
| つける | | v | to attach |
| 14. | | | |
| えらい | | adj | admirable |
| ぼうや | | n | dear litte boy |
| お礼言う | おれいいう | | [colloquial] to say thanks |
| しつけ | | n | discipline |

*Shinchan's mother does not exactly behave as an adult should either. She brags about herself when she says *Shitsuke ga ii mon de* 'We discipline him well' in response to the ship captain's compliment.

| 15. | | | |
| お返し | おかえし | n | (in) return |
| すね毛 | すねげ | n | hair on one's legs |
| そる | | v | to shave |

| 方法 | ほうほう | n | ways, methods |
|------|---------|---|---------------|
| 教える | おしえる | v | to teach |
| 肌 | はだ | n | skin |
| 対し | たいし | | against |
| 直角に | ちょっかくに | adv | at a 90 degree angle, vertically |
| あてる | | v | to place against |
| すべる | | v | to slide down |

16.

| やらす | | v | to make someone do |

17.

| 気持ちわり | きもちわり | | [colloquial] *kimochi ga warui* 'to feel sick' |

18.

| はしゃぐ | | v | to be very pleased, to romp around with joy |
| 釣り針 | つりばり | n | fish hook |
| ひっかかる | | v | to be caught |

19.

| かかる | | v | to catch |

20.

| 触る | さわる | v | to touch |

21.

| もっかい | | | [colloquial] *moo ikkai* 'one more time' |
| もどす | | v | to return, to restore |

*Modoshichao* is a colloquial expression of *Modoshite shimaoo* 'I will return this.'

22.

| ひっぱる | | v | to pull |

23.

| 負ける | まける | v | to lose |

*Makeru monka!!*, a colloquial expression of *makeru mono ka*, expresses negative determination and will, meaning 'I'm not going to lose.'

| | | | |
|---|---|---|---|
| 切る | きる | v | to cut |
| 24. | | | |
| やった | | exc | I did it! Got it! |
| 25. | | | |
| さしみ | | n | *sashimi* |
| かわいそう | | adj | poor, pitiful |
| やさしい | | adj | tender-hearted |
| 26. | | | |
| んまい | | | [colloquial] *umai* 'delicious' |
| 舌 | した | n | tongue |
| とろける | | v | to melt |
| 性格 | せいかく | n | character, personality |
| しとんのじゃ | | | [colloquial] *shiteiru n daroo* 'I wonder how he is...' |

## 4. Discourse notes

1. One of the sources of humor in this cartoon is the pun created by the use of homonyms; each of the two boats that appear in the cartoon is named *Genkaimaru*. *Genkaimaru* in frame 7 looks nice and safe as the name indicates (i.e., "Deep Sea") while *Genkaimaru* in frame 9 looks completely decrepit as its name indicates (i.e., "The Limited"). (See the original comic reproduced in the appendix.) As noted in Entry 29, the Japanese language contains a limited number of syllables and numerous homonyms, two conditions quite useful for creating puns and jokes. In actual text, since different *kanji* are used, the intended pun is rarely missed. Even when the homonyms are spoken, because of the contextual information, misunderstandings are infrequent.

2. Comics contain many exclamatory expressions that do not appear in other written texts. Because of the visual cues presented to us in comics, it is often

possible to understand what the fragmented verbal exclamations mean. Let me explain some of them appearing in R5; see if your interpretation matches the explanation. (Numbers correspond to the frames.)

| | | |
|---|---|---|
| 4 | *Oo!* | Yeah! (with surprise and excited willingness) |
| 6 | *Maa maa maa!* | Oh well, calm down, take it easy, lighten up (used when encouraging others to calm down or to relax) |
| 9 | *Waai!* | Wow! (pleased and impressed with something surprisingly good) |
| 13 | *Hee!* | I see! (surprise, finding out or learning something for the first time) |
| 17 | *Sore!* | Here it is! (calling out when starting some action) |
| | *To-oo!* | Here it comes! (calling out when throwing something) |
| 24 | *Yattaa!* | I did it! We got it! (declaring success) |

3.  Another linguistic feature prominent in comics and cartoons is the phonological (i.e., sound) variation of words. By lengthening vowels otherwise not lengthened, the speaker adds emphasis, and this is reflected in the written text; *waru-ui* instead of the standard *warui* and *sawarena-ai*, instead of the standard *sawarenai* in 20. Adding an additional vowel in *katakana* is another method of conveying the lengthened vowel. For example, *tsutchaoo ka na-a!!* in 5 and *yatta-a!!* in 24.

4.  Since we find many *giseigo*, onomatopoeic (i.e., sound-imitating) words and *gitaigo*, mimicry (i.e., action-imitating) words in comics and cartoons, let me list a few examples.

| | | |
|---|---|---|
| 1 | *kiii* | screeching (of cars) |
| 1,10 | *zazaan* | waves of ocean washing the shore |
| 10 | *pon pon pon* | boat engine making sounds of rhythmical rotation, exhaust coming out of chimney regularly |
| 17 | *shu shu* | fishing line released whispering in the air, sound of an item moving fast through the air |
| 24 | *pichi pichi* | young and lively body (in this case, of a fish), energetically jerking this way and that |
| 25 | *kyun* | heart aching with warm emotion, almost moved to tears |

5.  Occasionally one finds Japanese words written in *katakana*. Find *ora* in frames 4 and 11, *uchi* in frame 8, *pittarina* in frame 9, and *esa* in frame 13. *Katakana* presentation is used primarily to attract attention; it also helps give an impression that the words are contemporary and fashionable.

6. Study special graphological marks; a heart in frame 4, a wavy lengthening marker in frames 6, 11, 17, 20, 22, 23, and 26. The use of these marks is mostly limited to youth-oriented publications.

## 5. Discourse activities

1. Write a Japanese narrative that describes the incidents that occurred in R5. Include in the story: participants, time, place, for what purpose the participants did what, the results, and how the event ended. Develop a cohesive narrative plot by using appropriate cohesion devices.

2. Pretend you were one of the participants. Write a diary of that day in Japanese, organizing the events chronologically. Include in your writing the description of: (1) surprises, (2) worries, (3) joy, (4) anger, and (5) other emotional response.

3. Contrast the images of the ocean that Tawara (R1) and Usui (this reading) use in their writings. Describe in Japanese the different things each of the writers associate with the ocean. Use *danraku* divisions for highlighting the contrast.

## 6. Post-reading tasks

1. What do you think of Shinchan's behavior, toward his mother, in particular?

2. How did you like this comic? Does this comic portray an image of Japan different from what you have entertained so far?

3. Can you think of writers who use the image of the sea in their literary works? Yukio Mishima? Ernest Hemingway? Write a brief essay in Japanese.

## 1. Introduction

*Tensei Jingo* ( [literally] Heaven's Voice, Human Words) is a daily news-paper essay column written by an Asahi Shinbunsha employee. The column offers an (often philosophical) essay related to topical or current social issues, seasonal thoughts or any other items of concern to the writer. Started in 1904, its only absence a five-year period during World War II, this essay column continues to appear today. The *Tensei Jingo* column appears at the bottom of the first page in the morning *Asahi Shimbun*, and its English translation appears (since 1957) under the head-line of "Vox Populi, Vox Dei" in the same date's *Asahi Evening News*. The title of the column originates in a Chinese saying: There is a voice in the heavens and the voice is heard through the people. This column has been written by a number of essayists and/or commentators, some of whom have become popular with a substantial number of "fans" among news-paper subscribers.

Collections of *Tensei Jingo* are regularly published. Japanese collec-tions appear in two volumes per year, published by Asahi Shinbunsha, and the Japanese-with-English-translation version appears in four vol-umes per year, published by Hara Shoboo in Tokyo.

## 2. Pre-reading tasks

1. When you are in a pensive mood, do different seasons of the year make you ponder different things? What do you think when the fall arrives? When you see falling leaves? In the form of a short essay, write a few sentences in Japanese about your thoughts when you sense the arrival of the fall.

2. Think of five Japanese words associated with the fall season. Connect them in terms of cohesive relations and develop a Japanese text relevant to these relations. Use appropriate connectives.

### 3. Text and Vocabulary (*Asahi Shimbun*, November 28, 1994, p. 1)

天声人語

A:
1.　はらはらと葉の散る季節である。
2.　熊手やほうきで集めた落ち葉を、昔はよく焼いた。
3.　一般に焚き火が珍しくなかった。
4.　人々は尻などをあぶりながら雑談をし、子どもたちは火のおこし方や始末の仕方を覚えた。

B:
5.　そういえば、いまの子どもには、日常的には火をおこす機会がない。
6.　囲炉裏のほたびやおきの熱気などにも、なじみが薄いだろう。
7.　そういう、火の様子を示す言葉に接することもないかも知れない。
8.　煙たさも経験できず、焚き火で焼きいもをつくる楽しみも知らぬとすると、残念だ。

C:
9.　熱い焼きいもを灰の中から引っ張り出し、灰をはたき落としながら、ふうふう言って食う。
10.　そういう野趣が、いまの日常生活にはない。
11.　焚き火のあとの灰には水をかけた。
12.　灰は堆肥と同様、菜園の肥料にするために大切だった。

D:
13.　難しく言えば、炭酸カリウムだろう。
14.　いわゆるカリ肥料だ。

15. かつて農家には灰小屋があり、灰の売買をする灰問屋も存在し、灰市の立つ町もあった。
16. 灰という物質は、あく抜きにも使われ、生活に大きな役割を果たしていた。

E:

17. 灰は、物語や伝説にも登場する。
18. 「シンデレラ」は欧米の言葉では「灰かぶり娘」という意味である。
19. 台所の灰の中にすわって仕事をしていたからだ。
20. 不死鳥と訳される「フェニックス」は古代エジプトの想像上の鳥で、生命の終わりが近づくと香木を積んで火をつけ、自らを焼き、灰の中からよみがえる。

F:

21. 「花咲爺」の話で、よいおじいさんは犬が殺されたのを嘆き、葬り、そこに松を植える。
22. 成長した松で臼をつくるが、意地悪じいさんに焼かれてしまう。
23. 灰をもらって帰る時、風が灰を吹き上げると枯れ枝に花が咲く……

G:

24. 灰にまみれた娘が幸運をつかみ、灰から鳥が何度も蘇生し、灰をまいたら美しい花が咲いた。
25. いずれも思わぬ逆転劇である。
26. 落ちた葉が灰になるのも、来春の再生を期してのことであろうか。

Vocabulary:

1.

| | | | |
|---|---|---|---|
| はらはらと | | adv | steadily, incessantly |
| 葉 | は | n | leaves |
| 散る | ちる | v | to fall |

| 季節 | きせつ | n | season |
|---|---|---|---|

2.

| 熊手 | くまで | n | rake |
|---|---|---|---|
| ほうき | | n | broom |
| 集める | あつめる | v | to collect, to gather |
| 落ち葉 | おちば | n | fallen leaf |
| 昔 | むかし | n | old time |
| 焼く | やく | v | to burn |

3.

| 一般に | いっぱんに | adv | among the general public, among people |
|---|---|---|---|
| 焚き火 | たきび | n | fire, bonfire |
| 珍しい | めずらしい | adj | rare, unusual |

4.

| 人々 | ひとびと | n | people |
|---|---|---|---|
| 尻 | しり | n | buttocks, one's backside |
| あぶる | | v | to warm, to toast |
| 雑談 | ざつだん | n | chat, idle talk |
| 火 | ひ | n | fire |
| おこし方 | おこしかた | | ways of making fire |
| 始末 | しまつ | n | disposal |
| 仕方 | しかた | n | ways, methods |
| 覚える | おぼえる | v | to learn |

5.

| そういえば | | | speaking of that |
|---|---|---|---|
| 日常的 | にちじょうてき | | |
| | | adv | ordinarily, in everyday life |
| 機会 | きかい | n | opportunity |

6.

| 囲炉裏 | いろり | n | fire pit |
|---|---|---|---|
| ほたび | | n | fire (of burning wood pieces) |

| おき | | n | embers |
|---|---|---|---|
| 熱気 | ねっき | n | heat |
| なじみが薄い | なじみがうすい | | unfamiliar |

**7.**

| 様子 | ようす | n | the state of affairs, situation |
|---|---|---|---|
| 示す | しめす | v | to describe |
| 言葉 | ことば | n | words |
| 接する | せっする | v | to come in contact |

**8.**

| 煙たさ | けむたさ | n | smokiness |
|---|---|---|---|
| 経験する | けいけんする | v | to experience |
| 焼きいも | やきいも | n | roasted sweet potato |
| 楽しみ | たのしみ | n | pleasure |
| 知らぬ | しらぬ | | [old style] *shiranai* 'don't know' |
| 残念 | ざんねん | adj | regrettable, unfortunate |

**9.**

| 熱い | あつい | adj | hot |
|---|---|---|---|
| 灰 | はい | n | ashes |
| 引っ張り出す | ひっぱりだす | | to pull out, to drag something out |
| はたき落とす | はたきおとす | | to pat something off |
| ふうふう言って | | | [lit. utter *fuu fuu*] making a blowing sound (to cool things off) |
| 食う | くう | v | [blunt] *taberu* 'to eat' |

**10.**

| 野趣 | やしゅ | n | pleasure drawn from nature |
|---|---|---|---|

**12.**

| 堆肥 | たいひ | n | compost |
|---|---|---|---|
| 同様 | どうよう | | same as |

| 菜園 | さいえん | n | vegetable garden |
| 肥料 | ひりょう | n | fertilizer |
| 大切 | たいせつ | adj | important, precious |

13.

| 難しく言えば | むずかしくいえば | | (to put it) in technical terms |
| 炭酸カリウム | たんさんカリウム | n | potassium carbonate |

14.

| いわゆる | | adv | so-called |
| カリ肥料 | ひりょう | n | potassium fertilizer |

15.

| かつて | | adv | in the past, once |
| 農家 | のうか | n | farmer |
| 灰小屋 | はいごや | n | ash shack |
| 売買 | ばいばい | n | selling and buying |
| 灰問屋 | はいどんや | n | wholesale ash dealer |
| 存在する | そんざいする | v | to exist |
| 灰市 | はいいち | n | ash market |
| 立つ | たつ | v | to open (a market) |
| 町 | まち | n | town |

16.

| 物質 | ぶっしつ | n | material |
| あく抜き | あくぬき | n | reducing harshness (bitterness) of vegetables |
| 役割 | やくわり | n | role |
| 果たす | はたす | v | to play (a role) |

17.

| 物語 | ものがたり | n | story |
| 伝説 | でんせつ | n | legend |
| 登場する | とうじょうする | v | to appear |

18.

| | | | |
|---|---|---|---|
| シンデレラ | | prop | Cinderella |
| 欧米 | おうべい | n | Europe and the U.S. |
| 灰かぶり娘 | はいかぶりむすめ | | |
| | | n | ash-covered maiden |
| 意味 | いみ | n | meaning |

19.

| | | | |
|---|---|---|---|
| 台所 | だいどころ | n | kitchen |
| すわる | | v | to sit down |
| 仕事 | しごと | n | work, chore |

20.

| | | | |
|---|---|---|---|
| 不死鳥 | ふしちょう | n | the Phoenix |
| 訳す | やくす | v | to translate |
| フェニックス | | prop | Phoenix |
| 古代エジプト | | n | Ancient Egypt |
| 想像上 | そうぞうじょう | | imaginary |
| 鳥 | とり | n | bird |
| 生命 | せいめい | n | life |
| 終わり | おわり | n | end |
| 近づく | ちかづく | v | to come near |
| 香木 | こうぼく | n | fragrant wood |
| 積む | つむ | v | to pile up |
| 火をつける | | v | to light a fire |
| 自ら | みずから | n | self |
| よみがえる | | v | to resurrect |

21.

| | | | |
|---|---|---|---|
| 花咲爺 | はなさかじじい | | [title of a Japanese old tale] flower-blooming old man |
| 殺す | ころす | v | to kill, to murder |
| 嘆く | なげく | v | to lament, to mourn |
| 葬る | ほうむる | v | to bury (the dead) |
| 松 | まつ | n | pine tree |

| 植える | うえる | v | to plant |
| 22. | | | |
| 成長する | せいちょうする | | |
| | | v | to grow |
| 臼 | うす | n | wooden mortar |
| 意地悪 | いじわる | adj | wicked |
| 23. | | | |
| 風 | かぜ | n | wind |
| 吹き上げる | ふきあげる | v | to blow upward |
| 枯れ枝 | かれえだ | n | bare branch |
| 花 | はな | n | flower, blossom |
| 咲く | さく | v | to bloom |
| 24. | | | |
| まみれる | | v | to be covered with |
| 幸運 | こううん | n | fortune |
| 何度も | なんども | | (for) many times |
| 蘇生する | そせいする | v | to be born again, to resurrect |
| 25. | | | |
| いずれも | | | all of them |
| 思わぬ | おもわぬ | | surprising |
| 逆転劇 | ぎゃくてんげき | | |
| | | n | reversal drama |
| 26. | | | |
| 落ちる | おちる | v | to fall down |
| 来春 | らいしゅん | n | next spring |
| 再生 | さいせい | n | rebirth |
| 期する | きする | v | to anticipate |

## 4. Discourse notes

The original text appearing in the appendix contains *kanji* for *oki* and *hotabi* (line 6). These characters are not in daily use and I use *hiragana* instead in the sentence-by-sentence presentation.

1. Note the graphological mark of an upside-down triangle used as a *danraku* division marker appearing in the original text.

2. The flow of discourse of R6 presents an interesting case of the *ki-shoo-ten-ketsu* scheme, as presented below with *danraku* assignments.

*ki* (topic presentation)
    A: the season of falling leaves
*shoo* (topic development)
    A: custom of burning leaves a while back
    B: lack of this experience among today's children
    C: after burning, ashes were collected
    D: commercial value of ashes in old days
*ten* (surprise turn)
    E: ashes symbolize resurrection in Western fairy tales
    F: ashes in Japanese fairy tales symbolize rebirth
*ketsu* (conclusion)
    G: reversal drama – from ashes (of leaves) to rebirth

3. Closely associated with the *ki-shoo-ten-ketsu* framework are the *bunmyaku* and *danraku* types. The logical thread of R6 may be captured as shown in Table 15.

**Table 15** Logical thread of R6 with identification of *Danraku* types

| *logical thread* | *types* |
| --- | --- |
| introductory: | |
|   A (custom of burning leaves a while back) | introductory/background |
|   ↓ | |
| supplementary evidence, minor opinion: | |
|   B (lack of this experience among today's children) | background |
|   ↓ | |
| supplementary evidence, minor opinion: | |
|   C (after burning, ashes were collected) | background |
|   D (commercial value of ashes in old days) | background |
|   ↓ | |
| main evidence, concrete examples: | |
|   E (ashes symbolized in Western fairy tales) | main |
|   F (ashes in Japanese fairy tales symbolize rebirth) | main |
|   ↓ | |
| conclusion, presentation of opinion: | |
|   G (reversal drama – from ashes [of leaves] to rebirth) | concluding |

4. We are able to identify organizational principles as presented above partly because the text uses the strategy of repeated key phrases. In fact, R6 contains many words related to fire and ashes. These key phrases offer, through repetition and a sentence-chaining mechanism, obvious clues as to what the text talks about. Table 16 illustrates the repeated key phrases appearing in R6.

**Table 16**  Key phrases in R6 and their distribution by sentence

| sentence | key phrases | | |
|---|---|---|---|
| | *leaves, falling* | *fire and related phrases* | *ashes and related phrases* |
| 1. | *ha no chiru* | | |
| 2. | *ochiba* | *yaita* | |
| 3. | | *takibi* | |
| 4. | | *hi no okoshi kata, shimatsu no shikata* | |
| 5. | | *hi o okosu* | |
| 6. | | *hotabi, oki* | |
| 7. | | *hi* | |
| 8. | | *takibi* | |
| 9. | | | *hai* |
| 10. | | | |
| 11. | | *takibi* | *hai* |
| 12. | | | *hai* |
| 13. | | | |
| 14. | | | |
| 15. | | | *haigoya, hai, haidon'ya haiichi* |
| 16. | | | *hai* |
| 17. | | | *hai* |
| 18. | | | *hai kaburi musume* |
| 19. | | | *hai* |
| 20. | | *hi, yaki* | *hai* |
| 21. | | | |
| 22. | | *yakarete* | |
| 23. | | | *hai, hai* |
| 24. | | | *hai, hai, hai* |
| 25. | | | |
| 26. | *ochita ha* | | *hai* |

5. Study sentence-final strategies of R6. Recall the two types of sentence-final strategies – (1) descriptive presenting fact, (2) judgmental and communicative expressing opinions (as discussed in Entry 18). Let us focus on the last three *danraku* of R6 and see what we can learn from sentence-final forms.

*2R6: Sentence-final forms*

E

17. **toojoosuru**.

18. to yuu imi **dearu**.

19. shigoto o shiteita **kara da**.

20. hai no naka kara **yomigaeru**.

F

21. soko ni matsu o **ueru**.

22. **yakareteshimau**.

23. kareeda ni hana ga **saku**.

G

24. utsukushii hana ga **saita**.

25. omowanu gyakutengeki **dearu**.

26. kishite no **koto dearoo ka**.

Note the distinction between the description of facts and the expression of the writer's judgment and opinions. Sentences that take the nominal predicate *kara da* in 19 and *koto dearoo ka* in 26 express the writer's commentary while others describe facts (as least, the writer views them as facts). It is also interesting to note that fact sentences (lines 17, 18, 20, 21, 22, 23, and 25) all appear in non-past tense. Sentences 17 and 25 describe the fact in the writer's time; sentences 20, 21, 22, and 23 describe events as-if-being-there. The only fact sentence marked with the past tense, 24, appears in the last *danraku*, in which the writer now returns to the writer's time. The last two sentences (lines 25 and 26) express the writer's conclusion in non-past tense.

6. The reader may reach the central message of R6 from a few different perspectives. First, the repeated related phrases of "fire" and "ashes" suggest their importance as key concepts. Second, based on the sentence-final form, sentence 26 seems important for understanding what the writer wishes to say. Given the overall organization, the final *danraku* – the final sentence, in particular – seems important. Third, there is a conceptual correspondence between sentences 1 and 26, which leads to a philosophical interpretation of fallen leaves. The essay takes

us through the conceptual process of leaves → fire → ashes → resurrection, finally reaching the central message, nature's way of death leading to re-birth.

7.  Review the deletion of the subject/topic in R6, some of which was discussed in Entry 17.

8.  Study the cohesive relationship between sentences 18 and 19; 19 provides the reason for 18 through the predicate *kara da*.

## 5. Discourse activities

1.  Write a one-sentence summary for each *danraku* of R6. Identify the connection between each and insert connectives and organizational markers where appropriate.

2.  List all Japanese vocabulary items related to fire and ashes. Summarize the content of R6 by using some of these words. When writing a summary, follow the *ki-shoo-ten-ketsu* structural scheme and make an explicit conclusive statement in *ketsu*.

3.  Based on your memory, write the gist of the Cinderella story in Japanese. Incorporate in your story (1) narrative chronological sequencing, (2) quotations, and (3) similes and/or metaphors.

## 6. Post-reading tasks

1.  What do you think of the writer's philosophical point? Do you think this view toward life is culture-specific or universal?

2.  What intertextual commonality does the writer find between *Hanasaka Jijii* and Cinderella? If you know both stories, explain similarities and differences.

## 1. Introduction

R7 is a sample of a modern Japanese essay written by Tetsuroo Morimoto, a scholar and essayist. He has written extensively on the philosophy of traveling. The piece we read as R7 was published in his book titled *Subarashiki Tabi – Ningen, Saigetsu, Deai* "The Wonderment of Travel – Human Beings, Passing Time and Chance Encounter" in 1976 (Tokyo: Daiamondosha). Although students of Japanese will find many new vocabulary items, this essay, in its entirety, can be read with a basic grammatical background combined with the discourse knowledge gained by studying this book.

Since the essay is divided into five sections as shown in the original text in Appendix 1 – (1) *danraku* A, (2) *danraku* B to F, (3) *danraku* G to L, (4) *danraku* M to U, and finally (5) *danraku* V to Z – the reader may read each section separately. This strategy may help the reader not to be overwhelmed by the number of new vocabulary items.

## 2. Pre-reading tasks

1. Do you like to travel? Why do you travel? Why don't you travel? How do you decide where to go? List Japanese words you need in order to answer these questions.

2. What images and impressions do you have about the desert? The Mohave? The Sahara? Describe your images in Japanese in a memo format.

## 3. Text and vocabulary (Morimoto 1976, reproduced in Morimoto 1983:119–125)

砂漠への旅

A:
1.    「千里の旅、万巻の書」という中国のことばがある。
2.    その意味はいろいろに解釈できるが、私は自分で勝手にこう改釈している。

3. 　　——千里の旅をすることは、万巻の書物を読破するにひとしい。

B:

4. 　ところで、万巻の書物を読破するなどということは、私のような凡人にはとうていできないけれども、千里の旅なら、いまはジェット機の時代だから、けっしてむずかしくはない。

5. 　そこで私は書物を読むようなつもりで旅に出る。

6. 　そう思って出かけると、世界は一冊の巨大な本のような気がしてくる。

C:

7. 　たしかに世界は一冊の書物だ。

8. 　旅をするということは、その巨大な本のページを繰ってゆくことである。

9. 　私はこれまで、世界のかなりの地域を旅したが、それでも、まだ世界という書物の第一章も読み終えていないような気がする。

10. 　私はときどき旅先で、いったい、いつになったら読み終えることができるのか見当もつかないこの巨大な書物、世界そのものにめまいを覚えることがある。

11. 　そして、旅とは、このように途方に暮れることではないか、と考えてみたりする。

D:

12. 　なぜ旅が読書とひとしい意味を持つのか。

13. 　言うまでもあるまい。

14. 　旅は読書とおなじように、小さな自分の世界を大きくするからである。

15. 　旅とは自分の住む井戸から脱け出て、世界は広いんだなあ、と実感することだ。

16.　そのおどろき、そのとまどい、それがそのまま
　　　自分への反省につながってゆくのである。

E:

17.　日本人は井のなかの蛙のようなものだ。

18.　たしかに日本は小さな島国だから、世間知らず
　　　になりやすい。

19.　けれど、人間というのは、どこに住んでいよう
　　　と、じつは例外なく井のなかの蛙なのである。

20.　いや、そもそも、ひとつところに住むというこ
　　　とが、すなわち井のなかの蛙になるということ
　　　である。

F:

21.　むろん、井戸のなかでも、それなりの文化は生
　　　れるであろう。

22.　が、文明の歴史は、人びとが井戸から脱け出す
　　　ことによって文化を発展させてきたことを教え
　　　ている。

23.　人類はまさしく旅によって文化をつくりあげて
　　　きたのだ。

24.　広い世界に出て、途方に暮れることによって。

G:

25.　これは私の友人の探検家からきいた話なのだが、
　　　ニューギニアの奥地のある村では、若い未婚の
　　　男女が二人だけで食事をするなどということは、
　　　それこそ「とんでもない話」なのだそうである。

26.　そんなことをしたら、村じゅうがハチの巣をつ
　　　ついたような騒ぎになって、男は追放され、女
　　　はヨメに行けなくなってしまうのだという。

27.　ところが、若い未婚の男女が藪かげでいっしょ
　　　に寝て夜を過ごしても、それはべつになんの問
　　　題にもならないのだそうだ。

28.　つまり、食事を共にすることは許されないが、夜を共に過ごすことはかまわないというのである。

29.　友人の探検家はこの話をしながら、目をまるくして、「世界は広いねえ」と言った。

H:

30.　このような例は極端かもしれない。

31.　しかし、私自身、旅をしてみて、おなじ人間でありながら、こんなにもちがうものかと、いまさらのように思い知らされたことがしばしばある。

32.　たとえば、インドでは葬式に涙は禁物であると教えられた。

33.　古都ベナレスのガンジス河のほとりで、私は何組かの葬列にあい、葬式にも加わったが、たしかにだれひとりとして泣いていない。

34.　葬儀に女性の姿をあまり見かけなかったが、インドの友人の話によると、婦人はつい涙をこぼしてしまうので遠慮するのだ、とのことであった。

35.　なぜ泣いてはいけないのか。

36.　インド人にとって、死ぬということは母なるガンジスへ帰ってゆくことなのであって、泣くべきことがらではないからだというのである。

I:

37.　しかし、私がエジプトのカイロで目撃した葬列には、多勢の女たちが泣き叫びながら従っていた。

38.　あまりにも異様なその慟哭に、私は思わず立ちどまって凝視した。

39.　とたんに女たちは泣きやみ、私をきっと睨んだ。

40.　同行のエジプトの友は私にこう教えた。

41.　「あれは泣き女です。

42.　彼女たちは葬式に雇われて泣いてみせるのです」

J:

43.　そうした泣き女という風習は、かつては中国でも見られた。

44.　葬儀という人生の最も深刻な行事においてさえ、人間はこうもちがっているのである。

45.　ちょっとした仕草に至っては、そのようなちがいは無数にある。

K:

46.　日本人は子供の頭を撫でてかわいがるが、東南アジアの国々では、たとえ子供であろうと赤ん坊だろうと、頭に手をふれることをたいへんいやがる。

47.　頭は人間にとっていちばん大切な部分だから、そこに気安く手をふれることは侮蔑にひとしいのである。

48.　日本人はスープを音を立てて吸うが、ヨーロッパ人はその音をきくと眉をひそめる。

49.　ところが、そのヨーロッパ人は食事最中に音を立てて鼻をかむのをなんとも思わない。

50.　また、日本人やアメリカ人は、人と待ち合わせて定刻を五分も過ぎようものならイライラしはじめる。

51.　そして、相手を三十分も待たせるなどということは、腹を立てるのにじゅうぶんな仕打ちであると考える。

52.　けれど、アラビア人やラテン・アメリカ人にとっては、三十分などという時間は人を待たせる最低の単位にすぎない。

L:

53. このような例をあげてゆけば、きりがない。

54. 世界というのは、それぞれの井戸のなかに暮す蛙たちにとっては、それこそ"反世界"の集合体なのである。

55. 世界を旅するということは、反世界を旅することなのだ。

M:

56. 私は何度か砂漠へ出かけた。

57. 旅ということばをきくと、どういうわけか私の胸中には空と砂とがひとつに溶け合った果てしない砂漠の光景が浮かぶのである。

58. そのような光景が浮かぶと、つぎの瞬間、私はどうしてもそこへ我が身を置いてみたくなる。

59. こうして私はまるで砂にたぐり寄せられるように砂漠へ旅立った。

N:

60. なぜ砂漠にそんなに惹かれるのか。

61. 自分にもよくわからない。

62. しかし、おそらく、砂漠というものが、私にとってはまったくの反世界だからだろうと思う。

O:

63. たしかに砂漠は私たちの住む日本の風土の反対の極と言ってもいいであろう。

64. 和辻哲郎はあの有名な『風土』という書物のなかで、世界の風土をモンスーン型、牧場型、砂漠型の三つに分け、砂漠型を私たちの住むモンスーン型風土の対極に置いた。

65. そしてモンスーン型の日本人がインド洋を抜けてアラビア半島にたどりついたときの衝撃を記している。

66. その衝撃とは、「人間いたるところに青山あり」などと考えているモンスーン型日本人が、どこをどう見まわしても青山など見あたらぬ乾き切った風土に直面したおどろきだと言う。

P:

67. たしかに砂漠は、青山的な私にとって衝撃そのものだった。

68. そこにあるのはただ砂と空だけなのだから。

69. けれど、そうした砂の世界に何日か身を置いてみると、やがて砂は私になにごとかをささやきはじめる。

70. そして、不思議なことに、こんどは自分が住んでいるモンスーン型の日本の風土や、そこにくりひろげられている生活が、"反世界"のように思えてくるのである。

Q:

71. 砂漠には何もない。

72. 何もないということがとうぜんのようになってくると、逆に、なぜ日本の生活にはあんなにもたくさんのものがあるのか、奇妙に思えてくる。

73. あんなに多くのものに取り巻かれなければ暮してゆけないのだろうか、と。

74. もしかしたら、それらのものは、ぜんぶ余計なものではないのか。

75. 余計なものに取り巻かれて暮しているから、余計な心配ばかりがふえ、かんじんの生きる意味が見失われてしまうのではないか......。

R:

76. しかし、待てよ、と私は考える。

77. 生きてゆくのに必要なものだけしかないということは、文化がないということではないか。

78. 生きてゆくうえに必要なもの、それを上まわる
    余分のものこそが、じつは文化ではないのか。
79. 文化とは、言ってみれば、余計なものの集積な
    のではないのか。
80. だとすれば、砂漠を肯定することは、文化を否
    定することになりはしまいか……。

S:
81. それにしても――と私はさらに考えなおす。
82. 私たちはあまりにも余分なものを抱えこみすぎ
    ているのではなかろうか。
83. 余分なものこそ文化にはちがいないが、さりと
    て、余分なもののすべてが文化であるわけもな
    かろう。
84. 余分なもののなかで、どれが意味があり、何が
    無価値であるか、それをもういちど考えなおす
    必要がありはしまいか……。

T:
85. 砂漠とは、こうした反省を私にもたらす世界で
    ある。
86. 砂漠は現代の文明社会に生きる人びとにとって、
    一種の鏡の国と言ってもいいような気がする。
87. 私は砂漠に身を置くたびに、ある探検家がしみ
    じみと洩らしたつぎのことばをかみしめる。
88. 「砂漠とは、そこへ入りこむさきには心配で、
    そこから出て行くときにはなんの名残もない。
89. そういう地域である。
90. 砂漠には何もない。
91. ただ、その人自身の反省だけがあるのだ。」

U:
92. 私は砂漠に自分自身の姿を身に行くのである。

V:

93. 砂漠は、私たち日本人が考えがちなロマンチックな場所ではけっしてない。

94. 王子さまとお姫さまが月の光を浴びながら銀色の砂の上を行く——などというメルヘンの世界ではない。

95. 昼と夜とで温度は激変し、一瞬のうちに砂嵐が天地をおおってしまう、そういうおよそ非情な世界である。

96. 日本という井戸のなかに住む蛙である私は、こうした砂の世界に足を踏み入れたとたん、いつも後悔する。

97. よりによって、なんでこんなところへ来てしまったのか！

W:

98. だが、その後悔は、やがて反省へ変り、さらに希望へと移ってゆく。

99. 生きることへの希望へ。

X:

100. この意味で、砂漠こそ最もロマンチックな場所であり、メルヘンの世界だと私は思う。

101. なぜなら、そうした"反世界"へ行こうとすることこそが、現代ではいちばんロマンチックな行為のように思われるからだ。

102. メルヘンの世界とは、さかさまの国のことである。

103. だとすれば、砂漠行こそ、まさしくメルヘンの国への旅ではないか。

Y:

104. 千里の旅、万巻の書——旅とはいろいろに考えられよう。

105.　しかし私は、旅とは、さかさまな国で自分を発
　　　見すること、後悔の向うに希望を見出すこと、
　　　そして人間の世界は、かくも広く、かくも多様
　　　で、かくも豊かなのだということを実感するこ
　　　とだと思う。

Z:

106.　だからこそ、千里の旅は万巻の書に値するので
　　　ある。

Vocabulary:

| 砂漠 | さばく | n | desert |
| 旅 | たび | n | travel |

1.

| 千里 | せんり | n | [lit. one thousand *ri* (one *ri* = 2.44 miles)], long distance |
| 万巻 | ばんかん | n | [lit. ten thousand volumes of books], huge amount of books, many books |
| 書 | しょ | n | books |
| 中国 | ちゅうごく | n | China |

2.

| 解釈 | かいしゃく | n | interpretation |
| 勝手に | かってに | adv | as one pleases |
| 解釈する | かいしゃくする | v | to interpret |
| *改釈する | かいしゃくする | v | to interpret anew, to interpret in revised ways |

\*This *kaishakusuru* is an author's creation, emphasizing that his interpretation is a revised version of the known word *kaishakusuru* 'to interpret.'

3.

| | | | |
|---|---|---|---|
| 書物 | しょもつ | n | books |
| 読破する | どくはする | v | to finish reading completely |

4.

| | | | |
|---|---|---|---|
| ところで | | conn | by the way |
| 凡人 | ぼんじん | n | ordinary person |
| とうていできない | | | cannot possibly do |

\**Tootei* used with the negative of a potential verb [a case of adverb-predicate correspondence] expresses strong negation – 'cannot possibly.'

| | | | |
|---|---|---|---|
| ジェット機 | | n | jet plane |
| 時代 | じだい | n | era, time, period |
| けっして | | adv | [in negative sentences] never |

6.

| | | | |
|---|---|---|---|
| 世界 | せかい | n | world |
| 巨大な | きょだいな | adj | huge, giant |
| 気がする | | v | to feel (like) |

7.

| | | | |
|---|---|---|---|
| たしかに | | adv | certainly |

8.

| | | | |
|---|---|---|---|
| 繰る | くる | v | to turn (the page) |

9.

| | | | |
|---|---|---|---|
| かなりの | | | considerably many |
| 地域 | ちいき | n | area |
| 第一章 | だいいっしょう | | the first chapter |
| 読み終える | よみおえる | | to finish reading |

10.

| 旅先 | たびさき | n | travel destination |
|---|---|---|---|
| いったい | | adv | how in the world |

\**Ittai* used in an interrogative sentence is an emphatic marker – 'in the world.'

| 見当もつかない | けんとうもつかない | | cannot possibly guess |

\**Kentoo o tsukeru* means to make an estimate, to guess at something.

| そのもの | | n | the very thing, the thing itself |
| めまいを覚える | めまいをおぼえる | | to be dizzy |

11.

| 途方に暮れる | とほうにくれる | | to be at a loss |

12.

| 読書 | どくしょ | n | reading of books |
| ひとしい | | adj | equal, equivalent to |

13.

| 言うまでもあるまい | | | [written style] *yuu made mo nai daroo* 'there should be no need to mention' |

14.

| 大きくする | | | to expand, to enlarge |

15.

| 井戸 | いど | n | well |
| 脱け出る | ぬけでる | v | to get out, to come out of |
| 実感する | じっかんする | v | to experience the feeling |

16.

| とまどい | | n | bewilderment, perplexity |
| 反省 | はんせい | n | reflection |
| つながってゆく | | | to be connected to |

17.

| 井 | い | n | well |
| 蛙 | かわず | n | frog |

18.

| 島国 | しまぐに | n | island country |
| 世間知らず | せけんしらず | | person ignorant of the ways of the world |

19.

| 例外 | れいがい | n | exception |

20.

| そもそも | | adv | in the first place |
| ひとつところ | | | one place |
| すなわち | | conn | namely, that is to say |

21.

| むろん | | adv | naturally |
| それなりの | | | in its own way, as it stands |
| 文化 | ぶんか | n | culture |

22.

| 文明 | ぶんめい | n | civilization |
| 歴史 | れきし | n | history |
| 発展する | はってんする | v | to advance |

23.

| 人類 | じんるい | n | human race |
| まさしく | | adv | surely, really, no doubt |
| つくりあげる | | | to build, to complete |

25.

| 探検家 | たんけんか | n | explorer |
| ニューギニア | | prop | New Guinea |
| 奥地 | おくち | n | the interior |
| 村 | むら | n | village |
| 未婚の | みこんの | | unmarried |

| 男女 | だんじょ | n | man and woman |
| 食事 | しょくじ | n | meal, dinner |
| とんでもない | | adj | flagrantly wrong, totally wrong |

26.

| ハチの巣 | ハチのす | n | beehive |
| つつく | | v | to poke |

*Hachi no su o tsutsuita yoona* literally means 'like poking at a beehive'; this idiomatic expression describes the situation that is 'utter confusion, bedlam,' the result caused by poking at a beehive.

| 騒ぎ | さわぎ | n | uproar, furor |
| 追放する | ついほうする | v | to oust |
| ヨメに行く | | | to marry into the groom's family |

27.

| ところが | | conn | however |
| 藪かげ | やぶかげ | n | within the thicket |
| 寝る | ねる | v | to sleep |
| 夜を過ごす | よるをすごす | | to spend the night |
| べつに | | adv | (not) particularly |

*Betsuni* used in negation means 'not particularly.'

28.

| つまり | | adv | in other words |
| 共に | ともに | adv | together |
| 許す | ゆるす | v | to permit, to allow |

29.

| 目をまるくする | | | to open eyes wide (with surprise) |

30.

| 例 | れい | n | example |
| 極端 | きょくたん | adj | extreme |

31.

| 自身 | じしん | n | oneself; *watashi jishin* – 'I myself' |
| いまさら | | adv | anew, again |
| 思い知らされる | | | to be made aware |

32.

| 葬式 | そうしき | n | funeral (service) |
| 涙 | なみだ | n | tears |
| 禁物 | きんもつ | n | things forbidden |

33.

| 古都 | こと | n | old town, ancient city |
| ベナレス | | prop | Benares |
| ガンジス河 | ガンジスがわ | prop | the Ganges (river) |
| 何組か | なんくみか | n | several groups |
| 葬列 | そうれつ | n | funeral procession |
| 加わる | くわわる | v | to join, to attend |
| 泣く | なく | v | to cry |

34.

| 葬儀 | そうぎ | n | funeral |
| 女性 | じょせい | n | female, woman |
| 姿 | すがた | n | appearance |
| 婦人 | ふじん | n | female, woman |
| つい | | adv | inadvertently |
| 涙をこぼす | | | to shed tears |
| 遠慮する | えんりょする | v | to decline from |

36.

| 死ぬ | しぬ | v | to die |
| 母なる | ははなる | | [written style] *haha dearu*, (being) the mother |

37.

| エジプト | | prop | Egypt |

| | | | |
|---|---|---|---|
| カイロ | | prop | Cairo |
| 目撃する | もくげきする | | |
| | | v | to witness |
| 多勢の | たぜいの | | many (people) |
| 泣き叫ぶ | なきさけぶ | | to wail out loud |
| 従う | したがう | v | to follow |
| **38.** | | | |
| 異様な | いような | adj | unusual, strange |
| 慟哭 | どうこく | n | violent wailing |
| 立ちどまる | | | to pause, to stop |
| 凝視する | ぎょうしする | v | to stare at |
| **39.** | | | |
| とたんに | | adv | suddenly, as soon as |
| きっと | | adv | (to look at) sharply |
| 睨む | にらむ | v | to stare hard at, to stare fixedly at |
| **40.** | | | |
| 同行の | どうこうの | | accompanying |
| **42.** | | | |
| 雇う | やとう | v | to employ |
| **43.** | | | |
| 風習 | ふうしゅう | n | custom |
| かつて | | adv | once, at one time |
| **44.** | | | |
| 人生 | じんせい | n | one's life |
| 最も | もっとも | adv | most |
| 深刻な | しんこくな | adj | serious |
| 行事 | ぎょうじ | n | event |
| **45.** | | | |
| 仕草 | しぐさ | n | gesture |
| 至っては | いたっては | | when it comes to |
| 無数に | むすうに | adv | countlessly, innumerably |

46.

| 頭 | あたま | n | head |
| 撫でる | なでる | v | to pat, to softly touch |
| かわいがる | | v | to love and care, to show affection |
| 東南アジア | とうなんアジア | | Southeast Asia |
| 国々 | くにぐに | n | many countries |
| たとえ...であろうと | | | even if it is ... |
| 赤ん坊 | あかんぼう | n | baby |
| いやがる | | v | to dislike, to show dislike |

47.

| 大切な | たいせつな | adj | precious |
| 部分 | ぶぶん | n | part |
| 気安く | きやすく | adv | casually |
| 侮蔑 | ぶべつ | n | despising |

48.

| スープ | | n | soup |
| 音を立てる | おとをたてる | | to make noise |
| 吸う | すう | v | to suck in |

*Oto o tatete suu* means 'slurping (soup) while making a sucking-in sound.'

| ヨーロッパ人 | | n | Europeans |
| 眉をひそめる | まゆをひそめる | | to frown |

49.

| 最中に | さいちゅうに | | in the middle of |
| 鼻をかむ | はなをかむ | | to blow one's nose |

50.

| 待ち合わせる | まちあわせる | | to meet someone by appointment |
| 定刻 | ていこく | n | set time |
| 過ぎる | すぎる | v | to pass |

*Volitional form of the verb followed by *mono nara*, as in *sugiyoo mono nara*, is an emphatic conditional – 'if it ever did.'

| | | | |
|---|---|---|---|
| イライラする | | | to be annoyed, to be irritated |

51.

| | | | |
|---|---|---|---|
| 相手 | あいて | n | partner |
| 腹を立てる | はらをたてる | | to get angry |
| 仕打ち | しうち | n | punishment |

52.

| | | | |
|---|---|---|---|
| アラビア人 | | n | Arabs, Arabians |
| ラテン・アメリカ人 | | n | Latin Americans |
| 最低の | さいていの | | the least |
| 単位 | たんい | n | unit (of measurement) |

53.

| | | | |
|---|---|---|---|
| きりがない | | | endless, limitless |

54.

| | | | |
|---|---|---|---|
| 反世界 | はんせかい | n | opposite-world |
| 集合体 | しゅうごうたい | | assembly, collection |

57.

| | | | |
|---|---|---|---|
| どういうわけか | | | somehow, for some unknown reason |
| 胸中 | きょうちゅう | n | inside of one's heart |
| 砂 | すな | n | sand |
| 溶け合う | とけあう | | to melt into one |
| 果てしない | はてしない | adj | endless, boundless |
| 光景 | こうけい | n | scenery |
| 浮かぶ | うかぶ | v | to come to mind |

58.

| | | | |
|---|---|---|---|
| 瞬間 | しゅんかん | n | moment, instant |
| 我が身 | わがみ | n | one's own body |
| 置く | おく | v | to place |

59.

| | | | |
|---|---|---|---|
| たぐり寄せる | たぐりよせる | | to pull toward |
| 旅立つ | たびだつ | v | to leave for a trip |

60.

| | | | |
|---|---|---|---|
| 惹かれる | ひかれる | v | to be attracted to |

61.

| | | | |
|---|---|---|---|
| 自分 | じぶん | n | self |

62.

| | | | |
|---|---|---|---|
| おそらく | | adv | perhaps |
| まったくの | | | complete |

63.

| | | | |
|---|---|---|---|
| 風土 | ふうど | n | climate |
| 反対の | はんたいの | | opposite |
| 極 | きょく | n | pole, extremity |

64.

| | | | |
|---|---|---|---|
| 和辻哲郎 | わつじてつろう | | Watsuji Tetsuroo [philosopher, writer, 1889–1960] |
| モンスーン型 | | n | monsoon pattern |
| 牧場型 | ぼくじょうがた | | |
| | | n | pasture/meadow pattern |
| 砂漠型 | さばくがた | n | desert pattern |
| 対極 | たいきょく | n | opposite pole |

65.

| | | | |
|---|---|---|---|
| インド洋 | | prop | the Indian Sea |
| 抜ける | ぬける | v | to pass through |
| アラビア半島 | アラビアはんとう | | |
| | | prop | the Arabian Peninsula |
| たどりつく | | v | to arrive finally (after hardships) |
| 衝撃 | しょうげき | n | shock |
| 記す | きす | v | to write down, to record |

66.

| | | | |
|---|---|---|---|
| いたる | | v | to reach |
| 青山 | せいざん | n | [lit. green mountains] fertile land |
| 乾き切った | かわききった | | arid, bone-dry |
| 直面する | ちょくめんする | v | to be face-to-face |
| おどろき | | n | surprise, bewilderment |

67.

| | | | |
|---|---|---|---|
| 青山的な | せいざんてきな | | those who hold the view of the world being fertile land |

69.

| | | | |
|---|---|---|---|
| 何日か | なんにちか | | for some days |
| やがて | | adv | soon |
| なにごとか | | | something, things |
| ささやく | | v | to whisper |

70.

| | | | |
|---|---|---|---|
| 不思議なことに | ふしぎなことに | | strangely |
| くりひろげる | | v | to unroll, to unfold |

72.

| | | | |
|---|---|---|---|
| とうぜんの | | | natural |
| 逆に | ぎゃくに | adv | conversely |
| 奇妙に | きみょうに | adv | strangely |

73.

| | | | |
|---|---|---|---|
| 取り巻く | とりまく | v | to surround with |

74.

| | | | |
|---|---|---|---|
| 余計な | よけいな | adj | unnecessary, excessive |

75.

| | | | |
|---|---|---|---|
| かんじんの | | | really important, essential |
| 見失う | みうしなう | v | to lose sight of |

77.

| | | | |
|---|---|---|---|
| 必要な | ひつような | adj | necessary |

78.

| | | | |
|---|---|---|---|
| 上まわる | | v | to exceed, to be above and beyond |
| 余分の | よぶんの | | unnecessary, excessive |
| じつは | | | in reality, actually |

79.

| | | | |
|---|---|---|---|
| 集積 | しゅうせき | n | accumulation, collection |

80.

| | | | |
|---|---|---|---|
| 肯定する | こうていする | v | to affirm |
| 否定する | ひていする | v | to negate, to deny |

81.

| | | | |
|---|---|---|---|
| それにしても | | | even then, still |
| さらに | | adv | furthermore |
| 考えなおす | | | to re-think |

82.

| | | | |
|---|---|---|---|
| あまりにも | | adv | too much, excessively |

83.

| | | | |
|---|---|---|---|
| さりとて | | conn | even so |
| すべて | | n | everything |

84.

| | | | |
|---|---|---|---|
| 無価値 | むかち | n | of no value, worthlessness |

85.

| | | | |
|---|---|---|---|
| もたらす | | v | to bring about |

86.

| | | | |
|---|---|---|---|
| 現代 | げんだい | n | modern times |
| 文明社会 | ぶんめいしゃかい | | |
| | | n | civilized society |
| 人びと | | n | people |

| 一種の | いっしゅの | | a kind of, of sort |
| 鏡 | かがみ | n | mirror |

87.

| しみじみと | | adv | with deep-felt emotion |
| 洩らす | もらす | v | to utter, to reveal |
| かみしめる | | v | [lit. to chew on] to meditate on, to appreciate |

88.

| 入りこむ | はいりこむ | | to enter into |
| 名残 | なごり、 | n | reluctant feelings of parting |

93.

| 考えがちな | | | likely to think |
| ロマンチックな | | adj | romantic, dream-like |
| 場所 | ばしょ | n | place |

94.

| 王子さま | おうじさま | n | prince |
| お姫さま | おひめさま | n | princess |
| 月の光 | つきのひかり | n | moonlight |
| 浴びる | あびる | v | to be bathed in |
| 銀色 | ぎんいろ | n | silver color |
| メルヘン | | n | [German]Märchen, fairy tale |

95.

| 温度 | おんど | n | temperature |
| 激変する | げきへんする | v | to fluctuate drastically |
| 一瞬 | いっしゅん | n | one moment |
| うちに | | | while, during |
| 砂嵐 | すなあらし | n | sandstorm |

| 天地 | てんち | n | heaven and earth, everything |
| おおう | | v | to cover |
| およそ | | adv | entirely, quite |
| 非情な | ひじょうな | adj | cold-hearted, forbidding |
| **96.** | | | |
| 踏み入れる | ふみいれる | | to step into |
| 後悔する | こうかいする | v | to regret |
| **97.** | | | |
| よりによって | | | of all other possibilities |
| **98.** | | | |
| だが | | conn | but |
| 希望 | きぼう | n | hope |
| 移ってゆく | うつってゆく | | to transform, to change |
| **100.** | | | |
| こそ | | | [emphatic] the very thing |
| **101.** | | | |
| 行為 | こうい | n | action |
| **102.** | | | |
| さかさまの | | | inverse, inverted, opposite |
| **103.** | | | |
| 砂漠行 | さばくこう | n | desert-travel |
| **105.** | | | |
| 発見する | はっけんする | v | to discover |
| かくも | | | [written style] *sonoyooni*, to that extent |
| 多様な | たよう | adj | varied, diverse |
| 豊かな | ゆたかな | adj | rich |
| **106.** | | | |
| 値する | あたいする | v | to be worth, to be equivalent |

## 4. Discourse notes

1. We studied portions of R7 at various points of Part II. Here is the summary.
   1. cultural background knowledge in Additional Information of Entry 17
   2. *danraku*-final and sentence-final forms in Entry 18
   3. commentary predicate in Entry 19
   4. thought representation in quotation, constructed dialogue and idiomatic phrases using *yuu* in Entry 23
   5. proverbs in Entry 30

2. We find a pun (as discussed in Entry 23) in line 2 of R7 created through the use of a homonym. In fact the author creates this particular homonym. Normally, the first character *kai* for the word *kaishaku* is the one for "interpretation, division," but the author uses another character for "revision, renew." This way he implies that the interpretation is based on his revision, his personal creation. The fact that the author assigns the "wrong" *kanji* is indicated by *booten* or *wakiten*, a *ten* (dot) placed to the right-hand side of the character, as shown in the original text (see Appendix 1).

3. One can understand the discourse organization of R7 in the following way. The original Japanese text is visually divided into 5 sections marked by a skipped line. These sections correspond in general to the five-part organization as well as the *ki-shoo-ten-ketsu* structure as presented in Table 17.

**Table 17** Discourse organization of R7 in terms of the five-part and the *ki-shoo-ten-ketsu* organizations

| section | danraku | summary | five-part organization | ki-shoo-ten-ketsu |
|---|---|---|---|---|
| 1 | A | reading many books is equal to traveling many miles | *okori* | *ki* |
| 2 | B–F | traveling avoids provincialism; world cultures develop through traveling | *uke* | *shoo* |
| 3 | G–L | episodes of cross-cultural differences | *hari*-1 | *ten*-1 |
| 4 | M–U | the meaning of travel to the opposite-world | *hari*-2 | *ten*-2 |
| 5 | V–Z | endless desert makes one find truly important things just as does reading many books | *soe, musubi* | *ketsu* |

4. Table 18 illustrates the *bunmyaku* of R7, the logical thread in particular.

**Table 18**  Logical thread of R7 by section and its types

| *logical thread* | *types* |
| --- | --- |
| introductory<br>   A (reading many books is equal to<br>   traveling many miles)<br>   ↓ | introductory |
| opinion<br>   B–F (traveling avoids provincialism;<br>   world cultures develop through traveling)<br>   ↓ | main |
| evidence through examples<br>   G–L (episodes of cross-cultural differences)<br>   ↓ | example |
| further thought<br>   M–U (the meaning of travel to the<br>   opposite-world)<br>   ↓ | main |
| confirmation of opinion/conclusion<br>   V–Z (endless desert makes one find truly<br>   important things as does reading many books) | concluding |

5. Take a note of examples of the cataphoric relation; between lines 2 and 3, and between lines 40 and 41/42.

6. Finding the central message of R7 is not difficult. This is partly because the author presents the same idea in the initial and final segments of the text, namely, traveling many miles is educational as is reading many books. We also note that the third section (*danraku* G–L) merely provides examples; these *danraku* describe peripheral events in that they do not directly address the central issue. The author's thoughts expressed in the second and the fourth sections identify main ideas leading to the conclusion. By reading these sections we realize it is not the travel to the desert *per se* that the author writes about. Rather, the idea of traveling to the "opposite-world" providing a place for self-reflection offers the rationale for equating the concept of traveling many miles with the concept of reading many books.

## 5. Discourse activities

1.  List the Japanese vocabulary items related to the desert by dividing them into three groups: (1) climate, (2) the way the author describes what the desert is, and (3) the way the author describes what the desert is not. Create statements that contrast (2) with (3) by using appropriate connectives.

2.  Examine the sentence-chaining mechanism evident in *danraku* A, B, C, and D by focusing on key phrases including *tabi* and *shomotsu*.

3.  Identify all quotations in R7 and discuss who speaks to whom.

4.  Write a Japanese summary for each of the five sections.

5.  Describe in Japanese your image of the desert by using similes and metaphors. Compare your image with the author's image in R7. Discuss similarities and differences.

## 6. Post-reading activities

1.  What commonality do you find in reading books and traveling? Do you agree with the author's view?

2.  Write a Japanese essay on the meaning of travel. Why do you think people travel at all?

*Part IV*

**Appendices**

### R7 (Morimoto [1976] 1983: 119–125), page 7

が月の光を浴びながら銀色の砂の上を行く――などというメルヘンの世界ではない。昼と夜とで温度は激変し、一瞬のうちに砂嵐が天地をおおってしまう、そういうおよそ非情な世界である。日本という井戸のなかに住む蛙である私は、こうした砂の世界に足を踏み入れたとたん、いつも後悔する。よりによって、なんでこんなところへ来てしまったのか！

だが、その後悔は、やがて反省へ変り、さらに希望へと移ってゆく。生きることへの希望へ。

この意味で、砂漠こそ最もロマンチックな場所であり、メルヘンの世界だと私は思う。なぜなら、そうした"反世界"へ行こうとすることこそが、現代ではいちばんロマンチックな行為のように思われるからだ。メルヘンの世界とは、さかさまの国のことである。だとすれば、砂漠行こそ、まさしくメルヘンの国への旅ではないか。

千里の旅、万巻の書――旅とはいろいろに考えられよう。しかし私は、旅とは、さかさまな国で自分を発見すること、後悔の向うに希望を見出すこと、そして人間の世界は、かくも広く、かくも多様で、かくも豊かなのだということを実感することだと思う。

だからこそ、千里の旅は万巻の書に値するのである。

## R7 (Morimoto [1976] 1983: 119–125), page 6

きる意味が見失われてしまうのではないか……。

しかし、待てよ、と私は考える。生きてゆくのに必要なものだけしかないということは、文化がないということではないか。生きてゆくうえに必要なもの、それを上まわる余分のものこそが、じつは文化ではないのか。文化とは、言ってみれば、余計なものの集積なのではないか。だとすれば、砂漠を肯定することは、文化を否定することになりはしまいか……。

それにしても——と私はさらに考えなおす。私たちはあまりにも余分なものを抱えこみすぎているのではなかろうか。余分なものこそ文化にはちがいないが、さりとて、余分なもののすべてが文化であるわけもなかろう。余分なもののなかで、どれが意味があり、何が無価値であるか、それをもういちど考えなおす必要がありはしまいか……。

砂漠とは、こうした反省を私にもたらす世界である。砂漠は現代の文明社会に生きる人びとにとって、一種の鏡の国と言ってもいいような気がする。私は砂漠に身を置くたびに、ある探検家がしみじみと洩らしたつぎのことばをかみしめる。

「砂漠とは、そこへ入りこむさきには心配で、そこから出て行くときにはなんの名残もない。そういう地域である。砂漠には何もない。ただ、その人自身の反省だけがあるのだ」

私は、砂漠に自分自身の姿を見に行くのである。

砂漠は、私たち日本人が考えがちなロマンチックな場所ではけっしてない。王子さまとお姫さま

## R7 (Morimoto [1976] 1983: 119–125), page 5

るように砂漠へ旅立った。

なぜ砂漠にそんなに惹かれるのか。自分にもよくわからない。しかし、おそらく、砂漠というもの

のが、私にとってはまったくの反世界だからだろうと思う。

たしかに砂漠は私たちの住む日本の風土の反対の極と言ってもいいであろう。和辻哲郎はあの有

名な『風土』という書物のなかで、世界の風土をモンスーン型、牧場型、砂漠型の三つに分け、砂

漠型を私たちの住むモンスーン型風土の対極に置いた。そしてモンスーン型の日本人がインド洋を

抜けてアラビア半島にたどりついたときの衝撃を記している。その衝撃とは、「人間いたるところ

に青山あり」などと考えているモンスーン型日本人が、どこをどう見まわしても青山など見あたら

ぬ乾き切った風土に直面したおどろきだと言う。

たしかに砂漠は、青山的な私にとって衝撃そのものだった。そこにあるのはただ砂と空だけなの

だから。けれど、そうした砂の世界に何日か身を置いてみると、やがて砂は私になにごとかをささ

やきはじめる。そして、不思議なことに、こんどは自分が住んでいるモンスーン型の日本の風土

や、そこにくりひろげられている生活が〝反世界〟のように思えてくるのである。

砂漠には何もない。何もないということがとうぜんのようになってくると、逆に、なぜ日本の生

活にはあんなにもたくさんのものがあるのか、奇妙に思えてくる。あんなに多くのものに取り巻か

れなければ暮してゆけないのだろうか、と。もしかしたら、それらのものは、ぜんぶ余計なもので

はないのか。余計なものに取り巻かれて暮しているから、余計な心配ばかりがふえ、かんじんの生

## R7 (Morimoto [1976] 1983: 119–125), page 4

おいてさえ、人間はこうもちがっているのである。ちょっとした仕草に至っては、そのようなちがいは無数にある。

日本人は子供の頭を撫でてかわいがるが、東南アジアの国々では、たとえ子供であろうと赤ん坊だろうと、頭に手をふれることをたいへんいやがる。頭は人間にとっていちばん大切な部分だから、そこに気安く手をふれることは侮蔑にひとしいのである。日本人はスープを音を立てて吸うが・ヨーロッパ人はその音をきくと眉をひそめる。ところが、そのヨーロッパ人は食事最中に音を立てて鼻をかむのをなんとも思わない。また、日本人やアメリカ人は、人と待ち合わせて定刻を五分も過ぎようものならイライラしはじめる。そして、相手を三十分も待たせるなどということは、かれらにとっては、三十分などという時間は人を待たせる最低の単位にすぎない。

このような例をあげてゆけば、きりがない。世界というのは、それぞれの井戸のなかに暮す蛙たちにとっては、それこそ"反世界"の集合体なのである。世界を旅するということは、反世界を旅することなのだ。

私は何度か砂漠へ出かけた。旅ということばをきくと、どういうわけか私の胸中には空と砂とがひとつに溶け合った果てしない砂漠の光景が浮かぶのである。そのような光景が浮かぶと、つぎの瞬間、私はどうしてもそこへ我が身を置いてみたくなる。こうして私はまるで砂にたぐり寄せられ

### R7 (Morimoto [1976] 1983: 119–125), page 3

メに行けなくなってしまうのだという。ところが、若い未婚の男女が藪かげでいっしょに寝て夜を過ごしても、それはべつになんの問題にもならないのだそうだ。つまり、食事を共にすることは許されないが、夜を共に過ごすことはかまわないというのである。友人の探検家はこの話をしながら、目をまるくして、

「世界は広いねえ」と言った。

このような例は極端かもしれない。しかし、私自身、旅をしてみて、おなじ人間でありながら、こんなにもちがうものかと、いまさらのように思い知らされたことがしばしばある。たとえば、インドでは葬式に涙は禁物であると教えられた。古都ベナレスのガンジス河のほとりで、私は何組かの葬列にあい、葬式にも加わったが、たしかにだれひとりとして泣いていない。葬儀に女性の姿をあまり見かけなかったが、インドの友人の話によると、婦人はつい涙をこぼしてしまうので遠慮するのだ、とのことであった。なぜ泣いてはいけないのか。インド人にとって、死ぬということは母なるガンジスへ帰ってゆくことなのであって、泣くべきことがらではないからだというのである。

しかし、私がエジプトのカイロで目撃した葬列には、多勢の女たちが泣き叫びながら従っていた。あまりにも異様なその慟哭に、私は思わず立ちどまって凝視した。とたんに女たちは泣きやみ、私をきっと睨んだ。同行のエジプトの友は私にこう教えた。

「あれは泣き女です。彼女たちは葬式に雇われて泣いてみせるのです」

そうした泣き女という風習は、かつては中国でも見られた。葬儀という人生の最も深刻な行事に

## R7 (Morimoto [1976] 1983: 119–125), page 2

ことができるのか見当もつかないこの巨大な書物、世界そのものにめまいを覚えることがある。そして、旅とは、このように途方に暮れることではないか、と考えてみたりする。

なぜ旅が読書とひとしい意味を持つのか。言うまでもあるまい。旅は読書とおなじように、小さな自分の世界を大きくするからである。旅とは自分の住む井戸から脱け出て、世界は広いんだなあ、と実感することだ。そのおどろき、そのとまどい、それがそのまま自分への反省につながってゆくのである。

日本人は井戸のなかの蛙(かわず)のようなものだ。たしかに日本は小さな島国だから、世間知らずになりやすい。けれど、人間というのは、どこに住んでいようと、じつは例外なく井戸のなかの蛙なのである。いや、そもそも、ひとところに住むということが、すなわち井のなかの蛙になるということである。

むろん、井戸のなかでも、それなりの文化は生れるであろう。が、文明の歴史は、人びとが井戸から脱けだすことによって文化を発展させてきたことを教えている。人類はまさしく旅によって文化をつくりあげてきたのだ。広い世界に出て、途方に暮れることによって。

これは私の友人の探検家からきいた話なのだが、ニューギニアの奥地のある村では、若い未婚の男女が二人だけで食事をするなどということは、それこそ「とんでもない話」なのだそうである。そんなことをしたら、村じゅうがハチの巣をつついたような騒ぎになって、男は追放され、女はヨ

### R7 (Morimoto [1976] 1983: 119–125), page 1

砂漠への旅

森本哲郎

「千里の旅、万巻の書」という中国のことばがある。その意味はいろいろに解釈できるが、私は自分で勝手にこう改釈している。

——千里の旅をすることは、万巻の書物を読破するにひとしい。

ところで、万巻の書物を読破するなどということは、私のような凡人にはとうていできないけれども、千里の旅なら、いまはジェット機の時代だから、けっしてむずかしくはない。そこで私は書物を読むようなつもりで旅に出る。そう思って出かけると、世界は一冊の巨大な本のような気がしてくる。

たしかに世界は一冊の書物だ。旅をするということは、その巨大な本のページを繰ってゆくことである。私はこれまで、世界のかなりの地域を旅したが、それでも、まだ世界という書物の第一章も読み終えていないような気がする。私はときどき旅先で、いったい、いつになったら読み終える

**R6 (*Asahi Shimbun*, November 28, 1994, page 1)**

天声人語

はらはらと落葉の散るころ、焚き火をする季節である。散った落ち葉を熊手で集め、昔はよく焼いた。一般に

人々は火を見ながら雑談をし、子どもやりの始末の仕方を覚えた▶そういえば、日常的に火を見る機会が少なくなった。用炉裏の火や燃える薪の様子や火の扱い方も知らない。煙たさをも示す言葉ももう知らない。焚き火で焼きいもをつくる薬しみも知らぬまま、残念だ▶熱い灰の中から引っ張り出した焼きいもを頬張りながら食べる。もういう野趣あふれる日常生活のある灰は、同様にいた灰は、燃えた薪の肥料だ▶雛しく言えば、かつて農家にとって灰は大切な灰を買うする。灰はカリ肥料である。灰小屋を持つ農家もあり、灰問屋も存在したし、

灰がこうして生活に大きな役割を果たしていた▶灰は物語や伝説にも登場する。「シンデレラ」は、欧米の「灰かぶり娘」という意味である。台所の灰の中にすわって仕事をするからだ▶不死鳥と訳される「フェニックス」は、古代エジプトの想像上の鳥で、生命の終わりが近づくと青木を積んで火をつけ、自らを焼く▶おじいさんが、柴刈りに行った松で灰をつくるが、意地の悪い風が灰を吹き、枝にかれ灰から花が咲く……▶灰に殺された松で日をつくるが、灰を吹き上げると柏らに花が咲く……▶灰に娘が蘇り、美しい花が咲き、米春の再生を期したのであろうか。

わが町の立っ町であった。昔の物質は、生活に大きな役立て、灰ざらは役割を果たした。灰は

のか。劇であるから、落ちた薬が灰になるのも、来春の再生を期すのであろうか。

### R5 (Usui 1994: 98–100), page 3

**R5 (Usui 1994: 98–100), page 2**

**R5 (Usui 1994: 98–100), page 1**

**R4 (*Popeye* May 25, 1997: 65)**

愛すべき故郷。《プロケッズ》は永遠のアメリカン・ストーリー・テラーです。

みんな知らないケッズの功績を話してあげよう。
アメリカ中には、それまで確か19のメーカーがあって
それぞれが、"スニーカ"という無限の可能性を持った
この新しい商品で何とかひと儲けしようと
他人のやらない色々な工夫を凝らしていたわけさ。
でも、ある時誰かがこう言ったんだ。
「こんな高価な靴を買ってくれる金持ちが
アメリカ中にいったい何人居るんだい。
誰でも買えるくらいに安くする方法を考えよう」…と。
19のゴム底シューズ・メーカーの16社が賛同し

こうして生れたのが、ケッズ、プロケッズの母胎となった
"ナショナル・インディアンラバー・カンパニー"。
おかげで、それまでヘック＆スナイダーのカタログにも
6ドル50セント(!)で載ってたようなクロケット・サンダルが
1897年のシアーズのカタログでは
60セントで売られるほどに身近かになったってわけ。
あれからもう100年もたつけれど
だからアメリカ人にとってケッズは今も特別なのさ。
誰だって、まるで空気を呼吸するようにケッズをはいている。
日本で売られているよりもっと沢山の中から選んで…。

Tucson
Navy, White
23→28cm : ¥5,800

Sprinter
Royal Blue × Yellow
Green × Yellow
Red × Yellow
23→28cm
¥6,800

Jogette
Yellow × White
Royal Blue × White
Orange × Dark Green
23→28cm : ¥6,800

**R3 (*Asahi Shimbun*, October 31, 1995, page 3)**

千葉県の幕張メッセで第三十一回東京モーターショーが始まった。

今年は新車のお披露目も多いが、例年にも増して華やかだ。デザインや性能とならんで、エアバッグやＡＢＳなど、「安全」が一つのキーワードになっている。

交通事故による死者は、日本だけで毎年一万人を超える。考えてみると、毎年必ず一万人が死ぬような工業製品の使用が社会で許されているのは、不思議なことだ。

## 交通安全ソフト

それだけに、「安全」がセールスポイントになり、テレビのコマーシャルにも衝突実験の画像が登場してきたのだろう。安全のための技術開発はむしろ遅すぎたくらいだ。

日本の交通事故死は、一九六〇年代後半から急速に増え、七〇年に一万六千余人に達した。官民一体の事故撲滅運動の結果、七〇年代にはいったん減った。けれども八〇年代に転じて再び増加し、いまでは毎年一万人を超えている。

日本の交通安全白書によれば、日本の事故死者数を車の走行キロ数だけで欧米諸国と比べると、米国とはほとんど変わらない。ところが英国だと、半数近くの死者の差は大きいのだ。

英国の値が特別に安全というわけではない。英国人の運転が特にうまいとも思えない。車も、車からの道路とかの「ハード」ではなく、総合的な交通政策という「ソフト」の成果なのであろう。

日本の交通安全政策の所管は総理府だが、総合的な「ソフト」の研究を十分にしているとは思えない。英国のケースを徹底的に研究することで、毎年五千人の命を救えたかもしれないのだ。

車などハード面だけでなく、ソフトの研究にも力を結集したものである。

〈鉄〉

## R2 (Hoshi 1982: 9–11), page 3

つぎの春からこのアリたちは、地上に出ても働こうとせず、キリギリスのバイオリンにあわせて踊りまわるだけだった。ただ、おじいさんアリだけが慨嘆する。

「なんたることだ、この堕落。このままだと遠からず……」

そして、若いアリたちを理論で説得すべく、食料の在庫を調べ、あとどれくらいでそれが底をつくか計算しようとした。だが、あまりに貯蔵量が多すぎ、どうにも手におえない。あと数十年を踊り暮したって、なくなりそうにはないのだ。そこでつぶやく。

「世の中が変ったというべきなのか。わしにはわけがわからなくなった……」

おじいさんアリは信念と現実との矛盾に悩み、その悩みを忘れようと、酒を飲み、若い連中といっしょに踊りはじめるのだった。

教訓。繁栄によりいかに社会が変ったからといって、古典的な物語をこのように改作すること、はたして許されるべきであろうか。

### R2 (Hoshi 1982: 9–11), page 2

「だめなら、しようがない。じゃあ、よそのアリさんのとこへ行ってみるか……」

帰りかけるのを、若いアリが呼びとめる。

「ま、まって下さい……」

その一方、おじいさんアリに説明する。

「……おじいさん、考えてみて下さいよ。われわれ先祖代々の勤労愛好の性格によって、巣のなかはすでに食料でいっぱい。毎年のように巣を拡張し、貯蔵に貯蔵を重ねてきたわけですが、それも限界にきた。さっきも貯蔵のために巣をひろげたら、壁が崩れ、むこうから古い食料がどっと出てきて、それにつぶされて三匹ほど負傷しました。キリギリスさんに入ってもらって少し食べていただかないと、もう住む空間もないほどなんです」

かくして、キリギリスはアリの巣の客となった。その冬はアリたちにとっても楽しいものとなった。ジュークボックスがそなえつけられたようなものなのだ。曲目さえ注文すれば、なんでもバイオリンでひいてくれる。

このキリギリス、芸術家だけあって、頭のひらめきもある。アリの巣の貯蔵庫を見て回っているうちに、奥の古い食料が発酵し酒となっているのを発見した。アリたちに言う。

「あんたがた、これをほっぽっとくことはないぜ。飲んでみな」

アリたち、おそるおそるなめ、いい気持ちとなり、酒の味をおぼえる。酒と歌とくれば、踊りだって自然と身につく。どうくらべてみても、勤労よりこのほうがはるかに面白い。この冬ごもりの期間中に、このアリ一族の伝統精神は完全に崩壊した。

**R2 (Hoshi 1982: 9–11), page 1**

## アリとキリギリス

秋の終りのある日、アリたちが冬ごもりの準備をしていると、そこへバイオリンをかかえた

キリギリスがやってきて言った。

「食べ物をわけてくれませんかね」

おじいさんアリが、その応対をした。

「あなたはなぜ、夏のあいだに食料あつめをしておかなかったんだね」

「わたしは芸術家なんですよ。音楽をかなでるという、崇高なことをやっていた。食料あつめ

などしているひまなんか、なかったというわけです」

「とんでもない怠け者だ。ふん、なにが芸術だ。お好きなように歌いつづけたらどうです、雪

の上ででも……」

おじいさんアリはそっけない。しかし、キリギリス、さほど落胆もしない。

**R1 (Tawara 1988: 154)**

空の青海のあおさのその間（あわい） サーフボードの君を見つめる

夏の空。夏の海。二つの青が接するところを、サーフボードの彼がゆく。まるで一羽のカモメのように。〈白鳥（しらとり）はかなしからずや空の青海のあをにも染まずただよふ〉──若山牧水のこの一首を私は自然に思い出す。空の青からも、海の青からも、染め残されたカモメ。カモメのようなあなた。あなたはかなしくないですか。一枚の板に両足をのせ、両手にはつかまる何ものもなく、危ういバランスを保ちながら、私の視界を横切ってゆく。あなたは寂しくないですか。サーフボードの下は波。気まぐれでとらえどころのない、そのゆらゆらに身をまかせ、私の視界を横切ってゆく。サーフボード。それはあなたの生き方そのもののようで。

# Appendix 2  **English translations of discourse samples (DS1–DS7)**

**DS1 (Ishimori *et al.* 1985b:40)**

1. When we find discontent and worries inside our hearts, we inadvertently say (mumble) things to ourselves.

2. Why do we mumble to ourselves?

3. It is because by mumbling to ourselves, we calm our emotions down a little.

4. When angry, we sometimes kick at stones and calm our emotions.

5. This is a compensatory act which channels anger into things other than the direct cause, thus releasing one's feelings.

6. This unconscious compensatory act is life's wisdom given to human beings.

**DS2 (Mukooda 1984:101)**

*Once Burned, Always Burned*

A:

1. When I break in a new frying pan or wok for the first time, I am more nervous than when I put on a new dress.

2. After amply heating up the pan, and letting it cool a while, I pour in a little used oil, heat it and then empty the pan.

B:

3. After repeating this three times, I stir-fry (unusable) vegetable end-pieces and examine how the pan is cooking.

4. Of course, I throw the contents away.

5. Although it is a bit wasteful, since I am rearing my right-hand assistant in the kitchen from whom I will receive assistance for some years to come, I suppose this extent of waste should be tolerated.

C:

6. Even though I go to this much trouble, I sometimes end up burning the pan.

7. Burned pans are similar to traffic accidents; the accidents occur in a moment's carelessness and one suffers the consequences for many more months.

D:

8. I clean the burns with great care and just when I think, "Now perhaps everything is working out fine," I end up burning the same spot again.

9. Once a bad habit is formed, enormous time and effort is required before it (corrects itself and) returns to complete normalcy.

E:

10. Human beings may be the same.

**DS3 (Ishimori *et al.* 1985b:38–39)**

    1. In the old days when they wanted to retrieve information from books and preserve it, they used to copy it down by hand.

    2. If careless, they sometimes made mistakes in their copying.

    3. Because we can use copying machines today, we are able to accurately and quickly copy characters (text) as well as charts and figures (graphics) from newspapers, magazines, books and so on.

    4. By the way, this is something that I feel when traveling; driving around is convenient because we can go to many places in a short period of time, but impressions of the goings-on in the localities we visit do not stay.

    5. In contrast to this, when we walk around on foot, we can directly absorb the scenery and activities of the people.

    6. The same is true when collecting information; copying by machine certainly is convenient, but there are many cases where copying by one's own hand is better.

    7. Necessary information remains in one's memory for a long time and can be utilized later.

**DS4 (Hayashi 1987:5)**

*Color and Human Life*

    A:

    1. While walking along bustling city streets, we sometimes by chance happen to stop in front of a store.

    2. There, attractively displayed, are clothing items, bags, hats and handkerchiefs of various colors – such as red, blue, yellow and green.

    3. Looking at those pretty colors and hues makes me feel happy.

    4. These colors are mostly man-made and are dyed into the items.

    B:

    5. In old times, it was not possible to manufacture colors as freely as (we do) today.

    6. They used natural colors as they came, by using such things as plant extract and crushed minerals, which they used for dying other things.

    7. But in the mid-nineteenth century in England, the color purple was manufactured from coal tar.

    8. Since then it has become possible to manufacture colors.

    9. Today, it is possible to manufacture tens of thousands of colors.

C:

10. Colors, depending on the hues, create different impressions.

11. We utilize the effects that each of many colors brings about and make the best use of colors in our lives.

D:

12. Red strongly stimulates those who see it and it is the color that first catches our attention.

13. So, mailboxes, fire engines, fire alarms and so on are painted red; red lights are placed at the entrance of police boxes and hospitals.

14. In traffic signals placed in city intersections, red is the color that signals the message "stop."

E:

15. Blue is a color that gives cold and cool feelings and brings calmness to those who see it.

16. Thus, there are cases where office desks and work tables on which detailed work is conducted are painted pale blue.

17. We often find examples where the whole interior of a train operator's control room is painted pale blue.

F:

18. Yellow is bright and gives a feeling of expansiveness, and it also makes objects appear distinct and clear.

19. So yellow has become the standard color on children's school wear such as hats, caps, and umbrellas.

G:

20. Combining colors can result in various effects.

21. The combination of bright colors such as yellow and black stands out and catches people's attention.

22. Some road signs are painted in yellow and black to make use of that effect.

23. Furthermore, combinations of colors such as red and green or orange and blue and so on strengthen each color, making each more brilliant.

24. A red roof among green trees can be seen brightly from afar.

H:

25. Colors give various feelings to people; they are useful in our lives.

26. We should use colors effectively and make our lives richer and more enjoyable.

### DS5 (Akagawa 1995:7–10)
*Noisy Departure*

A:

1. Inside the bus it was very noisy.

B:

2. Well, that is something often expected.

3. They are going on a school excursion; on such occasions, it is usually the case that the inside of the bus on the way to the destination is filled with an air of excitement.

C:

4. "Hey, be quiet!"

5. Yuriko Yabuki yelled out.

6. "I can't sleep."

D:

7. "Trying to sleep here is ridiculous,"

8. said Akiko Kuwata, (Yuriko's) best friend who was seated next to her on the bus.

E:

9. "But I'm sleepy."

F:

10. Usually Yuriko would make a racket together with her.

11. But . . . oh well.

12. There are various reasons for staying up late.

G:

13. Surely it wasn't because Yuriko had spent the night alone with her boyfriend.

14. Yuriko was seventeen; she thought she was as feminine as one would expect for her age, but still she was motivated by a desire for food over a desire for a love affair.

15. No, in that regard, Akiko, sitting next to her, was the same.

H:

16. The bus is moving steadily.

17. Heading for Haneda Airport.

. . .

I:

18. Well (perhaps there is no need to be formal here), those riding the bus are juniors at Hanazono Gakuen, a private girls' high school.

J:

19. They are now on their way to a "ski school."

. . .

K:

20. At this point some of the readers may think "Wait!"

L:

21. "In addition to Yuriko Yabuki and Akiko Kuwata, isn't there another rather unusual (clique) member, Kyooko Hirono?"

### DS6 (Murano 1975:71)

*The Deer*

1. The deer, at the edge of the forest,

2. stood still in the evening sun.

3. He knew –

4. his small forehead is being aimed at.

5. But for him,

6. what was there to do?

7. He stood slim,

8. looking toward the village.

9. The time of living glittering like gold,

10. where he lived,

11. the night of the vast forest behind him.

### DS7 (Shinkawa 1985:126–128)

*Do Not Bundle Me*

1. Do not bundle me

2. like blooming stocks

3. like white green onions.

4. Please do not bundle me.

5. I am ears of rice plants

6. that, in fall, burn the bosom of the land,

7. golden ears of rice plants as far as the eye can see.

. . .

8. Do not punctuate me

9. by commas, periods and so many of the *danraku*

10. like a letter that would say "good-bye" at the end.

11. Please do not bring me to an end so carefully and diligently.

12. I am discourse without an end,

13. like a river

14. flowing endlessly, expanding, a line of a poem.

# Appendix 3 **English translations of readings (R1–R7)**

**_R1_ (Tawara 1988:154)**

1. The blue of the sky, the blue of the sea,
   Between the blueness, you, on the surfboard;
   On you, my eyes are fixed.

2. The summer sky.

3. The summer sea.

4. Where the two bluenesses meet, he moves on the surfboard.

5. As if he were a sea gull.

6. "The white bird, I wonder if it isn't sad,
   Against the blue of the sky, and the blue of the sea,
   completely unstained, drifting about."

7. This piece of *tanka* by Bokusui Wakayama comes naturally to my mind.

8. The sea gull, left alone without being touched by the blue of the sky, or the blue of the sea.

9. You are just like a sea gull.

10. You aren't sad, are you?

11. Placing both feet on a single board, with both hands having nothing to hold on to, keeping a precarious balance, you swiftly move across my vision.

12. You aren't lonesome, are you?

13. Beneath the surfboard are the waves.

14. Resigning yourself to the sway of the surge, whimsical and hard to hold on to, you swiftly move across my vision.

15. The surfboard.

16. Just like the way you live your life.

**_R2_ (Hoshi 1982:9–11)**

*The Ant and the Grasshopper*

A:

1. One day toward the end of the fall, when ants were making preparations for the coming winter, a grasshopper holding a violin came by and said,

2. "Could you spare me some food?"

B:

3. An elderly ant answered him,

4. "Why didn't you collect a sufficient supply of food during the summer?"

5. "I am an artist.

6. I was engaged in the noble act of playing music.

7. That's why I didn't have time to be bothered by collecting food."

8. "What terrible sloth!

9. So what if it is an art!

10. Why don't you just continue singing to your heart's content – even in the snow . . ."

C:
11. The elderly ant is unsympathetic.

12. But the grasshopper is not too disappointed.

13. "Oh, well, that's OK.

14. Maybe I should stop by another ant's place . . ."

D:
15. As the grasshopper is about to leave, a young ant calls out.

16. "Please, please wait for a moment."

E:
17. To the elderly ant, the young ant explains.

18. "Grandfather, please give it some thought.

19. Our colony is packed with food because for generations our ancestors have had the work-loving character.

20. Almost every year we expanded our colony and repeatedly stored additional food; we are at our limit now.

21. When I widened the colony for additional food storage a while ago, the wall collapsed and old food fell down from the other side and three ants were injured as the food crashed down on them.

22. Unless we ask a favor of Mr. Grasshopper to come in and eat some of our food, no living space will be left for us."

F:
23. Thus the grasshopper became the guest of the ant colony.

24. That winter turned out to be an enjoyable one for all the ants.

25. It was as if they had installed a jukebox.

26. The grasshopper plays on his violin whatever music the ants request.

G:

27. This grasshopper, being an artist, is also brilliant.

28. As he took an inspection tour throughout the storage houses of the colony, he discovered that some of the old food stored in the back had fermented and had turned into *sake*.

29. The grasshopper announces to the ants.

30. "Hey, everyone, you shouldn't leave it like this.

31. Here, take a sip."

H:

32. The ants tasted the *sake* hesitantly, began to feel good and learned to appreciate alcohol.

33. With *sake* and songs, they easily learned how to dance.

34. When closely compared, these activities are much more fun than working, they found out.

35. During this winter period, the traditional values of the ant tribe were totally demolished.

I:

36. From next spring on, even when the ants came out to the surface, they were unwilling to work; instead, they did nothing but dance to the music of the grasshopper's violin.

37. Except for . . . the elderly ant. He lamented.

38. "What decadence!

39. If we continue like this, soon . . ."

J:

40. And in order to convince the young ants logically, the elderly ant began to appraise the food storage and tried to calculate in how many years all the food would be consumed.

41. But the inventory was too massive to handle.

42. It would not seem to run out even if they spent tens of years doing nothing but dancing.

43. So the elderly ant mutters.

44. "Perhaps the world has changed.

45. I don't understand it any more . . ."

K:

46. The elderly ant agonized over the incongruity between his belief and the reality, and in order to forget this anguish, he drank some *sake* and ended up dancing with the young ants.

L:

47. Moral of the story:

48. Is it really permissible to modify, as I did here, a classic story such as this one simply because prosperity has immensely changed society?

### R3 (*Asahi Shimbun* 1995)

*Window*

*From the Office of the Editorial Committee: The "Soft"-Ware for Traffic Safety*

A:

1. The thirty-first Tokyo Motor Show has opened at the Makuhari Messe in Chiba Prefecture.

B:

2. This year many new cars are introduced and the site is even more spectacular than previous years, and along with the automobile design and performance, the word "safety" has become the key issue as represented by air bags and so forth.

C:

3. The number of deaths caused by traffic accidents surpasses ten thousand in Japan alone.

4. Upon pondering, one finds it peculiar that the use of an industrial product that would surely result in as many as ten thousand deaths every year is (even) permitted in our society.

D:

5. It is perhaps because of this (awareness) that "safety" has become the selling point and visuals of crash tests have begun to appear in television commercials.

6. The development of safety technology is indeed seriously overdue.

E:

7. The traffic death toll in Japan increased rapidly starting from the latter half of the 1960s and in 1970 it reached over sixteen thousand (per year).

8. As a result of the joint crusade against traffic accidents by the government, industry and people, in the 1970s the death toll decreased steadily and in 1979 it dropped to the level of eight thousand.

9. However, in the 1980s it again shifted toward an increase, and ever since 1988 the number of deaths has been surpassing ten thousand.

F:

10. According to a traffic safety white paper, when the number of traffic deaths is compared with Western nations after converting the number of deaths per total number of miles driven (per year), the total barely differs from that of the United States and Germany.

11. But, Great Britain differs significantly, boasting a death figure of roughly half the number.

G:

12. This is not because British cars are especially safe, nor do we hear that British people are exceptionally good drivers.

13. Perhaps, the issue is not related to the "hard"-ware such as the car or the road; the favorable result is perhaps the fruit of the "soft"-ware-like efforts such as integrated traffic policies.

H:

14. The traffic safety policy in Japan falls under the jurisdiction of the Prime Minister's Office, but I am not under the impression that they are conducting sufficient research on integrated traffic "soft"-ware.

15. For example, by thoroughly studying the British case, we may be able to save five thousand lives every year.

I:

16. It is necessary to gather all resources not only for developing the "hard"-ware of the automobile but also for research on its "soft" side.

### R4 (*Popeye* 1994:65)

*Dear Hometown*

*Pro-Keds is an eternal American story teller.*

1. Let me tell you a Keds' success story that nobody knows about.

2. In America, if I am correct, there were at one time nineteen rubber sole manufacturers, and each was working hard to devise something no one had ever tried before in the hope of turning a considerable profit through the limitless possibilities this new product "sneaker" might offer.

3. But one day someone said,

4. "How many rich people are there in America who can afford such expensive shoes?

5. Let's think of ways to make them inexpensive so that everyone can afford them."

6. As a result of the agreement between sixteen of the nineteen rubber sole manufacturers, the National Indian Rubber Company was thus created, which later came to be called Keds, and Pro-Keds companies.

7. As a result, Croquet sandals which were listed in the Peg & Schneider catalogue at $6.50 (!) (a pair) became accessible – the same pair was listed at only 60 cents in the 1897 Sears' catalogue.

8. More than 100 years have passed since then, but because of this, Keds are special for Americans even now.

9. Anyone and everyone wears Keds shoes so naturally, as naturally as they breathe.

10. They can choose from many styles of shoes, many more than those sold in Japan.

## R5 (Usui 1994:98–100)

*Sunflower Class versus Rose Class, a Heated Competition Begins, Part 4*
*Note: M stands for mother, F for father, S for Shinchan, SC for Ship Captain.*

1.  M:  Wow, the ocean.
    [car screeching]
    F:  Here we are.
    [sound of waves rushing the shore]

2.  S:  What are we going to do now?
        Are we jumping into the ocean as we are?
    F:  Stop kidding!

3.  M:  Think more like a kid.
        There are other things you can do at the shore, aren't there?
    S:  Hum . . . a "drowned body game."
    F:  Fishing!! We came to go fishing!!

4.  S:  Yeah! fishing, fishing.
        I'm going to catch whales and penguins!!
    M:  He sure is just a little boy.
        All of his thoughts are innocent.

5. M:  Then, maybe Mom will catch a mermaid!! [with a girlish expression of excitement]

6. S:  Mermaids are fictional creatures, so they aren't here.
       Misae, you are a middle-aged (woman), so don't say such childish things.
   M:  [being upset]
   F:  Oh, well, well . . . [suggesting to calm down . . . ]

7.  They decided to charter a boat.
    *Genkaimaru* [boat's name: literally "Deep Sea"]
    SC A:  30,000 yen for half a day.
    F:  Expensive, isn't it?

8.  SC B:  My offer is 9,000 yen for half a day.
    F:  (Okay) It's a deal!

9.  SC B:  Welcome aboard.
    *Genkaimaru* [boat's name: literally "The Limited"]
    M:  Perfect name for this boat. [laugh]
    F:  I should have brought an inner tube float.
    S:  Wow, it's a "ghost" boat.

10. [hum of the boat's engine, sound of waves]

11. M:  The sea is rather choppy.
        Hope we're going to be OK.
    S:  I'm scared.
    F:  What's the matter with you people? Aren't you cowards! [laugh]

12. Several minutes later.
    F:  Ugh
    [seasick]
    M:  Oh, no, he's useless.
    S:  Ugh, smelly feet.

13. SC B:  You set the bait like this.
    M:  Oh, I see.
    S:  I see.

14. S:  Thank you very much for teaching me.
    SC B:  Well behaving boy, aren't you; you know how to say thank you.
    M:  We discipline him well . . . [smile]

15. S:  For expressing appreciation, this person will teach you "how to shave your legs quickly."

M:  Place the razor at 90 degrees to the skin and shave as you slide down!!
Shave down!!

[shaving]

16. M:  What are you making me do here?

SC B:  Thank you very much for teaching me. [laugh]

17. M:  Here it is!

[casting fishing lines]

S:  Here goes.

F:  Ugh, I still feel sick.

18. F:  Aww. [hurting]

S:  Oh, Dad is fine now and he's having fun.
I'm glad I took him along.

M:  Your fishing hook caught him!!

19. M:  Ah, I caught one!!

F:  Oh.

20. [fish jumping]

M:  Yuck, feels awful, I can't touch it.

21. M:  I'll throw it back into the sea.

[fish splashing into water]

22. [pulling hard]

S:  Wow, someone is pulling this.

F:  Shinnosuke caught one, too.

23. S:  I'm not gonna lose this! [pulling hard]

F:  What are you going to cut that for?

24. [fish jumping]

M:  You caught it!!

25. SC B:  I'll prepare it right away as *sashimi*.

F:  Great!! Got some beer?

S:  Poor little fish . . .

M:  Ah, such a tender-hearted son of mine, you are . . . [heart aching with
warm emotion]

26. F:  Delicious!

S:  Oh, wow. Melts on the tongue, doesn't it?

M:  What kind of personality is that?

### R6 (*Asahi Shimbun* 1994)

A:

1. This is a season when leaves fall steadily.

2. In old times, we often used to burn the fallen leaves gathered by rakes and brooms.

3. Burning leaves wasn't an uncommon (sight) among the general public.

4. People chatted while warming their bodies including their backsides, and children learned how to make a fire and extinguish it.

B:

5. Speaking of that, today's children have no opportunity to make a fire in their daily lives.

6. They are probably unfamiliar with the fire in the farmhouse fire pit, and with the heat coming from the embers.

7. They may not have opportunities to come in contact with words that describe these conditions of fire.

8. It is regrettable if they cannot experience smokiness and cannot experience the pleasure of roasting sweet potatoes in the fire.

C:

9. To pull out roasted sweet potatoes from a fire, pat off the ashes, and eat them while cooling them by blowing.

10. Such natural pleasure is absent in today's daily lives.

11. We poured water over the ashes of the fire.

12. Ashes were, just like compost, valuable as fertilizer used for vegetable gardens.

D:

13. In technical terms, the ash material is potassium carbonate.

14. It is the so-called potassium fertilizer.

15. In the past, farms had ash shacks; there were wholesale ash dealers who bought and sold ashes, and there were towns where ash markets were opened.

16. Ashes, as material, were used to get rid of the harshness (of vegetables); they played an important role in our lives.

E:

17. Ashes appear in stories and legends.

18. In Western languages "Cinderella" means "an ash-covered maiden."

19. This is because she used to work, sitting down in the kitchen covered with ashes.

20. The Phoenix, the bird translated as *fushichoo* (literally "never-death-bird"), is an imaginary bird in Ancient Egypt; when the end of life approaches, the bird gathers and piles up fragrant branches and lights a fire to burn itself; and then the bird is resurrected from the ashes.

F:

21. In the story of "*Hanasakajijii*" (literally "flower-blooming old man"), a good old man mourns over his murdered dog; after burying it, he plants a pine tree there.

22. He makes a (wooden) *usu* (a large wooden mortar to pound cooked rice in) out of the grown pine tree, but an evil old man burns it down.

23. As the good old man returns home with the ashes, along the way, the wind blows the ashes away and then blossoms appear on the bare branches.

G:

24. A maiden covered with ashes seized a good fortune, a bird repeatedly was resurrected from ashes, and when ashes were scattered, beautiful blossoms opened.

25. In all cases, they are examples of an unexpected reversal in a drama.

26. I wonder if leaves turn into ashes only in anticipation of next spring's rebirth.

## R7 (Morimoto [originally 1976], 1983:119–125)

*Traveling to the Desert*

A:

1. There is a Chinese expression, "One thousand miles of travel, ten thousand volumes of books."

2. The meaning of this expression can be interpreted in many ways, but I understand it in my own renewed (selfish) way as follows.

3. To travel one thousand miles is equivalent to reading ten thousand books.

B:

4. Now, (to complete a task such as) reading ten thousand books is totally impossible for a common man, such as myself, but traveling one thousand miles, since this is the era of jet travel, is not difficult at all.

5. So, with a feeling as if reading books, I take off on a trip.

6. As I travel with this thought, when traveling, I feel as if the world is one enormous book.

C:

7. Certainly, the world is (like) one volume of a book.

8. To travel is to turn the pages of that enormous book.

9. I have traveled to many places in the world so far, but still I feel as if I haven't finished reading even the first chapter of this book named "the world."

10. At my destination, I sometimes feel dizzy because of the world – that is, this immense book of which I have absolutely no idea as to when I will ever be able to finish reading.

11. And I sometimes think that perhaps traveling means to experience this overwhelming sense of being lost.

D:

12. Why does traveling mean the same thing as reading?

13. Perhaps there is no need to elaborate.

14. It is because traveling, like reading, broadens one's small world.

15. To travel is to come out of one's own well and to deeply feel – how vast the world is!

16. The bewilderment and the perplexity; these (feelings) directly lead one to reflect on oneself.

E:

17. Japanese are like frogs in a well.

18. True, because Japan is a small island country, the Japanese are likely to be ignorant of the world.

19. The truth of the matter is that human beings are, no matter where they live, without exception, frogs in a well.

20. Or, rather, the very fact that human beings live in one location means that they turn into frogs in a well.

F:

21. Naturally, even within a well, culture will come into existence in its own way.

22. But the history of civilizations teaches us that people have developed their cultures by coming out of the well.

23. Indeed, the human race has created its culture through traveling.

24. By going out into the vast world, and by being overwhelmingly lost by it.

G:
25. This is a story I heard from my explorer friend; according to him, in one village deep in the mountains of New Guinea, for a young unmarried couple to share a meal alone is "totally outrageous."

26. If they did so, the entire village would be thrown into utter confusion; the young man would be ousted from the village, the young woman would not be able to get married.

27. However, according to him, even when a young unmarried couple sleeps together in the bushes and spend the night together, that poses no problem at all.

28. In short, having a meal together is forbidden, but spending a night together is permitted.

29. My explorer friend, with his eyes wide open, said, "The world is a vast place, indeed."

H:
30. An example such as this one may be extreme.

31. But when I myself travel, I often am reminded anew of the fact that, although we are all the same in terms of being human, we also differ to a great extent.

32. For example, I was taught that in India tears are forbidden at funerals.

33. I witnessed several funeral processions in the ancient city of Benares on the Ganges, and I attended some funerals, but there was not a single person shedding tears.

34. Women were rarely seen at funerals; according to my Indian friend, women sometimes cannot hold back tears and therefore they decline attending.

35. Why is it forbidden to cry?

36. I understand that for the people in India, to die is to return to the mother Ganges, and it is not something that one should shed tears over.

I:
37. But in the funeral processions I witnessed in Cairo, Egypt, many women followed as they wailed and wept out loud.

38. At such an unusual wailing, I unintentionally stood for a moment and watched them.

39. Suddenly the women stopped wailing and stared sharply (back) at me.

40. The accompanying Egyptian friend explained it to me this way.

41. "These people are wailing women.

42. They are hired to wail and cry at funerals."

J:

43. Such a custom of wailing women once existed in China as well.

44. Even at funerals, the most serious event in life, human beings differ to this extent.

45. We find unlimited differences regarding casual gestures.

K:

46. Japanese people show affection by softly touching a child's head, but in Southeastern Asian countries, they abhor touching heads, even a child's or a baby's.

47. Because the head is the most important part of the human body, to touch it casually means to despise it.

48. The Japanese make (slurping) noises while eating soup, but Europeans frown over that noise.

49. But those Europeans think nothing of noisily blowing their nose in the middle of dinner.

50. Furthermore, Japanese and Americans are easily annoyed when their companions do not show up after five minutes past the appointed time.

51. And they think that making one's companion wait for thirty minutes is sufficient cause for making one's companion angry.

52. But for Arabs and Latin Americans, thirty minutes is the minimal period of time someone could be made to wait.

L:

53. There is no end to these examples.

54. For each group of frogs living in wells, the (rest of the) world is defined as the assembly of "opposite-worlds."

55. To travel the world means to experience a world opposite from one's own.

M:

56. Countless times, I made the desert my travel destination.

57. When I hear the word "travel," somehow in my heart this endless desert scene appears, the scenery where the sky and the sand meet and melt into one.

58. When such scenery appears, the next moment, no matter what, I want to place myself there.

59. And so I traveled to the desert, as if I were pulled toward it by the sand.

N:
60. Why am I so strongly attracted to the desert?

61. I myself cannot quite understand it.

62. But I think it is perhaps because, to me, the desert is a complete opposite-world.

O:
63. It can be said that certainly the desert is the polar opposite of the Japanese climate we live in.

64. Tetsuroo Watsuji, in that famous book titled "Fuudo (Climate and Cultures)," divided the world climate into three patterns – monsoon, meadow, and desert – and placed the desert as the opposite of our monsoon.

65. And he describes the shock when the Japanese accustomed to the monsoon pattern arrived at the Arabian Peninsula via the Indian Sea.

66. That shock is the surprise felt among the Japanese, conditioned by the monsoon pattern – who believed that "wherever humans go, there will be green (fertile) mountains (land)" – the shock caused by the realization that when faced with the arid climate, however hard they looked, there were absolutely no green mountains.

P:
67. Certainly, the desert was nothing but a shock to myself, for I am one who holds the green mountains view.

68. All one can find there are the sand and the sky.

69. When I place myself in that world of the sand for several days, however, soon the sand begins to whisper things to me.

70. And strangely, when this happens, the climate of the monsoon pattern in which I live and the Japanese ways of life occurring there begin to look like the "opposite-world."

Q:
71. In the desert, there is nothing.

72. When the state of nothingness begins to appear as the natural state of being, ironically, one begins to find it strange as to why there are so many things in Japanese life.

73. Why is it that we cannot live unless we are surrounded by so many things?

74. It could be that all those things are unnecessary.

75. Because we live surrounded by unnecessary things, unnecessary worries only increase and the really important meaning of life may be lost.

R:
76. But, wait! – I think.

77. Doesn't having nothing but necessary things to live mean not having culture?

78. Things that are above and beyond what we need to sustain our life, aren't these things, in reality, culture?

79. Isn't culture something of an accumulation of unnecessary things?

80. If that is the case, doesn't affirmation of the desert mean the denial of culture?

S:
81. Even so – I think again.

82. Isn't it that we hold on to too many of the unnecessary things?

83. Unnecessary things are certainly part of culture, but even then, it cannot be that all unnecessary things are part of culture.

84. Perhaps it is necessary for one to think once again; among many unnecessary things, which ones are meaningful, and which ones are worthless?

T:
85. The desert is a world which brings this self-reflection to me.

86. I think it is reasonable to say that the desert is a mirror-like country, of sorts, for those who live in the modern civilized world.

87. Whenever I place myself in the desert, I ponder upon the following words that an explorer spoke with deep-felt emotion.

88. "The desert is a place where one worries before entering, and one never feels reluctant when departing.

89. Such a place, it is.

90. There is nothing in the desert.

91. Nothing except a person's self-reflection."

U:

92. I go to the desert in order to look at myself.

V:

93. The desert is not a romantic (dream-like) place we, the Japanese people, like to think of.

94. It is not a fairy-tale world where a prince and princess travel across the silver sand under the moonlight.

95. The temperature varies drastically between night and day, and in an instant, a sandstorm blankets everything; it is an entirely forbidding world.

96. As soon as I step into this world of sand, I, who am a frog living in the well called Japan, always feel regret.

97. Of all the possible places, why have I come to this kind of place?

W:

98. But the regret soon changes into self-reflection, and then it changes further into hope.

99. Hope for living.

X:

100. In this sense, I think the desert is the most romantic place, a world of fairy tales.

101. It is because, today, traveling to such an "opposite-world" seems to be the most romantic act.

102. The world of a fairy tale is a world that is upside-down.

103. If that is so, certainly, going to the desert is like entering into a fairy-tale world.

Y:

104. One thousand miles of travel, ten thousand volumes of books; one can think of traveling in many ways.

105. I think, however, that to travel means to discover oneself in the world of upside-down, to find hope beyond regrets, and to experience how broad, how varied and how rich the human world is.

Z:

106. That is exactly why one thousand miles of travel is worth ten thousand volumes of books.

Depending on whether the text is written horizontally or vertically, graphological marks sometimes take different shapes and locations. Refer to marks appearing in the readings (R1–R7) originally presented vertically, but reproduced horizontally in the sentence-by-sentence presentation. Lists (1) and (2) provide commonly used marks and their names in vertical and horizontal styles, respectively. Additionally, refer to the usage list with reference to samples contained in readings.

(1)

かぎかっこ
ふたえかぎ
かっこ
やまがた
ふたえやまがた
なかぐろ
ぎもんふ
かんたんふ
なかせん
てんせん
くてん（まる）
とうてん（てん）
いんようふ（ひげ）

（2）

| | | |
|---|---|---|
| 「 | 」 | かぎかっこ |
| 『 | 』 | ふたえかぎ |
| （ | ） | かっこ |
| ＜ | ＞ | やまがた |
| ≪ | ≫ | ふたえやまがた |
| ・ | | なかぐろ |
| ？ | | ぎもんふ |

！
———
. . .
　。
　、
〃　　〃

かんたんふ
なかせん
てんせん
くてん（まる）
とうてん（てん）
いんようふ（ひげ）

| name | usage |
| --- | --- |
| *kagi(kakko)* | direct quotation of speech, phrases calling for attention and emphasis |
| *futae kagi* | quotation within a quotation; title of books, plays and magazines (R7, sentence 64) |
| *kakko* | notes, additional explanation (R4, sentence 7) |
| *yamagata* | emphatic presentation of phrases (R1, sentence 4) |
| *futae yamagata* | emphatic marking of phrases (R4, headline) |
| *nakaguro* | listing nouns; simplified date/month/year presentation; also used to mark division between family and given names written in *katakana* (R4, headline) |
| *gimonfu* | a question mark, for questions, but not normally used in articles, theses and official documents (R5, frame 2) |
| *kantanfu* | exclamation, normally not used in articles, theses and official documents (R4, sentence 7) |
| *nakasen* | inserted portion; or to leave some things unsaid (R1, sentence 7) |
| *tensen* | dotted line (normally six dots) used for uncompleted sentence; or to mark silence (R2, sentence 10) |
| *kuten (maru)* | the end of a sentence |
| *tooten (ten)* | used for listing items, after connectives, to mark modifying clauses, to signal long modification clauses; for pause and break to facilitate reading; between subordinate clauses, usually more generously used than the English comma |
| *In'yoofu (hige)* | used as quotation marks for labeling phrases calling for attention (R4, sentence 2) |

# References

Abe, Kobo. 1968. *Tanin no Kao*. Tokyo: Shinchoosha.
*Aesop's Fables*. 1960. Told by Valerius Babrius, translated by Denison B. Hull. Chicago: University of Chicago Press.
Akagawa, Jiroo. 1995. *Kumo ni Kieta Akuma*. Tokyo: Koobunsha Bunko.
Akutagawa, Ryuunosuke. 1969. Torokko. In *Torokko, Ikkai no Tsuchi*, by Ryuunosuke Akutagawa, 5–12. Tokyo: Kadokawa.
*Asahi Shimbun International Satellite Edition*. 1994. *Koramu Watashi no Mikata*. January to April.
*Asahi Shimbun International Satellite Edition*. 1994. *Koramu Watashi no Mikata*. February 23, p. 2.
*Asahi Shimbun International Satellite Edition*. 1994. The *Tensei Jingo* column. November 28, p. 1.
*Asahi Shimbun International Satellite Edition*. 1995. The *Mado* column titled *Horaa*, October 22, p. 3.
*Asahi Shimbun International Satellite Edition*. 1995. An article titled *Kootaishi Gofusai Fukushima e*. October 22, p. 22.
*Asahi Shimbun International Satellite Edition*. 1995. The *Mado* Column titled *Kootsuu Anzen Sofuto*. October 31, p. 3.
Bain, Alexander. 1886. *English Composition and Rhetoric: A Manual*. London, New York: D. Appleton & Co.
Bellow, Saul. 1944. *Dangling Man*. New York: The Vanguard Press, Inc.
Birnbaum, Alfred. 1985. *Pinball, 1973* (translation of Murakami Haruki's *Senkyuuhyaku Nanajuusan-nen no Pinbooru*). Tokyo: Koodansha.
Carrell, Patricia. 1984. Evidence of a formal scheme in second language comprehension. *Language Learning*, 34, 87–112.
Fujishiro, Hiroko. 1996. Shiteita no moo hitotsu no kinoo. *Nihongo Kyooiku*, 88, March, 1–12.
Hall, Edward T. 1976. *Beyond Culture*. Garden City, NY: Anchor/Doubleday.
Hall, Edward T. and Mildred Reed Hall. 1987. *Hidden Differences: Doing Business with the Japanese*. Garden City, NY: Anchor/Doubleday.
Hanzawa, Kan'ichi. 1995. Nihongo no hiyu. *Nihongogaku*, 14, Nov., 22–31.
Hayashi, Shiroo. 1987. Bunpo o kangaeru – Koowa joshi no ron. *Nihongogaku*, 6, March, 4–10.
Hinata, Shigeo and Junko Hibiya. 1988. *Danwa no Koozoo*. Gaikokujin no Tame no Nihongo Reibun, Mondai Shiriizu, Vol. 16. Tokyo: Aratake Shuppan.
Hinds, John. 1990. Inductive, deductive, quasi-inductive: Expository writing in Japanese, Korean, Chinese and Thai. In *Coherence in Writing: Research and Pedagogical Perspectives*, ed. by Ulla Connor and Ann M. Johns, 89–109. Alexandria, Virginia: Teachers of English to Speakers of Other Languages, Inc.
Hoshi, Shin'ichi. 1982. Ari to kirigirisu. In *Mirai Isoppu*, 9–11. Tokyo: Shinchoo Bunko.

Ichikawa, Takashi. 1981. *Nihongo Kyooiku no Tame no Bunshooron Gaisetsu.* Tokyo: Kyooiku Shuppan.

Ikegami, Yoshihiko. 1981. *Suru to Naru no Gengogaku.* Tokyo: Taishuukan.

Ikegami, Yoshihiko. 1982. *Kotoba no Shigaku.* Tokyo: Iwanami.

Ikegami, Yoshihiko. 1988. What we see when we see flying cranes: Motion or transition. *The Japan Foundation Newsletter*, 15, 5–6, 1–9.

Ikegami, Yoshihiko. 1991. "DO-language" and "BECOME-language": Two contrasting types of linguistic representation. In *The Empire of Signs*, ed. by Yoshihiko Ikegami, 258–326. Amsterdam: John Benjamins.

Ishii, Satoshi. 1982. Thought patterns as modes of rhetoric: The United States and Japan. In *Intercultural Communication: A Reader*, ed. by Larry A. Samovar and Richard E. Porter, 97–102. Belmont, CA: Wadsworth Publishing Co.

Ishimori, Nobuo, *et al.* ed. 1985a. *Kokugo* II. Tokyo: Mitsumura Tosho.

Ishimori, Nobuo, *et al.* ed. 1985b. *Kokugo Hyoogen.* Tokyo: Mitsumura Tosho.

Kabashima, Tadao. 1979. *Nihongo no Sutairu Bukku.* Tokyo: Taishuukan.

Kaneoka, Takashi. 1989. *Bunshoo ni Tsuite no Kokugogakuteki Kenkyuu.* Tokyo: Meiji Shoin.

Kawabata, Yasunari. 1966. *Yukiguni.* Tokyo: Oobunsha.

Kern, Richard D. 1989. Second language reading strategy instruction: Its effects on comprehension and word influence ability. *The Modern Language Journal*, 73, 2, 135–149.

Kitagawa, Chisato. 1984. Hatsugen no kaisookoozoo to "kotoba" no shutaisei. *Nihongogaku*, 4, Aug. 31–42.

Kubota, Osamu. ed. 1990. *Nihongo no Hyoogen.* Tokyo: Soobunsha.

Langacker, Robert W. 1987. Nouns and verbs. *Language*, 63, 53–94.

Makino, Seiichi and Michio Tsutsui. 1986. *A Dictionary of Basic Japanese Grammar.* Tokyo: The Japan Times.

Makino, Seiichi and Michio Tsutsui. 1995. *A Dictionary of Intermediate Japanese Grammar.* Tokyo: The Japan Times.

Matsuki, Masae. 1992. Mirukoto to bunpoo kenkyuu. *Nihongogaku*, 11, August, 57–71.

Matsumoto, Seichoo. 1971. *Ten to Sen.* Tokyo: Shinchoosha.

Maynard, Senko K. 1990. *An Introduction to Japanese Grammar and Communication Strategies.* Tokyo: The Japan Times.

Maynard, Senko K. 1993. *Discourse Modality: Subjectivity, Emotion and Voice in the Japanese Language.* Pragmatics & Beyond New Series, Vol. 24. Amsterdam: John Benjamins.

Maynard, Senko K. 1997. *Japanese Communication: Language and Thought in Context.* Honolulu: University of Hawaii Press.

Miyaji, Yutaka. 1985. Kotengo to gendaigo. In *Kokugo II*, 96–100. Tokyo: Mitsumura Tosho.

Morimoto, Tetsuroo. 1976. Sabaku e no tabi. In *Subarashiki Tabi – Ningen, Saigetsu, Deai.* Tokyo: Daiamondosha.

Morimoto, Tetsuroo. 1983. Sabaku e no tabi. In *Nihon no Mei-zuihitsu*, Vol. 15, ed. by Hiroyuki Agawa, 119–125. Tokyo: Sakuhinsha.

Mukooda, Kuniko. 1984. Kogeguse. In *Yonaka no Bara*, 101. Tokyo: Koodansha.

Murakami, Haruki. 1983. *Senkyuuhyaku Nanajuusan-nen no Pinbooru*. Tokyo: Koodansha.

Murano, Shiroo. 1975. Shika. In *Gendai Kokugo* 1, *Shinshuuban*, ed. by Ryuu Kumazawa *et al.*, 71. Tokyo: Meiji Shoin.

Nagano, Masaru. 1986. *Bunshooron Shoosetsu*. Tokyo: Asakura Shoten.

Nagao, Takaaki. 1992. Bunshoo to danraku. *Nihongogaku*, 11, April, 26–32.

Nagara, Susumu and Naoko Chino. 1989. *Buntai*. Gaikokujin no tame no Nihongo Reibun, Mondai Shiriizu, Vol. 9. Tokyo: Aratake Suppan.

Nakamura, Akira. 1984. Yojooron. In *Hyoogen no Sutairu*, ed. by Akira Nakamura, 86–134. Tokyo: Chikuma Shoboo.

Nakamura, Akira. 1991. *Bunshoo o Egaku*. Tokyo: Nihon Hoosoo Shuppan Kyookai.

Natsuki, Shizuko. 1981. *Hikaru Gake*. Tokyo: Kadokawa.

Nishida, Naotoshi. 1992. *Bunshoo Buntai Hyoogen no Kenkyuu*. Osaka: Izumi Shoin.

Nishihara, Suzuko. 1990. Nichi-ei taishoo shuujihoo. *Nihongo Kyooiku*, 72, 25–41.

Noguchi, Yukio. 1995. *Choo-Benkyoohoo*. Tokyo: Koodansha.

Noto, Kiyoshi. 1980. *Bunshoo wa Doo Kaku ka*. Tokyo: K. K. Besuto Seraazu.

NTT. 1996. The constitution of Japan, @http://www.ntt.jp/japan/constitution/.

Oota, Minoru. 1971. *Chuuburarin no Otoko* (translation of Saul Bellow's *Dangling Man*). Tokyo: Shinchoosha.

Ozawa, Toshio. 1982. Hitoyo no taikenbanashi. *Gengo*, 12, September, 74–82.

*Popeye*. 1994. May 25th issue, p. 65. Tokyo: Magazine House.

Renkema, Jan. 1993. *Discourse Studies: An Introductory Textbook*. Amsterdam: John Benjamins.

Saunders, E. Dale. 1966. *The Face of Another* (translation of Kobo Abe's *Tanin no Kao*). New York: G. P. Putnam's Sons.

Segal, Ervin M., Judith F. Duchan and Paula J. Scott. 1994. The role of interclausal connectives in narrative structuring: Evidence from adults' interpretations of simple stories. *Discourse Processes*, 14, 27–54.

Seidensticker, Edward. 1964. *Snow Country* (translation of Yasunari Kawabata's *Yukiguni*). New York: Berkeley Publishing Corporation.

Shibata, Takeshi. 1992. Joohooka jidai no bunshoo. *Nihongogaku*, 11, April, 8–11.

Shimada, Sooji. 1991. *Kieru Suishoo Tokkyuu*. Tokyo: Koobunsha.

Shinkawa, Kazue. 1985. Watashi o tabane-nai de. In *Kokugo* 3, 126–128. Tokyo: Mitsumura Tosho.

Tannen, Deborah. 1989. *Talking Voices: Repetition, Dialogue and Imagery in Conversational Discourse*. Cambridge University Press.

Tawara, Machi. 1987. *Sarada Kinenbi*. Kawade Bunko. Tokyo: Kawade Shoboo.

Tawara, Machi. 1988. *Yotsuba no Essei*. Tokyo: Kawade Shoboo.

Tirkkonen-Condit, Sonja and Luise Liefländer-Koistinen. 1989. Argumentation in Finnish versus English and German editorials. In *Text-Interpretation-Argumentation*, ed. by Martin Kusch and Hartmut Schröder, 173–181. Hamburg: Buske.

Tokieda, Motoki. 1977. *Bunshoo Kenkyuu Josetsu*. Tokyo: Meiji Shoin.

Tokunaga, Sumiko. 1977. Kaguya-hime. In *Nihon no Otogibanashi, Ninensei*, 198–215. Tokyo: Kaiseisha.

Tsuji, Kunio. 1986. Tabi no owari. In *Shoowa Bungaku Zenshuu*, Vol. 24, ed. by Yasushi Inoue, *et al.*, 7–12. Tokyo: Shoogakukan.

Usui, Yoshito. 1994. *Kureyon Shinchan*, Vol. 7. Tokyo: Futabasha.

Utano, Shoogo. 1992. *Shiroi Ie no Satsujin*. Tokyo: Koodansha.

Werlich, Egon. 1982. *A Text Grammar of English*. Heidelberg: Quelle and Meyer.

Yasuoka, Shootaroo. 1972. Umibe no kookei. In *Gendai Nihon Bungaku Taikei*, Vol. 90, 185–231. Tokyo: Chikuma Shoboo.

*Zasshi Shinbun Sookatarogu*. 1995. Tokyo: Media Research Center, Inc.

# Index